Ukrainian Studies in Canada
Texts and Contexts

Proceedings of the CIUS Fortieth Anniversary Conference

14–15 October 2016

Edited by
Volodymyr Kravchenko

КІУС
CIUS

Canadian Institute of Ukrainian Studies Press
Edmonton • Toronto
2018

CANADIAN INSTITUTE OF UKRAINIAN STUDIES PRESS

University of Alberta
Edmonton, Alberta
Canada T6G 2H8

University of Toronto
Toronto, Ontario
Canada M5T 1W5

ISBN 978-1-894865-51-7 (softcover).—ISBN 978-1-894865-52-4 (HTML)

Library and Archives Canada Cataloguing in Publication

Ukrainian Studies in Canada: Texts and Contexts (Conference)
(2016 : Edmonton, Alta.)
Ukrainian studies in Canada : texts and contexts : proceedings of the CIUS fortieth anniversary conference, 14–15 October 2016 / edited by Volodymyr Kravchenko.

Includes bibliographical references and index.
Issued in print and electronic formats.
ISBN 978-1-894865-51-7 (softcover).—ISBN 978-1-894865-52-4 (HTML)

1. Ukraine—History—Study and teaching (Higher)—Canada—Congresses.
2. Ukraine—History—Study and teaching (Higher)—United States—Congresses.
3. Ukraine—History—Study and teaching (Higher)—Europe—Congresses.

I. Kravchenko, Volodymyr, 1957–, editor II. Canadian Institute of Ukrainian Studies. Press, issuing body III. Title.

DK508.48.U47 2017 947.70071'1 C2017-905470-8
C2017-906708-7

The publication of this book has been funded by a generous grant from the **Nestor Peczeniuk Memorial Endowment Fund** at the Canadian Institute of Ukrainian Studies (University of Alberta).

Book and cover design, including cover photos, by Halyna Klid.

Inside photographs by Halyna Klid (CIUS), Oliver Rossier (ACE), Oleksandr Pankieiev (ACE), and submitted by participants in the CIUS 40th Anniversary Conference (2016).

Printed in Canada

CONTENTS

CREDITS

CIUS 40th Anniversary Conference Proceedings Publication Committee

Serge Cipko	CIUS Assistant Director, Research
Halyna Klid	CIUS Communications and Research Assistant
Volodymyr Kravchenko	CIUS Director
Susanna Lynn	CIUS 40th Anniversary Project Coordinator
Ksenia Maryniak	CIUS Editor
Oleksandr Pankieiev	Media and Communications Assistant, Arts Collaboration Enterprise (ACE), Faculty of Arts
Marko R. Stech	Executive Director, CIUS Press
Viktoriya Yakovlyeva	CIUS Archival Assistant

Conference Proceedings Editorial and Technical Support

Roman Senkus (CIUS Senior Editor), Daria Storoshchuk, Myroslav Yurkevich

CIUS 40th Anniversary Conference Organizing Committee

(all CIUS unless otherwise indicated)

Jars Balan	Coordinator, Peter and Doris Kule Ukrainian Canadian Studies Centre
Steven Bello	Assistant Director, Finance and Administration
Serge Cipko	Assistant Director, Research
Iryna Fedoriw	Administrative and Finance Assistant
Bohdan Harasymiw	Research Associate, Contemporary Ukraine Studies Program
Ivan Kozachenko	Stasiuk Post-doctoral Fellow
Bohdan Klid	HREC Research Director
Halyna Klid	Communications and Research Assistant
Volodymyr Kravchenko	CIUS Director
Susanna Lynn	CIUS 40th Anniversary Project Coordinator
Frank Sysyn	Director, Peter Jacyk Centre for Ukrainian Historical Research
Alla Nedashkivska	Acting Director, Ukrainian Language Education Centre, and Professor, Dept. of Modern Languages and Cultural Studies
Oleksandr Pankieiev	Media and Communications Assistant, Arts Collaboration Enterprise, Faculty of Arts
Oliver Rossier	Senior Officer, Arts Collaboration Enterprise, Faculty of Arts

CIUS 40th Anniversary Conference Support

Diana Kondrat	Visiting student, Ivan Franko National University of Lviv
Ksenia Maryniak	CIUS Editor
Oleksandr Melnyk	Stasiuk Post-doctoral Fellow
Mark Minenko	Community volunteer
Iryna Sen	Visiting student, Ivan Franko National University of Lviv
Olena Sivachenko	ULEC Research Associate
Viktoriya Yakovlyeva	CIUS Archival Assistant

THANK YOU TO OUR CONFERENCE SPONSORS

BRONZE DONORS ($1,000–2,499)

Faculty of Arts Conference Fund, University of Alberta
Kule Dialogue Grant, Kule Institute for Advanced Study
Ukrainian Foundation for College Education (Edmonton)
Ukrainian Senior Citizens Association of Marko Boyeslaw (Edmonton)
Steve Fedchyshak
Ivan Harrakh

PATRONS ($500–999)

Peter Arabchuk
Bohdan Szuchewycz

SUPPORTERS ($100–499)

Walter and Stella Baydala
Irena Bell
Raymond Buciak
Andrij and Halyna Buhel
David and Mary Jane Burghardt
Michael Humnicky
Julian and Barbara Koziak
Ihor Kutash
League of Ukrainian Canadians Edmonton Branch
George and Orysia Lysyk
Oleh and Maria Maryniak
Maria Nebesio
Maria Roslak
Borys and Donna Sydoruk

The publication of these proceedings has been supported in part by the Ukrainian Canadian Foundation of Taras Shevchenko.

Shevchenko Foundation

UNIVERSITY OF ALBERTA
FACULTY OF ARTS

kias
KULE INSTITUTE
FOR ADVANCED STUDY

PREFACE

2016 was a year full of reasons to celebrate, reflect, and look toward the future in the Ukrainian-Canadian community. It marked not only the 125th anniversary of Ukrainian immigration to Canada and the 25th anniversary of Ukraine's independence but also the 40th anniversary of the Canadian Institute of Ukrainian Studies (CIUS), a leading centre of Ukrainian studies outside Ukraine and an integral part of the Faculty of Arts at the University of Alberta (U of A).

CIUS's milestone at the University of Alberta was marked alongside the special events across Canada and Alberta devoted to celebrating these landmark anniversaries in the community. Above and beyond CIUS's regular activities in Edmonton, nationally, and abroad, CIUS staff and colleagues organized and participated in a series of unique events and projects to highlight its forty years of service. Among them was a month-long display in the Rutherford Library Atrium, organized in co-operation with the Kule Folklore Centre and the U of A Libraries; it showcased CIUS's research areas (Ukrainian studies, Ukrainian-Canadian studies, and Ukrainian language pedagogical resources) and CIUS Press publications. The Institute also participated in several Edmonton festivals: Heritage Days, Ukrainian Day at the Ukrainian Cultural Heritage Village, and *Sviato 25* in Churchill Square. CIUS's fortieth also became a catalyst for ongoing initiatives such as the CIUS Digital Archive Project, which continues to digitize all CIUS materials and resources for public access.

CIUS's hallmark event for its 40th anniversary was a two-day conference titled "Ukrainian Studies in Canada: Texts and Contexts," held on 14–15 October 2016 at the U of A's Lister Conference Centre, on Treaty 6 / Métis Territory. Bringing together scholars and community members from across Canada, the United States, and Europe, this major event formed the basis of the present publication. These proceedings are a direct product of the transcripts, submitted papers, discussions, questions, and opinions that came out of CIUS's 40th anniversary conference.

The reader should note that the transcripts of the conference have been edited for clarity and accuracy. All footnotes have been added by the editor. Participants were given the opportunity to review their presentations before publication. Six of the participants chose instead to submit research papers that had been prepared prior to the conference, and these papers replace the transcripts of their presentations.

The views, opinions, and statements of fact expressed in these proceedings are those of the authors, participants, and speakers, and do not necessarily reflect or represent those of CIUS, the editors, the organizing committee, or the supporters of this conference.

Cyrillic names, particularly in the émigré context, are given in their historical version; others conform to the modified version of the U.S. Library of Congress Romanization system that is used by CIUS and the Ukrainian government.

Please visit www.cius.ca for complete audio and video recordings of the conference and for information about CIUS, including upcoming events and initiatives.

Susanna M. Lynn
CIUS 40th Anniversary Project Coordinator
University of Alberta, May 2017

Dr. Volodymyr KRAVCHENKO

Director, CIUS

Ukrainian studies in Canada: Searching for new ways

Introduction

Marking the fortieth anniversary of the Canadian Institute of Ukrainian Studies in 2016[1] presented us with the opportunity to discuss the current state and future prospects of Ukrainian and Ukrainian-Canadian studies in Canada. The political, social, institutional, and financial contexts of these fields of knowledge are as important as their texts (i.e., narratives, paradigms, concepts, interpretations, etc.). Hence we selected the title of the conference, "Texts and Contexts," with a view to bringing together not only world-renowned experts in the fields but also community activists, donors, and politicians. We tried to approach the issue of Ukrainian studies from different geographical perspectives, including North America, Canada, Ukraine, and Europe. At the same time, our goal was to create a space for interdisciplinary dialogue among specialists in the humanities and social sciences, including historians, philologists, and political scientists.

Our intention was to represent various generations of specialists and community activists. Unsurprisingly, the debates were dominated by the generation of scholars who promoted Ukrainian studies in Canada to the highest level in the West at the end of the 20th century. This generation had been formed during the 1960s, and its representatives are today themselves in their sixties, if not seventies, yet remain active in both their professional careers and their community participation. On the one hand, the absence of historical distance between the past and the present affected the course and nature of the corresponding discussions. Reading between the lines, the careful reader will easily detect traces of old debates and personal interactions between some of the scholars, and even biased or self-promoting presentations. On the other hand, the personal and professional experiences of the conference participants permitted them to address a broad spectrum of issues connected to both the texts and contexts of modern Ukrainian studies in North America and Europe.

Before the conference, participants were sent a list of questions crafted to focus their attention on issues that were, to our mind, the most important: Who needs Ukrainian studies in Canada? What challenges are they facing? What is their future? The conference was structured accordingly, to enable an overview of the history of Ukrainian studies in Canada and the United States during the last forty years, and an examination of the current state and future prospects of Ukrainian and Ukrainian-Canadian studies. We further aimed to highlight issues surrounding the teaching of such courses at Canadian universities and, finally, to evaluate the interrelationships between the academic milieu and the Ukrainian community as well as the Canadian political establishment. Below I will try to contextualize, summarize, and assess the debates, following the structure of the conference.

Background

The nature and directions of the conference discussions published in this volume will be better understood in a historical perspective. Given that none of the participants limited their presentations to a solely historical framework, with the reader's indulgence I will briefly describe my own view of this perspective.[2]

Ukrainian studies have generally traced the muddling way of modern Ukraine's nation-state building during the last one hundred years or so. The interaction of religious,

1 *CIUS: Forty Years of Excellence*, a special issue of the 2016 *CIUS Newsletter/Biuleten' KIUSu* edited by Marko Stech and Roman Senkus (posted online at https://is.gd/cius40yrs_pdf).

2 See also my article "Ukrainian historical writing in Canada after the Second World War," published in 2016 in *Storia della Storiografia* (vol. 69, no. 1).

regional, cultural, and political factors in this process has been complicated by Ukraine's "fatal geography," and also by specificities relating to its Byzantine-Rus' historical legacy. Until recent times, Ukrainians never had even a semblance of their own proper nation-state. Divided by historical circumstance as well as by geopolitics, various subgroups of the Ukrainian ethnos operated under the frameworks of different national discourses: Russian, Soviet, Polish, Austrian, Canadian, and others. Thus, a variety of local and diaspora Ukrainian identities emerged—often hybrid ones.

> *"Divided by historical circumstance as well as by geopolitics, various subgroups of the Ukrainian ethnos operated under the frameworks of different national discourses: Russian, Soviet, Polish, Austrian, Canadian, etc."*

The concepts of nation and national territory of modern Ukraine have fluctuated, depending on changing political and socio-cultural contexts. One hundred years ago, when Ukrainian statehood was established with its seat in Kyiv, two intersecting visions of Ukrainian national identity emerged, one ethnocultural and the other territorial-political. Correspondingly, in the ethnocultural case of national identity, its content was determined by the classical humanities disciplines: language, folklore, history. In the territorial-political case, it was based primarily on the social sciences, including, e.g., political science, economics, and sociology. Essentially, the different content populating the definition of "Ukrainian studies" depends on the context; meanwhile, there are no guidelines for its proper application.

In Canada, the Ukrainian nation-building process acquired its own specificity. The Ukrainian community here falls into two main components: that formed in Canada between 1891 and 1947, and the émigrés of the post–World War II wave of immigration. The differences between the political and cultural priorities of these two groups, as well as their visions for the future, were not catastrophic for the community overall, especially during the Cold War, but they were nonetheless significant. They were also exacerbated by the decentralization of political, cultural, and educational life in Canada—above all by the regional distinction between the west, which was historically dominated by older-generation Ukrainian Canadians, and the east, where the new Ukrainian immigrants were mostly based. While these nuances have not always been understood in Ukraine, nevertheless they affected the emergence of differing visions regarding Ukrainian studies in Canada. Quite naturally, the most representative among these visions were *Ukrainian-Canadian studies* and *Ukraine-oriented studies*.

For the Ukrainian-Canadian community, which had been established and institutionalized for several generations already, the most important objective was to assert its presence and facilitate successful integration into Canadian society. The collective identity of this community was largely formed during their decades already in Canada, with Ukrainian regional, political, and religious features melded with local Anglo-Saxon symbols and values. The result was a situation of cultural marginality, on the one hand, and a sort of hybrid or "not-belonging" identity,[3] on the other. This kind of collective identity of the Ukrainians in Canada dovetailed rather smoothly with (and in fact has probably contributed to) the overarching Canadian identity, which is still in search of its defining formula. Occasionally the Ukrainian-Canadian identity displays an ardent Canadian nationalism; this is particularly evident in the statements of Manoly Lupul (see the exchange between him and Professor Magocsi on p. 36–37). There is no doubt that for Ukrainian Canadians born in Canada, their past and future are tied to this country, not Ukraine.

From that point of view, the postwar Ukrainian immigrants in Canada differ substantially from the earlier Ukrainian Canadians. The former, as a rule, maintained a strong Ukrainian ethnocultural identity. It was Ukraine, not Canada, that remained at the centre of the world view of these immigrants and motivated their many activities. For the postwar immigrants, the most important objectives were to preserve the achievements and accomplishments of the modern Ukrainian national movement, as well as to represent to the world the "authentic Ukraine" that they

3 Skrypuch, M.F. "Am I Ukrainian?" in *Unbound: Ukrainian Canadians Writing Home*, eds L. Grekul and L. Ledohowski (Toronto 2016).

"took with them"[4] when fleeing their native land. They vigorously opposed the Communist regime in the USSR and strove to influence Canadian foreign policy in that direction. It was they who established the field of academic Ukrainian studies in Canada and did their best to legitimize it in the Western academic milieu.

The Canadian government chiefly aimed to integrate the Ukrainian immigrants successfully into Canadian society. Along the way, from time to time Canadian politicians tried to exploit the resources of the Ukrainian community for some concrete goal. The government facilitated the institutional structuring of the Ukrainian community in the creation in 1940 of an umbrella civic body—the Ukrainian Canadian Committee.[5] Canada's new multiculturalism policy created political conditions for maintaining, and even developing, the ethnocultural identity of the Ukrainian-Canadian community during the political crisis around Quebec at the beginning of the 1970s. For its part, the Ukrainian community played a prominent role in providing input regarding Canadian government policy toward Ukraine, and Ukrainian Canadians occupied important positions in the Canadian federal government. It could be said that the Canadian political and academic elite at the time tended to regard Ukraine, and the field of Ukrainian studies, through the eyes of the Ukrainian-Canadian community.

> *"This kind of collective identity of the Ukrainians in Canada dovetailed rather smoothly with (and in fact has probably contributed to) the overarching Canadian identity, which is still in search of its defining formula."*

I believe that the aforesaid permits us to better understand some of the nuances in the history of Ukrainian studies in Canada. To illustrate, the conference participants particularly emphasized their influence on Western academia. Bishop Borys (Gudziak) recounts:[6]

> The standards in Ukrainian studies were high, and the vision was broad. From the Huns to Byzantium, from literature to numismatics, from demographic studies to minute linguistic detail...in many of our places of study and research, people in Ukrainian studies set standards for other scholars in the number of languages they knew, and the number of points of view they could understand, and in the hard work they had to put in to overcome the biases (17).

Mark Von Hagen notes that "Ukraine has been...the most important factor in what we now call the 'imperial turn' in Russian and East European history. Ukraine's example has forced Russian historians above all (the most important audience for some of us) and Polish historians to rethink a lot of their own history" (54). I would also add to this list the phenomenon of modern nationalities studies, whose early development can be credited in significant measure to Ivan Lysiak Rudnytsky, John Armstrong, and Stepan Horak. Overall, the conference presentations on the history of Ukrainian studies are of a remarkably personal nature, and the discussion often focuses on current issues in the state of this field.

Ukrainian studies

Considering the positive growth dynamic of Ukrainian studies during the past four decades—not to mention the attention paid to Ukraine by Western mass media during the last 15–20 years—it is somewhat surprising to hear, according to Paul Robert Magocsi, that even today "Ukraine does remain a little-known or misunderstood country in today's world," and that still a "distorted view of Ukraine... seems to dominate public awareness in many parts of Europe and North America" (26). The reasons for this must be sought first of all in the situation that Ukrainian studies are currently going through a new stage of reorganization and reconceptualization that has resulted from political, generational, and intellectual changes as well as evolving academic priorities.

The context in which these changes are occurring is greatly affected by the general crisis in the humanities in the global scholarly milieu. Mark Von Hagen speaks of "the

4 This quote references the memoir *Z soboiu vzialy Ukraïnu* (We Took Ukraine with Us; Kyiv 2007) by Peter (Petro) Savaryn, one of the founders of CIUS, who was present at the conference. He died in April 2017 at the age of 90.

5 The UCC (www.ucc.ca, renamed the Ukrainian Canadian Congress in 1990) embraced all Ukrainian organizations in Canada except pro-Soviet ones.

6 Quotes in the Introduction are taken from the given speaker's main presentation or from discussions in which he or she participated. All ellipses are inserted, replacing omitted text; the page number is given in parentheses following the end of the quote or quote cluster.

decline of funding for the humanities, both in the West and in Ukraine, and together with the humanities, area-studies centres that focus on international relations and foreign cultures and societies....The humanities are being made less and less attractive, as is the teaching profession in general, all the way down to the primary school level" (55). This point of view is shared especially by Rory Finnin and Bohdan Kordan. Kordan says, "It is not just the field of Ukrainian studies that has suffered but, with few exceptions, the entire humanities and social sciences as well" (107). Most of the conference participants appear to agree with this assessment.

"The decline in classical humanities subjects is directly connected to the crisis in the classical university model, which itself is founded upon the principle of academic autonomy."

Since 1991, the entire system of production, dissemination, and application of scholarly knowledge about the former socialist world that was set up during the Cold War years continues to undergo profound institutional and disciplinary reorganization. Primarily this has affected Slavic studies, East European studies, Sovietology or Soviet studies, and also area studies—all these have traditionally included Ukrainian studies. Although the discussions of the conference participants testify that there is no alternative to an interdisciplinary approach to Ukrainian studies, significant problems with interdisciplinary dialogue within Ukrainian studies themselves are also evident.

Apparently Taras Kuzio is the only discussant who still believes that "Ukrainian studies did not become broader and more inclusive after 1991, nor did it bring in political science" (34). Mark Von Hagen objects, noting that "it is not that *we* have abandoned political science...political science has abandoned *us*." He also suggests that this problem emerges from a so-called "Las Vegas complex"—namely, the tendency of social and political sciences in the US to self-isolate with respect to "what happens in Ukraine stays in Ukraine"—and concludes, "It is going to take a reconstruction of political science before they can come back to us" (40).

Dominique Arel, a political scientist himself, disagrees with both colleagues, pointing out that "political scientists are in fact a very important component of the area studies discipline that we call Ukrainian studies" (106) and citing the example of the Danyliw Seminar at the University of Ottawa, where political scientists comprise about one-third of the presenters. However, he is convinced that Ukrainian studies today include not only political scientists but also sociologists and anthropologists. Apropos, the latter are less influenced by political affairs than professional political scientists are.

It could be said that the traditional conceptions of the disciplines that encompass Ukrainian studies are changing. Certainly these disciplines have been significantly influenced by cultural studies. Thus, the philologist Taras Koznarsky quite justifiably asserts, "Ukrainian culture and literature are capable of providing access and insight into the most relevant, complex, and powerful human experiences, and we should display them with the best, without apologies or reservations" (112).

The decline in classical humanities subjects is directly connected to the crisis in the classic university model, which itself is founded upon the principle of academic autonomy. This problem is mentioned by Borys Gudziak, Rory Finnin, Frank Sysyn, Roman Petryshyn, and Manoly Lupul. The latter comments that the freedom characterizing university life in Canada forty years ago "does not exist now; instead there is too much worry about simply picking up the money" (41). The accelerating bureaucratization of the university system throughout the world, and in Canada in particular, is damaging the humanities and diluting the values of professional ethics.

At the same time, the centralization and unification of the university environment virtually hands it over to incompetent administrators, further reducing the already low competitiveness of Canadian universities in liberal arts education compared to US and European universities. Notably, in addressing the issue of academic autonomy, Frank Sysyn finds a positive example of it being upheld not in Canada or the US but in Britain: "They have an academic spine in Cambridge to defend academic traditions, not to go along with whatever the last bureaucracy or dean says" (69).

Given their traditionally small size and enrolment, Ukrainian courses are the first to be sacrificed in the process of deterioration of university humanities and are on a disappearing trend—as discussed in particular by Manoly Lupul, Myroslav Shkandrij, and Alla Nedashkivska. Paul Robert Magocsi calls on us to be realists and admit that "Ukraine is never likely to attract a level of interest among North American university students that would sustain the several existing Ukrainian research institutes, endowed professorships, and departments that offer courses in Ukrainian-related subjects" (26). However, his own example demonstrates that on a nationwide level, teaching Ukrainian studies courses at Canadian universities is hardly a uniform scenario.

According to Professor Magocsi, the Ukrainian history

> *"The accelerating bureaucratization of the university system throughout the world, and in Canada in particular, is damaging the humanities and diluting the values of professional ethics."*

course at the University of Toronto is flourishing, attracting a significant number of students per year. Dominique Arel, Serhy Yekelchyk, and David Marples also present a rather optimistic picture when describing their respective teaching experiences. Bohdan Kordan offers an interesting observation about "those who were still committed to a traditional language and literature model and were prepared to fight a losing battle against senior administration in its defence" (108). Unfortunately the question of traditionalists versus innovators in the field of Ukrainian studies is not taken up by other conference participants.

As we know, the events of 2014 in Ukraine, and the repercussions abroad, had a significant effect on Western academia, splitting it into pro-Russian and pro-Ukrainian political camps. The polemics between them very often crossed the boundaries of academic discourse. Understandably, the topic of Ukrainian-Russian relations is not ignored in these proceedings either. Mark Von Hagen speaks of the necessity for scholars to "counter" and "dismantle" the Russian imperial narrative (65), while David Marples agrees that "there are so many scholars today who have supported, by and large, the Russian version of why Russia is waging war in Ukraine" (66), and tells us not to demonize and not to exaggerate Putin's influence on the academic environment.

The problem of Ukrainian-Russian relations is contextualized in the frameworks of the civilizational paradigm and comparative approach. The ideas of Samuel Huntington, despite being criticized or perhaps because of it, remain relevant in academia, especially in light of recent events in Europe and the US. Not surprisingly, Huntington's name is raised alongside that of the current POTUS. The discussion around the civilizational paradigm, touched on by Rory Finnin and David Marples, demonstrates that national identity is still very much an issue in Ukraine. Professor Marples also discusses the significance of historical legacy, primarily concerning the Second World War, and regional dimensions of Ukrainian studies. Mark Von Hagen puts forward an interesting thought that the Israeli model of a militarized democracy could be applicable to Ukraine in its relations with Russia.

Some inspiring ideas on the prospects for the future development of Ukrainian studies are fervently expressed by Yaroslav Hrytsak. His position is clearly different from that of most of his colleagues:

> We are still dealing with identity, with language...but they do not explain what is really going on in Ukraine....We are still very much stuck in the old agenda....But I would say that there are much more important things to discuss....You have to come up with a set of ideas, suggestions to help this country fight the historical legacy (not with historical memory per se)....Ukrainian scholars have a unique opportunity to formulate a new agenda for Ukrainian studies (68).

It is interesting that Hrytsak's pragmatic approach to Ukrainian studies resonates with Martha Bohachevsky-Chomiak's vision of Ukrainian society—"basically...a quintessentially bourgeois society that really wants a good, decent life, and forcing people to come to a decision of what *Weltanschauung*, or world view, they all have to accept is generally not top on people's agenda" (72).

Ukrainian-Canadian studies

The panel devoted to Ukrainian-Canadian studies is distinctive for its reflections on the professional identity of this sub-discipline. The definition of the term *Ukrainian-Canadian studies* contains the same element of ambivalence as in *Ukrainian studies*. Natalia Khanenko-Friesen considers the difference between the two:

> We can speak about Ukrainian studies or the Ukrainian legacy, culture, history *in* Canada, and that is often the pursuit of so many of us. But we can also think of the Ukrainian-Canadian legacy in broader terms and operate with the adjective "Ukrainian-Canadian" *through* the hyphen, as applied to Ukrainian-Canadian ethnicity, culture, heritage, history, and society (78).

If one continues along these lines, then certainly the virtual space of Ukrainian-Canadian studies could include scholarship carried out in Ukraine, in Poland, or eventually any country in the world.

The necessity of differentiating more clearly between "Ukrainian" and "Ukrainian-Canadian" studies is also mulled over by other conference participants. For example, for Dominique Arel "these are two different worlds that intersect at some level, but not always, as they are two different experiences" (122). Lubomyr Luciuk goes even further and emphasizes that between representatives of Ukrainian and Ukrainian-Canadian studies there is "very little coordination or co-operation, and in fact, sometimes there has been a barely concealed hostility" (85). Andrij Makuch seeks a compromise by saying that "one cannot really divorce Ukrainian-Canadian studies from Ukrainian studies. If you are dealing with Ukrainian-Canadian studies, you really do have to know about developments in Ukraine, because there is an interplay between them" (87).

If Ukrainian-Canadian studies are part of Ukrainian studies from the Ukrainian perspective, then from the Canadian perspective they belong in the territory of *Canadian studies*—although, as Natalia Khanenko-Friesen notes, they are on the margins of both. On the one hand, this kind of disciplinary ambivalence in Ukrainian-Canadian studies corresponds to the hybrid nature of Ukrainian-Canadian identity. Professor Luciuk's declaration is characteristic in this regard: "I am not a Ukrainian-Canadian studies specialist, and I am not a Ukrainianist; I am somewhere in-between" (81). On the other hand, Ukrainian-Canadian studies show much stronger links to the community than do Ukraine-oriented studies. For Professor Khanenko-Friesen, "this field, Ukrainian-Canadian studies, is an excellent example of what scholars nowadays call *community-engaged scholarship*...with a mandate to pursue scholarship and research in partnership and collaboration with communities" (78).

If we agree with the aforesaid, then the question of critical distance between the subject and object of research in Ukrainian-Canadian studies becomes one of principle. Namely, in the proceedings, the comments on this subject are mostly given by members of that very Ukrainian-Canadian community itself who are attending the conference. Regardless, some of the observations made by conference participants deserve a closer look. For example, Martha Bohachevsky-Chomiak notes: "What always struck me was the similarity between the Ukrainian diaspora organizations and the way Ukraine functions. Just multiply the Ukrainian diaspora organizations by a few million, and you have Ukraine" (46). Overall, it must be admitted that on Ukrainian-Canadian issues the conference brought up more questions than it answered.

Who, in fact, makes up the Ukrainian-Canadian community? Are they ethnic Ukrainians only, or also others (as raised by Paul Robert Magocsi) who emigrated from the territory of contemporary Ukraine? The Ukrainian-Canadian community in general remains distant from the "fourth wave" of Ukrainian (post-Soviet) immigrants, which in numeric terms is already nearly equal to the post–World War II "third wave." What are the factors at play in the mutual alienation of different components of the Ukrainian community in Canada? Which of them qualify under the definition of "diaspora"? Finally, to what extent are "open society" values and norms cultivated in Ukrainian-Canadian organizations? Are they able to cope with the controversial historical legacies of Communism, integral nationalism, or anti-Semitism? What can be done about deeply rooted traditionalism, mythological thinking, siege mentality, parochialism, and nepotism? Other questions could be added to this list, but another conference would have to be specially called to seek the answers.

Town and gown

What kind of dialogue is there between the community and academia? What is "the vision that the Ukrainian diaspora had developed for Ukrainian studies" (Serhii Plokhii, 21)? On the community side, Manoly Lupul pursued its formation with great verve: "As a group, academics in Ukrainian studies are not practitioners like the others. Theirs is a very special constituency....At the base of the special constituency for academics in Ukrainian studies is of course the Ukrainian community" (24). Essentially, Dr. Lupul adheres to a traditional view of the special mission of the intelligentsia and its service to the community. This idea appears to be shared by some of the other conference participants.

In one of the discussions, Jars Balan quotes UCC President Paul Grod saying that he [Grod] came to this conference with an idea of getting "all our institutes, all our academic bodies, as members of the UCC" (99). Mr. Grod subsequently moderated his position somewhat, and declared only that he supports the proposal to create a "loosely affiliated council" of Ukrainian studies scholars under the UCC (149). However, it is not clear to what extent the UCC's policies on Ukraine are based on information from experts. In this respect, the UCC appears to be following the example of the federal government.

> *"As we know, the events of 2014 in Ukraine, and the repercussions abroad, had a significant effect on Western academia, splitting it into pro-Russian and pro-Ukrainian political camps. The polemics between them very often crossed the boundaries of academic discourse."*

Canada might be considered by many to be an emerging global power, especially in light of its growing relations with European countries, on the one hand, and the increasing isolationism of US foreign policy, on the other. Former Canadian ambassador Derek Fraser informs the audience about "regional strategic centres at various Canadian universities," then avows that "what is required is a certain degree of dialogue between centres of area studies at various universities in Canada and the Canadian government" (39). From what was said at the conference, it could be concluded that the expert opinions of Ukrainianists have little influence on Canada's political players, with the government continuing to base its policy decisions on the recommendations of the Ukrainian community rather than on academia.

Roman Petryshyn presents a proposal to further develop endowments and agencies to support Ukrainian studies. He argues for the necessary creation of new administrative structures that would engage in coordination and centralization in the field of Ukrainian studies. It appears that these ideas are based on concepts that existed at the time when CIUS was founded. The founders imagined it in the role of an overall national coordinating centre for Ukrainian studies, but today it can be stated that the concept was utopian. One obtains the impression that the Ukrainian community proposes to respond to increasing pressure from the university bureaucracy by increasing its own control over academia. Thus, academia is stuck between the metaphoric Scylla and Charybdis, essentially verifying the deterioration of the principle of academic autonomy.

Lubomyr Luciuk reacts to this situation with rhetorical questions: "Are we here to please the *hromada*? Are we here *for* the community?...Or are we, as academics, possessed of the academic freedom to study whatever we want?" (84). The answers to these questions can vary, of course, especially when one considers the dual nature of the humanities between science and art. The response of each successive generation of intellectuals probably varies depending on the context. The explosive development of social media only exacerbates the problematic relations between "town and gown." The conference participants are unanimous in supporting the necessity of paying more attention to social media. But in this chorus, for example, Paul Robert Magocsi is more reminiscent of the classic academic scholar in his or her ivory tower, while Yaroslav Hrytsak rather evokes the classic dichotomy of citizen-poet, who nowadays can be recognized as a "public intellectual." Understandably, in this case not only generational differences but also the specific socio-political situation with the "Ukrainian question" predicates different concepts about the role of scholars in society.

What is the vision of Ukraine as seen from the Ukrainian-Canadian perspective? The image of a captive nation heroically struggling for centuries for its independence is classic for a multitude of nationalisms. In the case of Ukraine, it was shared by all waves of Ukrainian émigrés. Again, understandably, during the years of the Cold War it was the ethno-cultural concept of the Ukrainian nation that prevailed over the territorial-political one—to such an extent that it was espoused not only by the "third-wave" Ukrainian immigrants but also by the Ukrainian Canadians, who were conscious of the need to preserve their own identity. Thus, in contrast to the former contingent, whose loyalties were Ukraine-oriented, in the latter community they had to contend from time to time with a question of priority: what was more important, Canada or Ukraine?

After the collapse of the USSR and emergence of an independent Ukraine, the priority issue concerning community policy on Ukrainian studies came to the fore with renewed urgency. Energies expended on Ukraine were eroded and gave way to disappointment, while increased threats were felt vis-à-vis the Ukrainian-Canadian community as a result of assimilation processes and federal government changes to Canadian identity policy. These problems were not specifically discussed during the conference, but traces of exchanges on relevant topics can be found in presentations on establishing foundations and endowments (Olga Kuplowska, David Marples) and on institutional Ukrainian studies networks that have resulted from such initiatives in Canada and the USA (Nadia Jacyk).

It is no accident when Paul Robert Magocsi concludes that "at an organizational level, our field has not only reached its realistic limits but has gone beyond them" (26). The practice of creating a broad network of small institutions and Ukrainian studies programs which inevitably must struggle to maintain their existence—and compete among themselves—was roundly criticized by the Ukrainian Canadian businessman and philanthropist Peter Jacyk forty years ago, but little has changed since then. The money that has been spent by Ukrainian donors on small programs would together have been more than enough to establish a full-fledged university, like the U of A's Campus Saint-Jean or the Canadian Mennonite University. In Winnipeg such a project came close to implementation, but the plans remained unfulfilled. The same can be said about Ukraine, since the community's dealings with Ukrainian studies there are sometimes governed by the personal ambitions of local leaders, as well as by the purchasing power of the Canadian dollar over the Ukrainian hryvnia, rather than by academic priorities.

In lieu of conclusions

In sum, did the conference provide answers to the questions posed by the organizers? Perhaps these published proceedings will generate contradictory perspectives, somewhat like the "glass half-full, glass half-empty" scenario. Some will say that Ukrainian studies are in a cyclical downturn, waiting for new people, new ideas, and new funding. Others may interpret this conference as a farewell to the generation that established Ukrainian studies in Canada in its current incarnation. Still others will realize that they have in their hands a primary source for a first-class history of Ukrainian studies in the West during the last forty years. In my opinion, the conference proceedings reflect the true state of the field of Ukrainian studies in Canada. Even the absence of certain people and the tacit treatment of certain problems provide food for thought. For these reasons we decided to publish the conference proceedings in the form of transcripts, which convey the lively atmosphere of the presentations and discussions.

The proceedings of the CIUS 40th Anniversary Conference show that Ukrainian studies in Canada can indeed look forward to the future, and also that the field is greatly dependent on the Canadian and international contexts. On the one hand, in the past four decades the field of Ukrainian studies has amassed solid institutional, intellectual, and financial capital where there was none before. On the other hand, this capital sometimes looks quite inert and tends to stagnate. Further, on the one hand recent events in Ukraine and their consequences have created a favourable political climate for the development of Ukrainian studies. But on the other hand, negative developments on university campuses are threatening to nullify any progress. To my mind, the biggest threats to Ukrainian studies are not insufficient funds (there is never enough money) or even comparatively low enrolment (it was never really high) but the overall deterioration in the professional academic standards of university education.

In Ukrainian studies there is no lack of innovative thinkers or fresh ideas. They try to persuade us regarding the significant advantages of new centres and programs over institutions, such as CIUS, that were formed during a completely different period and have difficulty changing their structure and academic priorities. New scholarly projects very often take place not thanks to but in spite of the dominant policy trends of stakeholders in this field—that is, politicians, mainstream academia, and the community. Referencing the conference title, we could say that the academic Ukrainian *text* has a good dynamic and positive development prospects, while its political, institutional, and socio-cultural *contexts* leave something to be desired.

Moreover, at an individual level Ukrainianists in the West are wholly prepared to meet challenges such as new paradigms, social media, and interdisciplinarity. However, our organizations have perennially lacked the broad consolidation required to jointly defend our professional rights and corporate interests. As Paul Robert Magocsi remarks, "Consolidation, even retrenchment—not expansion—would seem to be the appropriate approach for Ukrainian studies in North America" (26). But the potential basis for such a consolidation appears illusory. The International Association for Ukrainian Studies—established, as we know, at the time of the USSR's collapse—is today "more dead than alive…hopeless," according to Yaroslav Hrytsak (69). The Canadian Association for Ukrainian Studies (CAUS),[7] officially constituted in 2002, was largely ignored during the conference. One can hardly wonder that proposals to create new structures like consortiums, an institute of institutes, or a "community of communities" are met with skepticism.

The future prospects of Ukrainian studies in Canada depend to a large degree on their flexibility and openness to intellectual innovation, and also on their capability to expand their intellectual horizons—"to focus on where Ukraine can shed light on some other issues…to develop courses other than courses *on* Ukraine, but *with* Ukraine…" (Martha Bohachevsky-Chomiak, 47), to apply "a global-minded approach to teaching about Ukraine" (Serhy Yekelchyk, 58), and to "integrate Ukrainian studies into the humanities" (David Marples, 61). Of course, one cannot deny the necessity of maintaining continuity with the legacy projects that put Canada on the map of global Ukrainian and East European studies.[8] However, in the future the influence of Ukrainian-Canadian studies (as part of Canadian studies), as well as Ukrainian diaspora studies (as part of global diaspora studies), on Ukrainian studies in general could be more pronounced.

Finally, whether we like it or not, Ukrainian studies in Canada will continue to be seen as the domain of the Ukrainian community—at least in the eyes of the local political and academic establishment. This means that Ukrainian studies are, and will be, at the periphery of the Canadian academic mainstream. One need only recall how few scholars from other disciplines and faculties at the University of Alberta felt it worth their while to come to the conference and participate in the broader debates that went beyond the Ukrainian framework.

Today the centre of gravity of Ukrainian studies is in Ukraine, which since the country's independence in 1991 has gradually developed its infrastructure, fostered a favourable social milieu, acquired a sensitivity to context, and cultivated a political demand for a national narrative. To be sure, academia in Ukraine still needs funding from the West in order to survive in the post-Soviet reality. However, it no longer beholds Ukrainian studies in the West as a revelation. Today, we must heed the words of Yaroslav Hrytsak: "Ukraine and Ukrainian scholars—I am talking about Ukrainian scholars *in* Ukraine, definitely—have to start speaking in their own voice" (68).

Dramatic events engulfed CIUS after the conference, revealing the depth and the scope of the problems within the "Ukrainian studies-University-Community" triangle. They have seriously affected projects already underway, as well as our plans for future development. To some extent, this explains why the path of the proceedings of the conference from transcription to publication was so long. Nevertheless, concerning the complexity of the work required, I would like to give credit to Halyna Klid for book and cover design and layout; to Ksenia Maryniak for compiling the footnotes and index and selecting the pull-out quotes, and to Oleksandr Pankieiev for producing the online edition as well as the archival video recordings. I believe readers will be satisfied with this text, which allows us to continue the discussion on Ukrainian studies in Canada.

Volodymyr Kravchenko
CIUS Director
University of Alberta, June 2017

7 An autonomous affiliate of the Canadian Association of Slavists (CAS, est. 1954).

8 Including CIUS's *Encyclopedia of Ukraine*, edited by Volodymyr Kubijovyč (vols 1–2) and Danylo Husar Struk (vols 3–5; Toronto 1984–93), now online at www.encyclopediaofukraine.com.

His Excellency Andriy SHEVCHENKO

Ambassador of Ukraine to Canada

Director Kravchenko and distinguished guests, it is a great honour for my wife, Hanna, and me to be at this very special event. It is meaningful in many ways.

Firstly, it is a great opportunity to show respect and thank several generations of scholars who have done so much to make the Canadian Institute of Ukrainian Studies the leading Ukrainian academic institution in the Western hemisphere. Thank you so much for what has been done in these forty years!

Secondly, this event is an important moment during which to celebrate the wonderful co-operation that made this institute's existence possible and fostered its success.

The Institute started as a very successful joint initiative of the Ukrainian-Canadian community and the government of Alberta. It shows us the results we can achieve together when the Ukrainian-Canadian community, which has made such a wonderful contribution to this great country, the government, and academia work shoulder-to-shoulder. When we have visionary leaders, when we have people who take responsibility, this is the wonderful result that we can achieve together.

Thirdly, it is also a meaningful opportunity to rethink what the field of Ukrainian studies is and contemplate what it can be.

As we witness the geopolitical drama in and around Ukraine, it becomes clear that Ukraine's experience is providing very crucial and important keys to understanding the future. If we understand Ukraine and what Ukrainians are going through, we can better understand the direction in which the world is travelling, why empires collapse, even the last of them, why nations survive, and what helps them survive.

> *"It is also a meaningful opportunity to rethink what the field of Ukrainian studies is, and contemplate what it can be."*

Siohodni—velyke sviato, tse sviato Pokrovy Presviatoï Bohorodytsi,[9] and as many of you know, in Ukraine we celebrate this holiday as the day when we pay our respects to the warriors, our defenders. It is fair to say that today our thoughts and prayers are with those who physically defend Ukraine and the free world in the east of Ukraine. However, in a broader sense, all of you are defenders of Ukraine because you are defending our identity; you are defending our mind and soul, and again, it is a great honour to see such a wonderful mix of individuals who have been doing so much in this field because, at the end of the day, this is what we fight for. Thank you very much for helping us assert the right to choose our own destiny.

On behalf of Ukraine, I would like to congratulate the Canadian Institute of Ukrainian Studies and all those associated with this institution, and I wish all of us a productive conference. ■

9 "Today is a major holy day, the Feast of the Protection of the Most Holy Mother of God."

Hon. Linda DUNCAN

Member of Parliament for Edmonton-Strathcona

Good morning, *dobryi den'*. In the eight years that I have been the Member of Parliament for this area, I have spent much time with my wonderful Ukrainian-Canadian friends. I am looking forward to maybe being an honorary Ukrainian Canadian, because I love the community so much.

Your Excellency Ambassador Shevchenko, it is always nice to have you here in Canada, and we know that we hold him dear because of the time that he spent here in Edmonton with the terrific newspaper that comes out of here.[10] Former Ambassador [Fraser] and Dr. Kravchenko, thank you so much, Associate Vice-President Hamilton, Dean Cormack, Bishop Borys, and all the Ukrainian scholars.

When I went over what the Institute has done for forty years, it is profound. That takes more than dedication; it takes a real dedication to the heart. You know, not only have you built an incredible institution here at my alma mater, the University of Alberta, you have inspired the development of scholarship in Ukrainian studies across Canada and around the world, and equally important, the relationship between Canada and Ukraine.

Having had the privilege now of visiting Ukraine four times, and in particular the time that I spent with Ukrainian interns,[11] I think some of the most important learning experience that we can offer in Canada to Ukraine is the hands-on experience of Ukrainian youth, or post-doctoral Ukrainian students, coming to Canada, spending time in our legislature and parliament, and spending time with you here, furthering research, sharing ideas, and then taking those back.

I know with absolute certainty of the young Ukrainians who have come to Parliament Hill to participate in our program, that they have gone back fully charged with determination to build the rule of law and democratic reform and are digging into research. I know that one young fellow I met in a human rights organization is struggling to preserve the archives of the Holodomor.[12] So, nothing could be more important than this Institute, and that all levels of government and the university continue to support it.

Scholarship is important, but I think that we also need to be making sure that in all fields of study, in film, in literature, more people of Ukrainian descent are encouraged to write and produce in those areas so that others can know the richness of the history of the Ukrainian people. I have met with some of the young Ukrainians who have been doing films at the front, and it is heartbreaking, but it is so powerful to bring my colleagues to those viewings, to see first-hand what is going on, to cut through the propaganda.

“You have inspired the development of scholarship in Ukrainian studies across Canada and around the world.”

I know that on Parliament Hill, we continue to be there for the Ukrainians as they fight to retain Ukraine. There have been so many changes in the eight years since I was elected, witnessing the tragedy that is going on there. But Canada needs to stand firm, and I know that you can count on the House of Commons to be there, including supporting scholarship. ■

10 *Ukraïns'ki visti / Ukrainian News* (www.newpathway.ca).

11 Canada-Ukraine Parliamentary Program (hosted at www.katedra.org).

12 See www.memorialholodomor.org.ua and www.holodomor.ca.

Dr. Susan HAMILTON

Associate Vice-President Research, on behalf of President David Turpin, University of Alberta

Ambassador Shevchenko, Honourable Linda Duncan, Professor Kravchenko, and my dean, Lesley Cormack, distinguished guests. My name is Susan Hamilton, and I am the Associate Vice-President of Research here at the University of Alberta. I am very pleased to bring greetings on behalf of our president, Dr. David Turpin. We honour and celebrate the Canadian Institute of Ukrainian Studies as one of the most important institutes here at the University of Alberta. Turning forty is quite an achievement, I say, on the other side of that number, and I should note that CIUS has now been in existence for more than a third of the history of the University of Alberta.

The government of this province gives the U of A the authority to develop, manage, and operate programs for cultural advancement. We take that responsibility very seriously. Resources are allocated only when we see both demonstrated need and broad academic support for the creation of a new centre or an institute. Creating and managing a large, complex institute like this one takes a dedicated team of academics, staff, students, and community champions. CIUS is so fortunate to have had champions from the Ukrainian community from its very early days, people like Manoly Lupul and Peter Savaryn, whose names appear all through the founding documents of this institute.

Our own institutional plan, "For the Public Good," reaffirms and recharges many of the efforts by our exceptional centres and institutes like CIUS. When we look at the strategic goals of that document, we can see specific ways in which CIUS is well positioned to continue to excel in the future. Our document says that we will build a diverse, inclusive community of exceptional students, faculty, and staff from Alberta, Canada, and the world, and CIUS can help us with that. Our document says that we will engage communities across our campuses, our city, our region, the province, the nation, the world to create reciprocal, mutually beneficial learning experiences, research projects, partnerships, and collaborations. We can see that broad academic and community representation right here today in this room.

A very recent strategic review of this Institute praised its international reputation as one of the strongest sites for Ukrainian studies and community outreach in the world. Looking forward to the next forty years, we can see great potential to build and engage for the public good, and hopefully also for the Ukrainian good. In closing, I would like to say *mnohaia lita* to CIUS. Wishing you many, many more years of success. ■

"Our own institutional plan, "For the Public Good," reaffirms and recharges many of the efforts by our exceptional centres and institutes like CIUS. When we look at the strategic goals of that document, we can see specific ways in which CIUS is well positioned to continue to excel in the future."

Dr. Lesley
CORMACK

Dean,
Faculty of Arts,
University of Alberta

Dobryi den'. I am aware that I am the person who is standing between you and the actual work of this conference, so I will try to be brief. I do want to say that I am so pleased to be a part of this special day and this special conference, honouring one of our top research institutes at the University of Alberta.

The Canadian Institute of Ukrainian Studies is truly a jewel within our Faculty of Arts, and within the wider university, and I think in fact what makes it a jewel is that it doesn't belong to the Faculty of Arts or to the University of Alberta: It belongs to you, to the community, to the international world.

> *The Canadian Institute of Ukrainian Studies is truly a jewel within our Faculty of Arts, and ... what makes it part of that jewel is that it doesn't belong to the Faculty of Arts or to the University of Alberta: It belongs to you, to the community, to the international world.*

For forty years, CIUS has been leading the way in Ukrainian and Ukrainian-Canadian scholarship, something that I think is vital as Canada continues to evolve into an increasingly multicultural society, and as we welcome new generations of Ukrainian Canadians. Although CIUS has only been in the Faculty of Arts since 2011, I'm very proud that such a nationally and internationally recognized centre is attached to our faculty.

As you have already heard, CIUS has been a powerhouse of historical research over its first forty years, and of course there is much more to come in the next forty years. You have already heard Dr. Kravchenko talk about the *Encyclopedia of Ukraine*, which is now online.[8] We have had a number of important research projects, such as the Mykhailo Hrushevsky classic ten-volume *History of Ukraine-Rus'*.[13] These are just two of CIUS's projects that have made vital contributions to an understanding of Ukrainian history and culture.

However, the time is exactly right for us to think about the next steps. What can CIUS do that will move the conversation on, that will make Ukrainian studies even more important in Canada, in the world, that will make an intervention for good in a situation that is so volatile and so important? We heard some conversation that maybe we need to think about teaching, which I think is probably a very interesting idea. Dr. Kravchenko and I have talked about the idea of summer schools for our students to go to Ukraine to learn the language, to learn the culture, to be in internships or projects in Ukraine. I think this could be a very exciting initiative that our students would be very interested in.

I have also been pleased to see—and would encourage CIUS to continue—good research that makes interventions in events of the day and helps governments make decisions about what they need to do. I think those are going to be important as well. CIUS has been a leader, both in research and in its strong connections to the wider Ukrainian community, not only in Edmonton but also nationally and internationally. Of course, this work could not be possible without the generosity of our donors.

One of the strengths of CIUS has been the large number of people, over many, many years, who have supported CIUS through their work and their advocacy, but also through their hard-earned finances, and so I want to give a heartfelt thank-you to all our donors—especially those in the room today but also to those who have given over the years—for placing your trust in CIUS and for your

13 Annotated translation produced by CIUS's Peter Jacyk Centre for Ukrainian Historical Research and published by CIUS Press (www.ciuspress.com).

> *I have also been pleased to see—and would encourage CIUS to continue—good research that makes interventions in events of the day and helps governments make decisions about what they need to do.*

continued commitment to its important work. Of course, I also extend my thanks to the staff and faculty of CIUS, both past and present, because there are many of you here, and many of you in the ether as well: congratulations. You should be extremely proud of the fruits of your labours. I wish you continued success over the next forty years, and much beyond that. ■

VOLODYMYR KRAVCHENKO:

Now I am delighted and honoured to give the floor to Bishop Borys, eparch of the Ukrainian Greek Catholic Eparchy of Paris. He is a well-known historian who is published internationally and is the author of numerous scholarly works. Eparch Borys was awarded the National Order of the Legion of Honour of France and the Ukrainian Award for Service (a governmental award of the second and third degree granted by the Ukrainian president, Viktor Yushchenko), as well as the Antonovych Prize and the Order for Intellectual Courage.

Dr. Borys GUDZIAK

BISHOP BORYS (GUDZIAK), president of the Ukrainian Catholic University and a historian active in higher education reform, is today engaged primarily in pastoral and community leadership. He serves as bishop of the Paris Eparchy of St. Volodymyr the Great for France, Switzerland, and Benelux and as head of the Department of External Church Relations of the Ukrainian Greek Catholic Church. He studied biology and philosophy at Syracuse University and theology at the Urbaniana University in Rome while living in the circle of Patriarch Josyf Slipyj. He received a doctorate in Slavic and Byzantine Cultural History from Harvard University. In 1992 he moved to Ukraine, where he founded the Institute of Church History in Lviv and later served as rector of the Ukrainian Catholic University. Bishop Borys is the author of numerous scholarly works, among them *Crisis and Reform: The Kyivan Metropolitanate, the Patriarchate of Constantinople, and the Genesis of the Union of Brest* (1998).

Texts and contexts: The global framework of Ukrainian studies

Professor Kravchenko, I want first of all to thank you for this invitation, which was a complete surprise for me. The process began earlier, but when I was appointed a bishop in Paris, it finally reached its culmination. I had become a scholar *déclassé*, and to be invited to speak at a scholarly conference before my teachers, my colleagues, my friends, our donors, and community leaders who were already great when I was a toddler is a very great privilege and pleasure for me, and I thank you for this invitation.

I greet all the dignitaries from the university, the provincial political leaders. In a special way, I would like to salute Peter Savaryn, who is one of those leaders I saw as a child in the newspapers that my parents subscribed to, and who was so instrumental in the development of Ukrainian studies at the University of Alberta.

I would also like, in a special way, to mention the directors. I think we all are aware of the unique opportunity that we can have at least four of the directors—Manoly Lupul, Frank Sysyn, Zenon Kohut, and Volodymyr Kravchenko—here with us. I do not know if it is going to happen again. I hope it does. I hope that there will be a meeting of the five, and I hope I can be there, but I think that is not very likely.

At this time of celebrating a fortieth anniversary, we should remind ourselves of some of the context for Ukrainian studies in the modern period, which helps us understand how important the Canadian Institute of Ukrainian Studies is in a much broader context—how much it has served for social justice, for the recognition of the dignity of people, for giving people the wings of their language, their literature, their history, their identity.

Most Ukrainians in the middle of the nineteenth century were in Ukraine; there were very few emigrants. And in the first half of the century, most of them were serfs. They did not have freedom and dignity, they did not own their life, they could not move freely, they could not read or write. The abolition of serfdom in the Austrian Empire and then in the Russian Empire, the latter happening only in 1861, shows us how long the Ukrainians did not have basic human rights. We cannot even imagine it today. That is why Shevchenko is so prominent in our legacy—someone who emerged from that impossible situation to paint, to write, to speak the myths and legends of the people, to read their moral history. This occurred in the absence of institutions, with the legal prohibition of institutional life in fact, of the very language—we remember the Valuev Circular of 1863, which said that there *is* no "Little Russian" language, there *was* no "Little Russian" language, and there *can never be* a "Little Russian" language. It was followed by the Ems Ukase of 1876, which forbade all publishing in Ukrainian; this prohibition lasted until 1905.

This was the time when the great North American universities were taking off—the end of the nineteenth century and beginning of the twentieth. This great institution [the University of Alberta] was founded, as I understand, in 1908. At the same time, Ukrainians were forbidden to use their language in print, and most Ukrainians were illiterate.

Ukrainian studies have not emerged in modern times as a purely academic discipline. One of the themes pervading the subsequent century, and now a century and a half, of history of Ukrainian studies, is the theme of *Art for Art's Sake*—really pursuing objective research and science, as it was framed in the time of a prevailing positivistic mindset—*and* a very immediate sense of need to be with the marginalized people, the poor, the oppressed, whose language was taken away, whose literature was negated, whose history was stolen.

These are passionate words, but it is that passion that was behind the development of Ukrainian studies through institutions like the Shevchenko Scientific Society,[14] created in 1873 in Galicia as a language and literature organization: "Let us speak, let us have our word!" With its reorganization in 1893, having no state, no nation, and no government budget, a veritable academy of sciences was created, including not only the humanities—literature, language, history, philology—but also the social sciences, mathematics, and natural sciences. This happened without government support, as Ukrainians were a third-class people in the Austrian Empire, one rung below the Poles—who were, after all, themselves lorded over by the Austrians.

> *I am proud to say that I think in many of our places of study and research, people in Ukrainian studies set standards for other scholars.*

The short period of Ukrainian independence at the time of World War I opened new possibilities for Ukrainian studies, which had a period of development even in the Soviet Ukrainian Republic in the 1920s. But this was soon crushed most brutally, during a period in which Ukraine was the most dangerous place on the globe: when the famine, the Holodomor, was perpetrated, and when, with World War I, the purges, and World War II, between ten and fifteen million Ukrainians were killed or lost their lives in an unnatural way. In Western Ukraine, outside the Soviet Union, in the newly reconstituted Polish state, various efforts were made by the Ukrainians to foster, develop, and begin again the study of their identity. An underground university existed from 1921 to 1925 in Lviv, and the Ukrainian Free University, first in Vienna, then in Prague, and later in Germany, now settled in Munich. In Lviv, Metropolitan Andrei (Sheptytsky) in 1928 founded the Lviv Theological Academy, which was to become a Ukrainian university but could only do so three generations later.

14 www.ntsh.org.

Many of our founders and scholars, including some here present, were raised in a context in which these factors were a part of the Ukrainian consciousness. These were the issues, these were the challenges, this was the history—and there was a hope for free study, to be yourself, to know your heritage, to speak your language, to write your poetry, to develop your own philosophy. After the cataclysms of World War II, which brought many more immigrants from Ukraine to the Western world, many people who now had educations, people who had institutional academic experience, the Ukrainian community strengthened its commitment to scholarship on Ukraine. The émigré Shevchenko Scientific Society,[15] the Ukrainian Free Academy of Sciences,[16] the Bound Brook centre for the Orthodox community,[17] the Ukrainian Catholic University established in 1963 by Patriarch Joseph (Josyf Slipyj)[18]—all were examples of this commitment.

In speaking of Ukrainian studies in North America, allow me also to speak from a very personal experience. I grew up in the home of a Ukrainian studies donor. Not only a donor but a fundraiser. My father would go house to house in Syracuse to raise money for the Ukrainian Studies Chair Fund. I distinctly remember as a teenager when Adrian Slywotzky, now the world-famous business guru, came to our house as a Harvard law student to push the campaign for Ukrainian studies in Syracuse, New York.

It was also as a teenager that I met Patriarch Joseph and, still as a teenager, went to Rome to live and study with him at a university that at that time had eleven students. We were too young not to believe what he told us. He said, "You have to work for the change. It will come. Evil will not prevail. The Soviet system will fall. You have to develop Ukrainian ecclesiastical scholarship, theology. I am signing you up for the Lviv Archeparchy." It was like becoming a seminarian

15 In the USA since 1948 (www.shevchenko.org) and in Canada since 1949 (www.ntsh.ca), coordinated since 1955 by a Supreme Council that reunited with the revived organization in the homeland following Ukraine's independence.

16 Ukrainian Academy of Arts and Sciences (www.uvan.org; Ukrainian acronym: UVAN).

17 In South Bound Brook and Somerset, New Jersey; see www.uocofusa.org and www.ukrhec.org.

18 Today the Pope Saint Clement Institute in Rome (www.rome.ucu.edu.ua).

for an eparchy on the moon. You could not go there. I was refused a visa. But in this little community—which was presided over by a man who walked straight out of the Bible, as those of you who remember Josyf Slipyj and his visage can attest—we had the great privilege of serving cocktails to the different scholars and professors in Ukrainian studies the world over who came to pay homage to the Patriarch. It was a school in itself.

And one of the people I met in Rome—actually it was in St. Peter's Square, through the mediation of Vasyl Markus—was Omeljan Pritsak as he was coming out of the apostolic palaces, where he had just had an audience with John Paul II. Many at Harvard would hear the stories of Professor Pritsak, and when he said, "You know, I went to communion at the Pope's mass," people would say, "Yes, Professor Pritsak had his first Holy Communion." But there I met the man who encouraged me to come and do graduate work at Harvard. I said I wanted to do a Master's, and he said, "Come, come." When I came, I found out there was no Master's program in the humanities at Harvard. I said, "I don't really know how to apply, you know, I have a degree in biology, another in philosophy, I am finishing a degree in theology, I have no undergraduate degree in Slavic studies." "That's all right." "Can you review my application?" "Yes, yes, just apply." The old school was not concerned with bureaucracy but was guided by a passion for study, for teaching, for research, and so I came and visited and met with Ihor Ševčenko. Those of you who remember him can imagine: the conversation ended with the words *"Pane Gudziak, shkoda shcho vy ne pravoslavni."*[19] [Laughter.]

I emerged bewildered after a conversation with Horace Lunt, who said, "You know, you really should go to Vienna for what you are interested in." And then I met Frank Sysyn, who took me under his wing, and took me to lunch, and started to explain the ways of this world. It was all there, incredible standards: Pritsak, who read sixty languages and did not think you were finished until you were approaching his standards. Ihor Ševčenko, who would say to a graduate student in a seminar, "You know, Mr. So-and-So"—it wasn't actually to me, because I was not old enough—"You know, by your age, Byron was already dead. [Laughter.] What have you accomplished?" An émigré who grew up speaking Ukrainian and Russian, in Warsaw, in a French lyceum, who studied in Prague—Nazi Prague, German-occupied Prague—speaking perfect German and Czech, who did a second doctorate in Brussels, in French, spoke perfect Italian, and who knew Greek probably better than any person on earth, if you take it from Homer to *demotiki*, picking up some Turkish and Arabic along the way. The standards in Ukrainian studies were high, and the vision was broad. From the Huns to Byzantium, from literature to numismatics, from demographic studies to minute linguistic detail—I am proud to say that I think in many of our places of study and research, people in Ukrainian studies set standards for other scholars in the number of languages they knew, in the number of points of view they could understand, and in the hard work they had to put in to overcome the biases. You always had to be better if you wanted to make Ukrainian studies part of the scholarly mainstream. During our conference, many of you who know this much better than I will detail the achievements, the books, the research projects; you will describe the study programs that embrace so many students and people, members of the community.

I would like to say a few words on how Ukrainian studies in North America, Ukrainian studies in Canada, Ukrainian studies at this university have had a global impact. Volodymyr Kravchenko already mentioned how the histories written here in Canada by Orest Subtelny, Paul Robert Magocsi, the different publications of this Institute, the project at the Jacyk Centre headed by Frank Sysyn, the exchanges organized at the Institute under Zenon Kohut, how they galvanized Ukrainian studies in Ukraine. I do not think Volodymyr Kravchenko would be in Edmonton if it were not for almost two decades of co-operation of Edmonton with Kharkiv, something that was supported by donors who were not scholars but had an intuition, had a largeness of heart. Yaroslav Hrytsak came to this Institute—was it 1989 or 1990?—and read Ivan Lysiak Rudnytsky. He [Rudnytsky] was one of the early stars here, in Edmonton, who had emerged out of a strong centre, *seredovyshche*, in Philadelphia, whose essays on Ukrainian history have become a methodological manual for a whole generation of scholars. But it was the Canadian Institute of Ukrainian Studies that brought Yaroslav Hrytsak here, opened up this legacy to him, and he then opened it up to the rest of Ukraine.

The work in folklore, the work in Ukrainian dance, the teaching of Ukrainian language and literature—something

19 "Mr. Gudziak, it is too bad you are not Orthodox."

that emerges out of that sense of mission, the desire for dignity, the need for social justice. No other institution outside Ukraine taught Ukrainian language as much as this university. And that became part and parcel of the program of multiculturalism, of which Canada can be proud, a program that can be a model for other countries at a time when the rhetoric of Trump attracts millions. When the populism spawned by fear and hatred extends from the Philippines to Poland, teaching Ukrainian language has a meaning besides the number of students that are in the classroom. This sense of mission, this dedication to real, critical scholarship was a source of great inspiration for scholars in Ukraine in the late eighties and after Ukrainian independence in 1991.

> *I venture to say ... ten years ago, there was no place that had such a sophisticated community of Ukrainian historians as the University of Alberta—scholars of the early modern period, the modern period, the Soviet period, and contemporary history who are second to none.*

Few were the scholars in Ukraine who had access to your publications before *perestroika*, but even they had a glimmer of hope, knowing that somewhere at the end of this ideological tunnel—which in many ways was a continuation of the prohibitions of the nineteenth century, which were themselves a continuation of the serfdom, the slavery—a glimmer of hope that you could have free scholarship, that you could think freely, speak freely, that you could name things and people by their names, recognizing their God-given dignity. Those of us who had the privilege to travel to the Soviet Union and meet these scholars will never forget those images. From Yaroslav Dashkevych I heard how, in his little home in Lviv, which was not well heated, when visited by Omeljan Pritsak, they both just crawled into bed, covered themselves with quilts, and kept talking. It was very romantic, it was dangerous, but Ukrainian scholarship was on a mission.

Ukrainian studies had a true cause. So much in terms of methodology, so much in memory was brought or returned to Ukraine through the work of the Canadian Institute of Ukrainian Studies, through the chairs in Toronto, the professorships occupied by specialists in Ukrainian studies all over North America, through the Fulbright Program led by, among others, Martha Bohachevsky-Chomiak.[20] We worked very hard. The institutes that emerged in North America were first spurred by students who in the 1950s started saying, "We need institutionalization. Only through our presence in the establishment will our language, literature, and history gain full respect." Omeljan Pritsak's proposal in the 1960s to create three chairs and an institute at Harvard, which happened in the late 1960s and early 1970s, was followed by the initiative here. In some ways, maybe Harvard legitimized the notion that was taken to a new level in a province, in a country where Ukrainians had a profile, a presence, some political clout. At that time, the global network and the relationships were strengthened. The gradual completion of the Ukrainian encyclopedia project in Sarcelles in the mid-eighties was followed by the translation of the encyclopedia into English in Toronto. Sarcelles is part of my pastoral mandate. Those of you who know what it is, I would like to call upon you to save Sarcelles, at least the archive there.

Building on the *bursy*[21] that the Ukrainian community established in Saskatoon, Winnipeg, and Edmonton, scholars and students together established communities of Ukrainian studies, the study of language. The policy of multiculturalism created the bilingual schools that fed into the undergraduate programs, and the undergraduate programs fed into a top-notch PhD program—here, at the University of Alberta.

I venture to say, maybe it could be an exaggeration, but ten years ago there was no place that had such a sophisticated community of Ukrainian historians as the University of Alberta; scholars of the early modern period, the modern period, the Soviet period, and contemporary history, second to none. These programs, created in Canada, became a place to which PhDs flocked from other places. They found jobs at a time when the job market was very difficult. My colleagues from Harvard—Victor Ostapchuk, Maxim Tarnawsky, Uliana Pasicznyk, Olya Andriievska [Olga Andriewsky], Roman Koropeckyj, and others that I might fail to mention—all came to Canada and continued this

20 www.fulbright.org.ua.

21 *Bursa*: boarding school.

marathon. These achievements, this sense of community mission, this sense of responsibility to the community needs to be recognized and cherished.

One of the most beautiful aspects of Ukrainian studies is the relationships that are developed. In 1988 I went, as the only American PhD student at the time, to Ukraine for a six-month internship, and I was placed in a dormitory on Lomonosova [street in Kyiv], where already there was a colleague whom I did not yet know, Bohdan Klid, resident in this dorm. I had the privilege to be a witness at his wedding, and then he and Halyna took great care of me. I did not have anything but a teapot for six months. We would go to the so-called milk bars, *molochni bary*, where everything was white, and you had a sense that it could be clean, whether the milk, the cheese, or the *manna kasha*.[22] And then one time, I remember, it was the second anniversary of the Chornobyl disaster, I was followed from a demonstration by the KGB, and unfortunately, I had just received a few volumes of underground literature from Lviv that I was to deliver to Moscow, and I was pretty scared. I did not come home, I did not come back to the dorm for a day or two, and when I finally returned, Bohdan and Halyna embraced me, and Halyna said, *"My vzhe pytaly, chy ne postupyv iakyis' amerykanets' v morh."* They had been checking the morgues already to see if I had not perished somewhere. A great solidarity, in a context that cannot be, and hopefully will not be, recreated.

A few years later, in 1993, already after independence, during the second international congress of the International Association for Ukrainian Studies, a big enthusiastic celebration was being held in Lviv for our little Institute of Church History, the cornerstone for the revival of the Theological Academy and, later, the creation of the Ukrainian Catholic University. And Frank Sysyn, Olya Andriievska, and Mark Von Hagen brought me, to Lviv, by plane, paper plates and paper cups for this gala event hosting three hundred people. These are little details of the connections, the willingness to help, to serve, to accompany, to be in solidarity, because there was a sense of cause, there was a sense of mission. Now, not all the time, in all situations, were we on a high moral level. There was some nasty competition once in a while, a bit of backbiting, some devious deeds. Maybe an anniversary is a time to forgive, to be grateful for the solidarity that we have enjoyed, but also to recognize where we did not use to the utmost the opportunities that we have had, to say "I'm sorry."

I also want to say "thank you," in a special way, to the donors. Peter and Doris Kule have been so generous to this university.[23] And without them the Institute of Eastern Christian Studies[24] would be unthinkable. Peter and Nadia Jacyk have established programs that are bringing the best of scholarship to the attention of the broader English-speaking world. The translation of the Hrushevsky *magnum opus*[13] is only one aspect. The co-operation with historians in Lviv is touching the lives of so many young people. Jim Temerty, who is not here, with the Ukrainian Jewish Encounter[25] and the Holodomor Research and Education Consortium, is really making waves. I have already mentioned the program in Kharkiv sponsored by the Kowalsky family. There are many, many other donors, many generous people. How moving it is to remember the lists at the end of the individual volumes of the *Encyclopedia of Ukraine*![26] Do you remember those, in the Ukrainian version? Three dollars, five dollars from Edmonton, fifteen dollars from Shenandoah…At Harvard, the administration was floored. Never in the history of Harvard University was a chair endowed by so many donors. It was American oligarchs who endowed chairs, not the widow with her mite, not the factory worker who was semi-literate. These are the people who have stood behind us for the last decades.

Today I hope many of you will raise the questions on how to go forward. We are heirs of a great legacy. You are creators of a great legacy. We have received, in this history, many indications, signposts, the inspiration to work together, realizing that it is not just academic. It needs to follow the rules of the academy, it needs to be real, critical in dialogue and in discussion, but it also needs to serve. When we remember that our Ukrainian studies make a difference in the world, we get great energy. Today Ukraine is in a

22 Cream of wheat.

23 *Champions of Philanthropy: Peter and Doris Kule and Their Endowments*, edited by S. Cipko and N. Kononenko (Edmonton 2009).

24 Metropolitan Andrey Sheptytsky Institute of Eastern Christian Studies (www.sheptytskyinstitute.ca).

25 www.ukrainianjewishencounter.org

26 *Entsyklopediia ukraïnoznavstva*, a project of the Shevchenko Scientific Society, published by Molode Zyttia [Zhyttia] as vol. 1 (3 books, Munich–New York 1949–52), edited by Volodymyr Kubijovyč [Kubiiovych] and Zenon Kuzela [Kuzelia], and vol. 2 *Slovnykova chastyna* (10 books, Paris–New York 1955–84; book 11, suppl edn, Paris–New York 1995), ed. Kubijovyč.

geopolitical hotspot. There is a war in Ukraine, and today we are saluting those who are dying in this moment on the front, defending the dignity and freedom of the Western world. But the greatest war is a war of information. There is a hybrid war that is being conducted through falsification of history, of sociology, of politics, and it is only through good scholarship disseminated by students, by the media, by political structures that this hybrid war can be won. Again today we are reminded about the crucial importance of our vocation. What a privilege to be here to celebrate the fortieth anniversary of the Canadian Institute of Ukrainian Studies at the University of Alberta. What a privilege it is to serve together. Let us go forward again. ■

SERHII PLOKHII

Moderator, Harvard Ukrainian Research Institute

SERHII PLOKHII is the Mykhailo S. Hrushevs'kyi Professor of Ukrainian History and director of the Ukrainian Research Institute at Harvard University. A leading authority on the region, he has published extensively in English, Ukrainian, and Russian. Plokhii is the author of several influential monographs, including *Yalta: The Price of Peace* (2010), *The Last Empire: The Final Days of the Soviet Union* (2014), and *The Gates of Europe: A History of Ukraine* (2015). His books have won numerous prizes and awards, including the Lionel Gelber Prize for best English-language book on international relations, Pushkin House Book Prize (London), Antonovych Foundation Award, Ambassador of New Europe Prize (Poland), and Historia Nova Prize (Russia).

The first round table is on the foundations of the Institute and on Ukrainian studies in North America in general. My name is Serhii Plokhii, and I am the director of the Harvard Ukrainian Research Institute. I spent approximately fifteen years here, some of the best years of my life, at CIUS and the University of Alberta, and I am really very happy to be back for this marvellous event, for this conference.

I would like to start with greetings from my colleagues at the Harvard Ukrainian Research Institute to the university, the Canadian Institute of Ukrainian Studies, numerous associates, colleagues, and friends of the Institute. We are really very proud to be a sister institution, in a certain way, of CIUS.

The way CIUS was founded has very distinct Alberta roots, and Ukrainian studies started to develop here even before the founding of the Institute. But while having distinct Alberta roots from the very inception, CIUS was also an all-Canadian enterprise. The two major centres of studies and research and teaching were located here in Edmonton, in Alberta, and also at the University of Toronto with Professors George S.N. Luckyj and Danylo Husar Struk, who played an active part in putting the program together and making the Institute work.

> *The way CIUS was founded has very distinct Alberta roots, and Ukrainian studies started to develop here even before the founding of the Institute. But ... from the very inception, CIUS was also an all-Canadian enterprise.*

If you think about Ukrainian studies in North America, CIUS has not just an all-Canadian mandate but also an all-American mandate. This mandate is especially clear and obvious today, when you look at the participants of today's conference and this panel in particular. Close relationships have been established between Ukrainian studies at Harvard and those here, at the University of Alberta, in terms of concepts, ideas, division of labour, and also in terms of the exchange of cadres and people going back and forth across the Canadian-American border. This brings me to the point that was already made very eloquently by Bishop Gudziak about the vision that the Ukrainian diaspora had developed for Ukrainian studies and for university studies in general. Indeed, it was an all-American—and, in many senses, an all-Ukrainian—undertaking that brought together not only North America but also Europe and, in particular, Britain. Ukrainian studies in Britain—starting of course with Bohdan Krawchenko and represented today by Taras Kuzio (the commentator for this round table) and by Rory Finnin from Cambridge University, whom we are really happy to welcome here—stress that the global connections were there from the very beginning.

The vision of the CIUS founders was to transform Western scholarship about Ukraine. It also transformed the community by making a very important leap from the émigré institutions, like the Shevchenko Scientific Society[15] and the Free Academy of Sciences,[16] to Western academia. It helped to bring Ukrainian expertise, interests, and scholarship to the universities and to start the research and study of Ukraine at the university level.

I want to say that it was not just Ukrainian studies that benefited from coming to Western and North American universities but also the universities themselves that benefited enormously from that development.

I have at the same time an easy and a difficult task of introducing people today on the panel, in the sense that these are people who need no introduction. I just want to stress that they all have not just Albertan ties but also a global reach and global academic credentials.

The founder and first director of the Institute: Professor Manoly Lupul. Professor Lupul got his PhD at Harvard, and I also understand that you [Lupul] were one of the donors to the Orthodox church to which my family and I belong [St. Andrew Ukrainian Orthodox Church of Boston]. Even though CIUS was not conceived in terms of direct ties or connection with Harvard, that connection emerged with time and is certainly there for historians to study.

Bohdan Krawchenko, who is on the program but unfortunately will not be able to join us via Skype today, got his doctoral degree and postgraduate education in the UK. Professors Magocsi, Sysyn, and Kohut of course have extremely strong American ties and credentials, coming in one way or another from Harvard, and I already talked about Taras Kuzio, who received his doctoral degree from the University of Birmingham.

Before I invite our first speaker, Professor Lupul, I want to give a general idea of how we are going to proceed. Each of the participants will speak for approximately ten minutes, and afterwards the discussant will have ten minutes to present his questions and views. We will then have thirty minutes for questions from the audience and discussion among the round-table participants, and additional time for public discussion. I was also informed that we have a number of students here who came to Alberta from across Canada, and was asked to positively discriminate in favour of those students, if and when they have questions or comments. That is how we will proceed with our discussion. ■

MANOLY R. LUPUL

Founding CIUS Director, 1976–86

MANOLY R. LUPUL graduated with a BA and a BEd from the University of Alberta (U of A), an MA from the University of Minnesota, and a PhD from Harvard University, specializing in the history, philosophy, and sociology of education with a minor in political studies. Dr. Lupul published two books, including his memoir *The Politics of Multiculturalism*, edited five other books, and contributed numerous chapters and articles in books and scholarly journals. At the U of A he was the founding director (1976–86) of the Canadian Institute of Ukrainian Studies; to assist CIUS he co-established the Canadian Foundation for Ukrainian Studies in 1975. Lupul was an executive member of the Canadian Consultative Council on Multiculturalism (1973–79), and as a delegate of the Ukrainian Canadian Committee he wrote and presented a brief to the Joint Parliamentary Committee on the Canadian Constitution (1980). He also played a large role in the establishment of the Ukrainian bilingual education programs in Edmonton's two school systems. For his scholarly and community work, Professor Lupul was awarded the Order of Canada in 2003.

About the foundations of the Canadian Institute of Ukrainian Studies

I have entitled this talk "About the foundations of the Canadian Institute of Ukrainian Studies" because it is not the whole story by any means.

In April 1970, the Royal Commission on Bilingualism and Biculturalism recommended "university studies in the humanities and the social sciences related to languages other than English and French." The other fifteen recommendations, many again in education, practically begged for implementation once a federal policy of multiculturalism was enacted. The Commission was the federal government's response to Quebec's Quiet Revolution, which had insisted that the Québécois were not a people like the others, faced as they were with the steady erosion of their language and culture. This really aroused the organized Ukrainian-Canadian community, which declared that we too are not a people like the others, being rapidly assimilated in Canada and deliberately Russified in the hermetically sealed Soviet Union.

In the spring of 1970, the Ukrainian Canadian Students' Union, SUSK, obtained a federal grant for several field workers to press the ethnic communities to agitate for a federal policy of multiculturalism. One of the field workers somehow found me, and I was gently persuaded to participate in a multicultural conference at the University of Alberta in August 1970, followed immediately by another one, a SUSK conference at St. Andrew's College, University of Manitoba. Under its then-president Bohdan Krawchenko, SUSK was a dynamic organization, politically sophisticated, with media smarts, and quite brazen in tight situations. Most students were second-generation youths from the postwar Ukrainian emigration, some quite interested in Ukrainian studies.

To match their enthusiasm, I contacted the Ukrainian Canadian Professional and Business (P & B) Club[27]—a more effective political pressure group, I thought, to push for a policy of multiculturalism than the largely émigré-led Ukrainian Canadian Committee of that time. The P & B membership was largely Canadian-born, a few were politically active, and a good number were even rich. In Edmonton, almost immediately I became an *ex officio* member of the club's executive and attended its and the members' monthly meetings for the next ten years. In the process, the Ukrainian Canadian Professional and Business Federation was revived, and I even became its president for two years, 1973 to 1975.

In October 1971, the pressure, mainly by Ukrainians, paid off when the federal government introduced its policy of multiculturalism within a bilingual English-French framework, and provincial governments followed suit, especially on the prairies and in Ontario.

It was quickly evident that neither the P & B clubs nor their federation had any specific cultural or ideological identity. In 1973, our federation executive in Edmonton decided to tie the professional and business sector to education. We would build, we said, a national educational ladder out of the Ukrainian kindergartens already underway in Edmonton's public and separate schools, followed by the anticipated English-Ukrainian bilingual classes at the elementary school level and the Ukrainian classes already in place at the secondary level. The ladder was to be capped by a research and publication institute of Ukrainian studies at the university, the entire ladder hopefully to be fully funded by government.

With Peter Savaryn's political help, in July 1976 the provincially funded institute came into being. Peter, who was part of our federation executive, had been a member of the university's board of governors since 1972. He was prominent in the community and in the Progressive Conservative Party then in power, earning "brownie points" and political IOUs that eventually catapulted him into the chancellorship of the University of Alberta's Senate. His phone calls were returned by those in the corridors of power, and he was a very good man to know.

Far more important for our purposes than any of CIUS's earlier relationships within the university, or with the Harvard Ukrainian Research Institute, or Soviet Ukraine, was the future of Ukrainian studies in Canada. One could note, however, that despite the initial open hostility of the deans of the Faculty of Arts and of the Faculty of Graduate Studies and Research, the university president, Harry Gunning, and the two chairs of the all-important Academic Development Committee, Henry Kreisel and his successor, Myer Horowitz, all favoured the Federation's proposal for an institute and ensured its viability when it counted most. In drawing up the proposal, I saw CIUS and the bilingual classes as the first step in institutionalizing multiculturalism, similar to the institutionalized French-English bilingualism then being created by the federal government. As I put it in my memoirs on CIUS's first decade:

> To me, multiculturalism meant broadening the ethnic base of Canada's mainstream institutions [...] and at least in public education; the implication was quite clear. The English-Ukrainian bilingual classes, begun in September 1974, and the Institute were both visible, public manifestations of the Ukrainian fact in Canada. If the other ethnic groups did not wish to accompany the French Canadians into the country's public institutions, that was their affair. For me, the larger the Ukrainian presence became, the better, for that ensured the kind of professional or *quality* institutions and results that alone could impress and engage the Canadian-born of Ukrainian ancestry. The latter had to acquire an objective understanding of their circumstances in Canada, in the interest of both an enlightened multiculturalism and an appreciation of Ukraine's unfortunate fate as a politically submerged nation.

In the new multiculturalism, the song and dance, the colourful costumes, and the ethnic cuisine of the past—the cultural pluralism hitherto favoured by most Canadians—

27 Today the UCPBA (Ukrainian Canadian Professional and Business Association, www.ucpba.ca).

was not enough. What was needed was the lifting of the Ukrainian cultural agenda into the state's schools and the state's universities, to mention no other public institutions. Unfortunately, however, once the bilingual classes, the Institute, and other Ukrainian studies centres—the Chair at the University of Toronto, and similar positions elsewhere—came into being, the Ukrainian community appeared to fall asleep. The sheer success seemingly made further activism unnecessary. Yet in the 1990s, and in subsequent years, much quickly changed, with all the new developments but one affecting the Ukrainian community negatively.

The one positive event was of course the collapse of the dreadful Soviet Union and the birth of a free and independent Ukraine. Among the negatives, however, was, first, the rise of the ethnically hostile neo-conservative political movement, most evident in Preston Manning's Reform Party, whose sustained attacks on state funding of multiculturalism led to the demise of official multicultural policies and programs. Second, immigration from the Third World moved the social and political needle from a concern with ethnic diversity to how best to accommodate the new religious and racial diversity. Third, the Ukrainian Canadian Professional and Business Federation, and such formerly large clubs as that in Edmonton, collapsed. Fourth, the English-Ukrainian bilingual classes in Edmonton's public schools simply disappeared. Fifth, few of the retired or about-to-retire professors in Ukrainian studies were likely to be replaced. Sixth, university courses were limping or disappearing altogether because of an apparent lack of interest and low enrolments.

Now, what role did the academics in Ukrainian studies play in all this? Well, certainly the situation in Ukraine received a lot of attention, but as already indicated, for the academy the task was double-barrelled. It was not just to convey a better public appreciation of Ukraine's many difficulties in the enormous task of building a state almost from scratch, it was also to convey an objective understanding of the changing circumstances of Ukrainian group life in Canada. But regarding the latter, the academics were nowhere to be seen. They said nothing publicly about the disastrous impact of the terrible neo-conservative movement on institutionalized multiculturalism, nor did they say anything about the state's movement away from ethnic studies to the new racial and religious challenges; nor did they comment on the collapse of the P & B Federation, or the important future viability of P & B clubs, or the disappearance of the bilingual classes in Edmonton's public schools, or the looming crisis in retaining the hard-won academic gains of the past.

"The task ... was not just to convey a better public appreciation of Ukraine's many difficulties in the enormous task of building a state almost from scratch, it was also to convey an objective understanding of the changing circumstances of Ukrainian group life in Canada."

I know, of course, that academics generally like to be left alone to pursue their specialties, and Ukrainian academics are no different. But just as Ukrainians had earlier insisted that they were not a people like the others, it is also true that as a group, academics in Ukrainian studies are not practitioners like the others. Theirs is a very special constituency because their specialities are on the margin of mainstream university studies—especially in Arts faculties, which themselves have been almost outcasts for at least a decade now, given the economic and political preoccupation with STEM courses (science, technology, engineering, and mathematics).

At the base of the special constituency for academics in Ukrainian studies is of course the Ukrainian community, and for many years now it has not been cultivated much by the academics, either through membership in its organizations or by giving its problems much attention. There are many very able and intelligent professional and business people of Ukrainian background out there who are simply not being reached. Academics in professional Ukrainian studies have not mixed with them, informed them, or advised them, or occasionally even led them when necessary. And to do that well, it is of course as important to be familiar with their cultural and political history, and that of Canadians generally, as it is to understand the usual nuanced maze of mainstream academic culture on Canadian campuses. So how, really, did we end up with such little apparent interest in Ukrainian studies, and this at a time when there is more endowment money for such studies than ever before? What share of the blame must the academic leadership bear? I would insist that the gap between town and gown is largely responsible for the bitter fruit that has brought this very conference into being, and one is left wondering whether it is now even too late to try to close that gap. ■

PAUL ROBERT MAGOCSI
University of Toronto

PAUL ROBERT MAGOCSI is a professor of history and political science at the University of Toronto, where since 1980 he has also held the John Yaremko Chair of Ukrainian Studies. He completed his education at Rutgers University (BA 1966, MA 1967), Princeton University (MA 1969, PhD 1972), and Harvard University (Society of Fellows 1976). Among his publications are 37 books, including *The Shaping of a National Identity: Subcarpathian Rus', 1848–1948* (1978); *Historical Atlas of East Central/Central Europe* (1993, 2002); *A History of Ukraine: The Land and Its Peoples* (1996, 2010); *Ukraine: An Illustrated History* (2007); *This Blessed Land: Crimea and the Crimean Tatars* (2014); and, as co-author, *Jews and Ukrainians: A Thousand Years of Co-Existence* (2016). He is also the editor-in-chief of the *Encyclopedia of Canada's Peoples* (1999) and co-editor and main author of the *Encyclopedia of Rusyn History and Culture* (2002, 2005). Professor Magocsi has taught at Harvard University, the Hebrew University in Jerusalem, and Prešov University in Slovakia, and on five occasions was historian-in-residence at the Max Planck Institute for Social Anthropology in Halle (Germany). In 1996 he was appointed a permanent fellow of the Royal Society of Canada, and has been awarded honorary degrees from Prešov University in Slovakia (2013) and Kamianets-Podilskyi National University in Ukraine (2015).

Ukrainian studies in the West: Challenges of the present, views of the future

For this panel the participants were supplied with a list of questions, which I think is a very good way not just to come up and express whatever comes to mind, which is often the case with academics. Of those nine questions, most of them had to do with the past, and this is in many ways what we were urged to address. But after hearing the opening remarks, I felt it inappropriate to kind of rain on our parade, or snow on our commemoration, and so instead of looking at the past, with some of the unpleasantness that was alluded to, I thought it might be more useful to say something about the future. And actually, it addresses the last of those nine questions that were given to us: How do you see the future of Ukrainian studies in the West?

Now, this question seems to be asked almost by rote every decade or so. It has been addressed at conferences, whether in Canada or the United States, actually for the last forty years. At those conferences or meetings, practitioners of our craft cobble together answers and proposals that are in the end supposed to make us feel that we have been and still are on the right track. You have just heard that I guess we are not. The last of these exercises took place in 2013 in Cambridge, Massachusetts, under the auspices of the Harvard Ukrainian Research Institute, using the antique Roman (or Hollywood) formulation *Quo vadis?* "Where are you going?"

My view about the future has always been based on the challenges of the present, and I would say that those challenges have not changed since the early days of the Harvard experience in the 1970s. My concerns then are my concerns today. In short, we have too many university-based Ukrainian studies centres and have trained too many Ukrainian specialists in North America. Quite simply, we have exceeded what the market can bear.

This was obvious, or should have been already, in the early 1970s. The Harvard program prided itself on creating new cadres of Ukrainian historians and literary specialists with, it seems, little concern for practical reality. In short, where were the members of that first cohort—Subtelny, Sysyn, Hajda, Kohut, Magocsi—to find jobs? In those days there were no positions in Ukrainian history in the United States other than at Harvard. And considering that reality, I remember being somewhat surprised that the inspiration behind Harvard's Ukrainian program, Omeljan Pritsak—a tenured full professor in Turkic languages—himself took up, in 1973, the Mykhailo S. Hrushevs'kyi Professorship of Ukrainian History [at Harvard]. He certainly did not need that position, which was then closed off for several decades to any possible successor among the younger scholars whom he had helped to train. Aside from the self-serving nature of that academic move, neither Pritsak nor his successor in the Hrushevs'kyi Chair, Roman Szporluk, were historians of Ukraine. And neither did much for the field in terms of publications.

The first person to hold the Hrushevs'kyi Chair who has actually done research and published works on topics central to Ukrainian history is the present Harvard incumbent, Serhii Plokhii. Despite the absence of any employment future in their field of choice, Harvard continued to accept and train a second generation of specialists, not only in Ukrainian history but also in Ukrainian literature. And then, when the reality of joblessness sank in, and when, by the 1990s, North American applicants were fewer and fewer, Harvard and its sister institutions in Canada (Toronto and Alberta) began to accept graduate students from Ukraine. Most of them were desperate to experience life in North America; most never finished the rigours of the PhD process, left academia, and often were fated to lead a precarious economic existence in either Canada or the United States.

> *Why should Ukrainian studies have two institutes and several endowed professorial chairs in history, literature, language, and ethnography? At an organizational level, our field has not only reached its realistic limits but has gone beyond them.*

Now while Harvard, Toronto, and Alberta produced a fair number of newly minted PhDs in history and literature, these often talented young scholars added a further strain to the competition for the few jobs available in Ukrainian studies. Fortunately for the first cohort of Ukrainianists trained at Harvard in the 1970s and 1980s, there was a safety valve, a saving grace: Canada.

With no job prospects in the United States, many flocked to Canada, with the result that Harvard products took up some of the leading Ukrainian-related academic positions at the University of Toronto and the University of Alberta. However, that rather fortunate fate for those individuals did not change the long-term reality, and one must face that reality.

Despite the Orange Revolution, the *Maidan*, and Russia's invasion and continued aggression, Ukraine is never likely to attract a level of interest among North American university students that would sustain the several existing Ukrainian research institutes, endowed professorships, and departments that offer courses in Ukrainian-related subjects. Ukraine is not France, Germany, Italy, or Russia. Ukraine is more like Spain or Portugal or Sweden, and I ask: where in North America is there a university-based institute for the study of Spain, or of Portugal, or of Sweden? Are not those countries and their civilizations at least as historically important as Ukraine? Now, in that context we might ask: Why should Ukrainian studies have two institutes and several endowed professorial chairs in history, literature, language, and ethnography? At an organizational level, our field has not only reached its realistic limits but has gone beyond them. Consolidation, even retrenchment, not expansion, would seem to be the appropriate approach for Ukrainian studies in North America.

Having said that, Ukraine does remain a little-known or misunderstood country in today's world. Politically inspired propaganda from Russia has only contributed to the distorted view of Ukraine that seems to dominate public awareness in many parts of Europe and North America. It is also a reality that has not gone away. How, then, to correct this situation? If we remember what I just said before, what I am now about to say might sound like a blatant contradiction. But let us fantasize.

We need yet another Ukrainian institution—academically inspired but not necessarily university-based. What I have in mind is something that could be called an international centre for the study of Ukraine, to be comprised of five research institutes, each devoted to an aspect of Ukraine that has never been properly addressed, if at all, outside Ukraine. Those institutes would focus on five areas: Ukrainian statehood, the peoples of Ukraine, the religions (plural) of Ukraine, the art of Ukraine, and the music of Ukraine.

Since Ukraine is a state, should not the origins, evolution, and future of that state be a topic for research, public debate, and proposals for its proper functioning? Hence, an institute for the study of Ukrainian statehood. Since Ukraine is a multinational country, should not peoples other than ethnic Ukrainians be studied and given a voice in the country's political and social discourse? Hence, an institute for the study of the peoples of Ukraine.

As for religious life, Ukraine's citizens are not only Eastern Christians, Greek Catholics and Orthodox but also Protestants, Roman Catholics, Muslims, about whom we know little, if anything. Hence, an institute for the study of the religions of Ukraine.

Ukrainian arts do not consist only of folk embroidery and pottery. The country's painters and sculptors have been part of general European development, or in the case of the early twentieth-century avant-garde, they set the standards that the rest of Europe followed.

As for music, Ukraine is not only a land of folk songs and dances but also produced first-rate orchestral and operatic composers in the nineteenth and twentieth centuries who, alas, are virtually unknown to the outside world. Hence, an institute for the study of the music of Ukraine.

A body such as this proposed institute, an International Institute for the Study of Ukraine, would not only provide a base for scholars to carry out their research and publications but would also provide the mechanisms to preserve and promote, through exhibits and recordings, the artistic and musical heritage still hidden from the rest of the world. Ukraine is a real country, with a rich political, ethnic, religious, artistic, and musical culture. These are the elements that should become the face of Ukraine to the rest of the world. Fantasies, intellectual or otherwise, are fine. To be realized, they need concrete funds. These I have not yet found, but perhaps someone after me will take up this challenge. ■

FRANK SYSYN
CIUS

FRANK SYSYN is the director of the Peter Jacyk Centre for Ukrainian Historical Research at the Canadian Institute of Ukrainian Studies and editor-in-chief of CIUS's Hrushevsky Translation Project. He is a co-editor of *Culture, Nation and Identity: The Ukrainian-Russian Encounter (1600–1945)* (2003) and author of *Between Poland and Ukraine: The Dilemma of Adam Kysil, 1600–1653* (1985) and *Mykhailo Hrushevsky: Historian and National Awakener* (2001). He graduated from Princeton University (1968), the University of London (1969), and Harvard University (PhD 1976), taught at Harvard University (1976–85), and was an associate director of the Harvard Ukrainian Research Institute (1985–88). He served as acting director of CIUS in 1991–93 and currently serves as head of its Toronto Office.

Legitimizing Ukrainian studies in the US—Canadian contrasts—Pivot to Ukraine

As my predecessors have turned to the future, and there is going to be much to discuss about their presentations as well as subsequent ones, I will, for this purpose, stick to the past and two specific times in Ukrainian studies that come out of my own experience—that is, when I was involved and eventually wound up as a graduate student and junior faculty member at Harvard, during the time of the formation of the Ukrainian Research Institute there, and the initial period when I came to CIUS between 1990 and 1993.

My first topic is what I will call "Legitimizing Ukrainian studies in the US." This topic has already been mentioned earlier in our presentations, but I think it is essential for understanding what the Harvard Institute meant and what that project brought about. I would like to start with the role of émigré scholarly institutions. I think we have a tendency to rush ahead to the universities and mainstreaming into North American academia, and sometimes forget how great their contribution was.

In the New York metropolitan area, where I grew up, during the 1950s and 1960s the Ukrainian Academy of Arts and Sciences (UVAN) was formed, the Shevchenko Scientific Society was re-established in the US,[15] and the Bound Brook Center was built,[17] whose church was a memorial to the Holodomor (or the *Great Famine*, as we called it). I would add one more institution associated with the emigration (but I think chiefly funded by the CIA), and that was Prolog.[28] By the time I came into this field in the mid-1960s, there was a vibrant Ukrainian intellectual academic life going on because of these institutions. They provided a counter-narrative to most of what academia was doing. They certainly were institutions that were reaching out to the academic world. Not only did Prolog put out the *Digest of the Soviet Ukrainian Press* in English, but UVAN was able to put out the *Annals of the Ukrainian Academy of Arts and Sciences in the United States*, which for that period produced much of the valuable literature in English. I propose in our discussion we talk about that émigré phase and what it meant. I think

28 Prolog Research and Publishing Association (est. 1953 in New York).

it would be a valuable topic.

Academically, Ukrainian studies in the US and in Canada developed very differently. Ukrainian language and literature were taught at the University of Saskatchewan starting in the 1940s, and they already had a place here in Canada. The existence of a large number of people virtually not speaking English in the Canadian West around 1900 meant that small Ukrainian-English dictionaries were published in Canada around the First World War, and the University of Saskatchewan already published a major academic dictionary in 1955.[29] In Canada, the society, government, and academia had to be aware that Ukrainian was a language, because they had to deal with the Ukrainian community—this was much less so in the US, where Ukrainian studies there were largely Sovietology in political science departments. We think of the early-phase professors—Adams, Armstrong, Sullivant, Reshetar, Bilinsky—putting out their books, and research on Ukraine could find a place as long as it fit in Sovietology.

> *"In 1970, I believe, Franklin Ford, dean of Harvard, writes to Omeljan Pritsak. I have that letter, which says, "We are amazed at how you have shown that Ukrainian studies are a way of understanding world history and world affairs. You have shown that it is not a narrow field.""*

I remind you that "Soviet history" largely did not exist in the 1950s and 1960s in history departments: almost everywhere courses on the Soviet Union was taught in political science or government departments. It would move to history departments only later, especially when Soviet archives were opened to some Western scholars. Even in my own career as a Princeton undergraduate, I wrote a thesis at the Woodrow Wilson School of Public and International Affairs, with an advisor from sociology, on the contemporary Ukrainian intelligentsia of the 1950s and 1960s. Ukraine therefore had found a place in social sciences, but had a much more difficult time finding a place in history departments. It would have been much harder for me to go to Cyril Black or James Billington, our professors of history, as an undergraduate with a historical topic. It is true that Bob Magocsi was able to work on a Ukrainian topic as a graduate student, though he dealt with the Habsburg Empire and Transcarpathia, but I still maintain that history as a field was more resistant to Ukrainian topics. This in part explains the model that Omeljan Pritsak came up with to meet the needs of Ukrainian legitimization in North America, that is, the formation of what might be called a "traditional" research agenda.

The history, language, and literature initiative came about—at least by urban legend, and I am trying to verify this—because around the mid-1950s Ukrainian students at New York University asked that the Ukrainian language be taught. The then-Russian (I assume, if not Slavic) Department said that "we teach languages, not dialects." This was the stimulus for the Ukrainian Student Society in New York to begin the so-called *"Fond katedr ukraïnoznavstva"* (Ukrainian Studies Chair Fund). Now, I do not know if this account is accurate—I do not sell this as necessarily true, yet it does convey attitudinally the situation at that time—but as we know, it was SUSTA[30] and the student *hromady* that began the *koliada*[31] campaign. By the mid-1960s they raised $250,000, largely to form what they saw as a needed chair in Ukrainian studies that would give Ukrainian subjects some recognition.

It was at this time, when George Shevelov was at Columbia, that the endowment might have gone there, but as we know, for a number of reasons it did not. At that time, I believe a chair at Columbia cost $900,000, and one at Harvard $600,000; Harvard was a bargain in those days. But really it was Omeljan Pritsak and his proposals—which were definitely for a European research institute, three traditional chairs, in many ways meeting both the pattern of the Shevchenko Scientific Society, where he had begun his scholarly career, and the concept of chairs at universities that goes back to Austrian times—that won out. The plan was to have a journal and to carry out research projects. It was evidently not American in its conceptualization; and

29 *Ukrainian-English Dictionary*, compiled by C.H. Andrusyshen and J.N. Krett (Saskatoon 1955; Toronto 1957).

30 Ukrainian acronym for the Federation of Ukrainian Student Organizations of America (www.cycta.org).

31 Student groups raising funds by Christmas carolling at supporters' homes.

at Harvard, because professors in those days particularly had tremendous latitude within the university, he was able in many ways to accomplish this, although it did not fit the model of the American-type regional studies centres terribly well.

But it did have one great success, and one I would bring up. In 1970, I believe, Franklin Ford, the dean of Harvard, writes to Omeljan Pritsak. I have that letter, which states (this is a paraphrase not a direct quote), "We are amazed at how you have shown that Ukrainian studies are a way of understanding world history and world affairs. You have shown that it is not a narrow field."

> *Reading the material from Harvard made Paul Hollingsworth rethink "Kievan Russia" and make it "Kyivan Rus'."*

I might add that one of the things I found very troublesome was that a PhD from this university once wrote that the problem with Ukrainian studies was the existence of the two "ethnic institutes," CIUS and Harvard. I really thought that the Harvard institute, as it was formed, was something to reach far beyond any ethnicity, in the way that both Pritsak and Ihor Ševčenko conceptualized it. Certainly anyone who examines the *Minutes of the Seminar in Ukrainian Studies* published in the 1970s can see what an international array of scholars, in particular from Poland and Israel, participated in the Ukrainian studies initiative at Harvard. Did it have impacts that were important? Yes, I think, many.

Let me give one example. Paul Hollingsworth, who was for some time at Harvard, points out (in an introduction that will be published in volume 2 of Hrushevsky's *History of Ukraine-Rus'*) how in his own career as a graduate student at Berkeley, reading the publications from Harvard made him rethink "Kievan Russia" and understand it as "Kyivan Rus'." There were areas—medieval and early modern studies—where HURI had great impact; certainly the journal[32] did. The Institute also was embedded in an entire world of Ukrainian academics throughout the US and in Canada. There were scores of academics who were associated with Harvard (we could count them up by checking the Ukrainian professors' association numbers); they no longer exist in such numbers. Bob Magocsi has very well described the collapse of the academic market that brought many Ukrainian specialists to Canada. And therefore, in my three minutes left, I will describe my arriving at CIUS in 1990.

I came to CIUS at a point where the Institute had greatly benefited from the official Canadian multiculturalism policy. I arrived in 1991 just as the centennial of the Ukrainian immigration and community in Canada was being celebrated. Because Bohdan Krawchenko, who is not here today, then left immediately on my arrival for a two-year sabbatical and leave of absence in Ukraine, I was the acting director of the Institute. At the Royal Ontario Museum we had a huge Shevchenko lecture in 1991, sponsored by the then very active P & B club,[27] at which William Thorsell got up and basically said, "Forget this multiculturalism nonsense. You know, I spent my life leaving my Alberta Norwegian roots." So it was an interesting moment, because you had the editor of the *Globe and Mail* telling a hometown community that he did not believe in multiculturalism. This was also the year that Prime Minister Brian Mulroney came to Edmonton to address the community for the centennial of immigration, and the Ukrainian community basically made a *fait accompli* by giving him a letter from the Ukrainian government (which CIUS arranged) asking for recognition of Ukraine as an independent state. The action evoked a positive response from a prime minster who saw Ukrainian Canadians as a major political force. This indeed was also a high point of the contact of CIUS with a dynamic, organized community that Professor Lupul discussed. It was a period when a number of grand projects were coming to an end, above all the *Encyclopedia of Ukraine*,[8] in which the Institute was totally involved, including the Edmonton office, where we had to review fifty pages a day of that encyclopedia.

So it was ending a period of what might be called pioneer projects and multiculturalism, but it was a time just after the matching of endowments—and double-matching from the Government of Alberta—when the Institute received a large number of endowments, the largest of them being that of the Jacyk Centre, which brought me here. The Institute was adapting, in a way, to this new source of funding, which proved in the 1990s to be extremely important, above all

32 *Harvard Ukrainian Studies* (www.huri.harvard.edu/pubs/hus).

because when cuts hit the university, the Institute was somewhat cushioned.

What emerged from all this was a period that I will call the "pivot to Ukraine"—that is, in practice, the Institute became very involved with Ukraine, and this shaped it for its future. We had tremendous freedom in those days to work in Ukraine, and we are grateful to the University of Alberta administration of those days, above all the Office of the Vice-president for Research, that they encouraged us to be involved in Ukraine. We opened up a CIUS office in Kyiv. These were times, you remember, when you had to put money in a pocket and take it to Ukraine. There was no way to transfer money. We had to find ways of doing things very rapidly, and we also were able to provide assistance for many institutions. Some of the projects were big successes in those days; we should talk about what it meant for Ukraine. For example, the Jacyk Centre arranged for twenty or thirty historians from Ukraine within two years to go to Warsaw, to work in archives and libraries, and see how normal academia works. We funded the Institute of Historical Research at Lviv University out of the Stelmach endowment,[33] and we also worked closely with eminent scholars such as Professors Yaroslav Dashkevych and Yaroslav Isaievych—which made, in some ways, Lviv a centre of our activity. I will discuss later whether this was a good strategy; I think it was. We also witnessed the arrival of Serhii Plokhii in Edmonton, who was our link to Ukraine for those years, from then on for the next fifteen. Coming from the then Dnipropetrovsk, he brought us another Ukraine, what was then Eastern and now may be Central Ukraine. And we had new projects, such as the Hrushevsky project,[13] that were no longer carried out in isolation from scholars in Ukraine. The Ukrainian community responded to our initiatives, establishing many new endowments for our work in Ukraine, the largest of which being the Michael and Daria Kowalsky Fund to support projects in Eastern Ukraine.

If the institutes in both Harvard and CIUS had become international in outreach earlier, they became Ukraine-connected in this period. I cannot picture how we would have put out the Hrushevsky volumes without our Ukrainian colleagues; it has been a wonderful symbiosis. I was just at a Hrushevsky conference in Kyiv, and I was told that editors in Kyiv will be using our English version as a model for a new edition of Hrushevsky's original *Istoriia Ukraïny-Rusy* in Ukrainian. That is, all the work we have done on bibliographies, footnotes, and new material is now going to be put to use there in the new edition. The period of the early 1990s was one in which Ukrainian studies changed because of Ukrainian independence. This was a period when we acquired new constituencies, both government and media, and encountered new opportunities but also new demands on the Institute, some of which it had problems meeting while others it met quite well, down to the twenty-first century. ■

33 Institute of Historical Research (IHR) at the Ivan Franko National University of Lviv, founded in 1992 thanks to an endowment established in 1989 by Petro and Ivanna Stelmach of Mississauga, Ontario.

ZENON KOHUT

CIUS Director, 1994–2012

ZENON E. KOHUT is a professor emeritus of history at the University of Alberta and a former director of the Canadian Institute of Ukrainian Studies (1994–2012). He specializes in the history of Ukraine, Ukrainian-Russian relations, and questions of early-modern political culture and identity. Dr. Kohut is the author of *Russian Centralism and Ukrainian Autonomy: Imperial Absorption of the Hetmanate* (1988; Ukrainian translation 1996), *Korinnia identychnosty: Studiï z rann'omodernoï ta modernoï istoriï Ukraïny* (2004), and *Making Ukraine: Studies on Political Culture, Historical Narrative, and Identity* (2011), and co-author of the *Historical Dictionary of Ukraine* (2005, 2013).

My early career and the development of Ukrainian studies

I am also going to follow the instructions I received and talk entirely about the past, and particularly about the interplay between the diaspora institutions' life and the development of Ukrainian studies. I am going to use my own career as an example of how these things evolved. There is an interplay, and it should illustrate many of the points brought out—again, both the problems of doing Ukrainian studies, as well as to what extent the community was an asset in developing these studies.

Like many of my colleagues, I grew up in two parallel universes: the Ukrainian and American, which became linked and intertwined. I grew up in Philadelphia, in a Ukrainian family. My parents were not part of some intelligentsia; my father was a cabinetmaker, and my mother was a seamstress and homemaker. No one in my family had any university education. I participated in the usual community activities in Philadelphia, and that included Ukrainian Saturday school, Plast,[34] endless concerts, commemorations, *akademiï*, and so on.

At the same time, I went to American schools, I had American friends, I attended American sports events, concerts, and so on. So you really live in two parallel universes all the time. I went to college locally, La Salle College, now La Salle University. It was a feeder school for the Catholic school system in Philadelphia, but, like many of these small Catholic colleges, it provided a surprisingly good basic liberal arts education. La Salle had a second plus. Like many of the small colleges, it absorbed some of the many European academics displaced after World War II who could not get employment in the major universities. At La Salle they had John Lukacs, a Hungarian who was writing a book a year and became quite famous, actually; and, more importantly for me, Ivan Lysiak Rudnytsky, who of course subsequently taught here, at U of A. By the time I graduated from La Salle, there was an additional large contingent of Ukrainian professors: Leonid Rudnytzky in literature, Miroslav Labunka in history, Eugene Lashchyk in philosophy, and George Perfecky in language.

While these instructors introduced me to new topics and ideas in Ukrainian studies, it was Ivan Lysiak Rudnytsky who introduced me to works in Ukrainian history. I had no Ukrainian courses with him at La Salle because no course ever dealt with Ukraine there, but I took courses in European history [with Ivan Lysiak Rudnytsky], with Lukacs and others. However, Ivan Lysiak Rudnytsky invited me into his home, where for the first time I saw a huge library dedicated to Ukrainian history. He made me his teaching assistant, which was quite unusual in an undergraduate situation, but which really meant that I was grading his other students so he did not have to grade, and I would correct the student exams.

Ivan Rudnytsky also introduced me into a Ukrainian intellectual world in Philadelphia. It hovered around Rudnytsky and Ivan Koropeckyj, an economist at Temple University, and recruited several, I would say, generations of students pursuing graduate studies or trying to become literary figures; among these I would include Wsevolod Isajiw in Toronto, Martha Bohachevsky-Chomiak, Orest Subtelny, Marco Carynnyk, and Sonia Sluzar, who later edited *Problems of Communism*. This Philadelphia core was supplemented with a New York contingent, headed by Vsevolod Holubnychy, the well-known economist, and his wife, and also included Martha Bohachevsky-Chomiak, who was doing her work at Columbia University, and her husband, Rostyslav. They now became sort of New Yorkers, and the link between them was Professor Koropeckyj and his wife, who lived in New Jersey and arranged these parties, soirees, whenever there was some interesting visitor, scholar, some poet, or someone in town, and the guests from New York and Philly would meet halfway in New Jersey in the Koropeckyj household.

> *"I was denied a visa ... it brings out an important point: the ability of the Soviets to shape the field of Russian and Soviet studies in the United States by determining who went and what topics could be studied."*

Now the parallel Ukrainian sort of academic universe in Philadelphia also extended to more formal institutions. In 1963, when I was just starting at La Salle, the Lypynsky East European Research Institute was founded. It was the academic arm of the Ukrainian Hetmanite movement (Pavlo Skoropadsky was briefly hetman of the Ukrainian State in 1918, and supporters of the *Hetmanat* thought that monarchism was the real future of Ukraine). The Institute boasted of having the archive of Hetman Skoropadsky. It also had the papers of its patron, Viacheslav Lypynsky, another very important figure as both a historian and a sociologist but also an ideologist of the Hetmanite movement. Well, Ivan Rudnytsky got me involved in that because he was a monarchist, a Hetmanite. I helped to issue English-language leaflets for that, and through the Lypynsky Institute

34 Ukrainian scouting organization, est. 1912 (www.plast.org).

I also met Professor Jaroslaw Pelenski and Maksym Pyziur, a historian and a political scientist, who would take their summers off and work at the Institute, while teaching at their university during the academic year.

While engaged in the parallel Ukrainian community and academic life, I participated in normal American academic pursuits. After obtaining a Woodrow Wilson Scholarship, I was actually recruited by a number of universities for graduate studies, and for a variety of reasons I chose the University of Pennsylvania, which was also in Philadelphia. At that time, Pennsylvania had two specialists in Russian history, that is, Alexander Riasanovsky for the early period and Alfred J. Rieber for modern Russia. Before I left Penn, we already had Moshe Lewin, who was added for Soviet history, which was coming in as a field just at that time. Also, they had the rather distinguished Czech historian Otakar Odložilík, who was covering East-Central Europe. My progress was normal in course work, general exams, and then came thesis time. In one of my seminars with Rieber, I produced a large work on the beginning of modern Ukrainian political thought in the nineteenth century, and one of the elements of this was the role of Cossack autonomist literature, such as *Istoriia Rusov* and other works. Soon I ended up in eighteenth-century studies, with my thesis on the abolition of Ukrainian autonomy. Somehow Rieber looked favourably on such a topic; maybe he was afraid that with a more modern topic my nationalism would come out. Nevertheless, I was moving on that, but then how could one do this at the University of Pennsylvania, where not a single faculty member knew anything about the topic and the Penn library did not have the resources to support such a research project?

At this time, the Harvard project was just beginning. The chairs were not yet founded, but a program had been initiated by Professor Pritsak. And Professor Rieber allowed me to explore the possibility of engaging Harvard in my research project. At the same time, Professor Pritsak was searching for students, disciples really. You really had to be a disciple of his project, a practitioner of the newly revised Ukrainian studies he was promoting.

With my arrival at Harvard in 1969, I was thrust fully into the Harvard project, from coursework to fundraising. For the first time, I took courses at a university level in Ukrainian history, with Professor Pritsak and, more importantly for me, Professor Oleksander Ohloblyn, who at this time would be the leading authority on Cossack Ukraine anywhere, including Soviet Ukraine. I became first secretary of the seminar in Ukrainian studies held at Harvard University, an editor of its minutes, and then also editor-in-chief of *Recenzija*, a review of Soviet Ukrainian publications, in 1973–74. Those years at Harvard were absolutely formative for me: at Penn I became a historian, but at Harvard I became a historian of Ukraine.

Thus the Harvard project was very important. First of all, it legitimized my research interest and it gave me the wherewithal to pursue it. During this time I was gradually doing my dissertation work. It was proceeding rather slowly because of all the other things I was doing at Harvard, at the initiative of Professor Pritsak. My university was accommodating, even appointing Professor Ohloblyn as an additional thesis advisor, but everything did not work out so smoothly.

As part of my research I was supposed to go to Ukraine on the IREX[35] program and was accepted for this. Two weeks before my trip I was denied a visa to the Soviet Union. I was hardly shocked by this denial, but it brings out an important point: the ability of the Soviets to shape the field of Russian and Soviet studies in the United States by determining who went and what topics could be studied. It was crucial that you have this first-hand experience to be really a legitimate scholar, at least to get to the first tier of universities. Where could you do this kind of research but over there? Combined with the fact that Russian history was saturated by the students of Michael Karpovich of Harvard—who from the late 1940s to the early 1950s produced a whole array of scholars—these two factors also made any breakthrough for Ukrainian studies very problematic.

I will just mention one other thing that is illustrative. I was writing my thesis, producing chapters, and everything was going smoothly. Then, on my fifth chapter (so I was well into my thesis on the Ukrainian reactions and aspirations of the legislative commission of 1767–68, which was Catherine's legislative commission, when various elements of society were asked to write petitions about their needs and desires, and so on), this chapter was suddenly rejected by my thesis committee, and the answer was that Alex Ria-

35 A US non-profit granting agency, the International Research and Exchanges Board (www.irex.org).

sanovsky had grave reservations about it and its "nationalist approach." No examples were given; I was simply told to rewrite the entire chapter. It was a very strange chapter to make a stand on, because it was a highly technical chapter and not a broad, interpretive one. I mean, you had these points, from these people, and they all accumulated and so on. So how to rewrite it? Well, I retyped some pages that had corrective white-out on them (this was the pre-computer age) and handed in exactly the same chapter a year later, and the response from Professor Rieber was that the rewritten chapter was like night and day. [Laughter.] It was clear that Alex Riasanovsky, the scion of a White Russian émigré family, just could not accept what was happening and attempted to slow down, if not stop, the process. I do not know whether he even looked at the rewrite. I will stop now, but it shows you both the problems and the great opportunities that came up with the Harvard Ukrainian Research Institute. ■

SERHII PLOKHII:

We covered a lot of space in terms of the themes, topics, geography, and history of the foundations of Ukrainian studies here at the University of Alberta and in North America in general, and it presents a challenging task for our discussant to comment on all that.

TARAS KUZIO

Discussant, CIUS

TARAS KUZIO received a BA in economics from the University of Sussex, an MA in Soviet and Eastern European studies from the University of London, and a PhD in political science from the University of Birmingham (UK), and was a post-doctoral fellow at the MacMillan Center for International and Area Studies at Yale University. Kuzio is a research associate at CIUS and a non-resident fellow at the Center for Transatlantic Relations, School of Advanced International Studies, Johns Hopkins University. Kuzio has been a consultant to different branches of the US government, including team leader on a USAID assessment in spring 2015 of democracy, governance, and human rights in Ukraine. His most recent books are *Ukraine: Democratization, Corruption and the New Russian Imperialism* (2015) and *Putin's War against Ukraine: Revolution, Nationalism, and Crime* (2017).

Ukrainian studies should change to meet new challenges

This has to be probably one of the most difficult panels I have ever had to discuss, because of the huge variety and because it is difficult to discuss issues of personal memory and history.

There are some common themes, for example, the American influx into Canada, and three of the four speakers are Americans. [In a forthcoming paper titled "On becoming a Ukrainianist,"] Professor Magocsi brings out the point that to be a Ukrainianist in the 1970s–80s, you had to be somebody with a Ukrainian background. It could not be the case that somebody without a Ukrainian background could actually work in Ukrainian studies, which I thought was a very interesting point because it makes it very different from political science, where the majority of people working on Ukraine do not have a Ukrainian background.

I also thought it was interesting, and I think it is a very valid point that Frank Sysyn brought up, about the other institutions we should not forget. I worked for Prolog[28] from the early 1980s until 1991, when the US government money ran out, and I have written an academic article about Prolog. The US government archives about Prolog until the 1970s have been opened. This was an incredible institution in that because it was not tied to Ukrainian diaspora funding, particularly from the nationalist community, it could publish what the Ukrainian diaspora could not. For example, write and publish books on national communism, books on Jewish-Ukrainian relations, on Polish-Ukrainian relations, and there was a great relationship with the very influential and also US government-funded [Instytut Literacki] Kultura publishing house in Paris. Thus, this is a very important topic to bring out, and an area worth researching for young scholars. The range of publications and books produced by Prolog is really astounding. I just interviewed Anatol Kaminsky in Kyiv; he is over ninety now, he is working at the former KGB archives in Kyiv, and he was one of the founding members of Prolog and then went on to head the Ukrainian Service of Radio Liberty—a fascinating individual.

I thought there was also a common theme in the panel that back then, at both the University of Toronto and the University of Alberta nobody was interested in Ukraine.

There was in fact hostility to the idea of creating Ukrainian studies, both here and in Toronto. In Professor Magocsi's paper there are some interesting nuances that include references to two other people on the panel.

Where of course Professor Magocsi [and the Chair of Ukrainian Studies at U of T] stands out—making him different from other Ukrainian studies institutions—is that he was isolated from the Ukrainian diaspora. There were no other organizations. And why that was the case is a separate question we can discuss, but as he points out, he was isolated from the Ukrainian diaspora until about 2007, and he was also taboo in independent Ukraine for about the first two decades. These things changed in the case of Professor Magocsi, from 2007 to about 2011–12, with the publication of his new books.

> *If you want to assist Ukraine today, then assist it in the field of political science, as you helped it in the intellectual development of history writing in Ukraine in the two decades after 1991.*

If we can think of the impact of the Ukrainian diaspora on Ukraine in the 1990s, then Orest Subtelny had a massive impact, particularly because he was there at the right time in the right place, with the publication of his history of Ukraine[36] in Toronto in 1988, and then the Ukrainian and Russian editions were published in Kyiv in 1991 and 1993. Then it was massively reproduced in hundreds of thousands of copies in Ukraine. I remember going to Donetsk in 1994, to the university, and Orest Subtelny's history of Ukraine was being used there.

But the next decade was Magocsi's decade, with the publication of the first edition of his history[37] in 1996. Subsequently the second edition was published, Ukrainian translations, other similar books on Ukrainian history, and the more recent book on the history of the Crimean Tatars.[38] [...] In 2009 I helped to organize a panel of scholars—Dominique Arel (University of Ottawa), Alexander Motyl (Rutgers), and Serhii Plokhii and George Grabowicz (Harvard)—at the St. Vladimir Institute in Toronto. There, as an outsider not from Canada, I saw that the isolation of Magocsi from the Ukrainian community was rather ridiculous, and this, I think, broke the ice. Daria Darewych came up to me after the panel and said, "This should have been done long ago!" Magocsi mentions in his paper that in 2010 I introduced him to Borys Wrzesnewskyj, then a Liberal MP; he was one of those opposed to Magocsi being appointed to the Chair [of Ukrainian Studies] in 1980, and of course by then this was long water under the bridge. Thus, as he puts it in his paper, Magocsi's relationship with the Ukrainian diaspora went from alienation to co-operation and everything in between. But I think there is a fascinating bit in this paper about the whole question of his relation to Ukraine and how that opened up new opportunities. At the same time, there was much suspicion about Magocsi for his interest in Transcarpathia and, of course, the Rusyn movement. It was a very strange thing for me to see how somebody who was ostracized by the Ukrainian community for so long at the same time had attracted a very large number of students, who all have extremely fond memories of his teaching. There had always been a strange dichotomy there.

You are right to point out the changes at Harvard, where Magocsi now finally has a competitor in terms of publishing: Serhii Plokhii. I think we will leave to the discussion the question he raised about whether there are too many Ukrainian institutions today.

Talking about the collapse of the Soviet Union is an interesting factor where I would like to make my comments. Professor Magocsi talks about how the disintegration of the Soviet Union and coming about of an independent Ukraine "changed the rules of the game," finally making Ukrainian studies normalized. Ukrainian scholars in the West could no longer be smug and intellectually superior to scholars in Ukraine. I would agree with that only up to a point, because I think there has been, and Frank Sysyn and others have talked about this, incredible interaction between Ukrainian studies in the West and in Ukraine in various fields, particularly history. If you go to a bookstore, say, in Kyiv, you will see a huge selection of books on Ukrainian history, particularly on the Holodomor, on the 1940s. But that is not the case in political science.

I think it is fair to say that Ukrainian studies did not

36 Subtelny, O. *Ukraine: A History* (Toronto 1988).

37 Magocsi, P.R. *A History of Ukraine* (Toronto 1996).

38 Magocsi, P.R. *This Blessed Land: Crimea and the Crimean Tatars* (Toronto 2014).

become broader and more inclusive after 1991, nor did it bring in political science. This is something I would like to ask Zenon Kohut about, because he was the director during most of the period from 1991. Why was that the case? Why was political science not incorporated into Ukrainian studies?

One understands why it was not part of Ukrainian studies prior to 1991, but why have Ukrainian studies still not included political science since 1991? Of course, there is an exception within the University of Ottawa, opened more recently. We have seen tremendous progress in the field of historical writing in Ukraine, but what we have in political science is practically a disaster zone. Serhiy Kudelia wrote a few years ago that there was no political science discipline in Ukraine. There is not a single political science journal in Ukraine. There were two or three in the 1990s, but today there are none. In fact, of the five weekly political magazines, three are in Russian and two are in Ukrainian. Political science scholars in Ukraine are pretty mediocre, and very few of them get published in the West, unlike historians. There is, I would say, a high level of provincialism, they are inward-looking, and they have very little contact with the Western world. There is a project for us, if we want, to assist with political science in Ukraine—the same as we did with history in Ukraine in the 1990s. Although we have our own problems here: *East/West: Journal of Ukrainian Studies*,[39] for example, has not covered the Crimea or the Donbas, the Ukrainian-Russian war, or the Euromaidan Revolution. I cannot talk about the Harvard journal[32] because the last issue was in 2014. This is important, because one of the functions of Ukrainian studies I remember from that era of the 1970s and 1980s was to create these institutions and combat Russophilia in the West. I remember a leaflet from the Harvard Ukrainian Institute saying, "It is not Russia; it is the Soviet Union. You should not mix the two entities up." Today we have a massive onslaught of Russian propaganda, literally massive, in Vladimir Putin's information warfare. In the last three years, on the Ukraine-Russia crisis, on the war, on the Euromaidan, over three hundred academic articles and think-tank papers, the largest number ever [since 1991], have been published. [...] But the problem is that most of them are written by Russianists, Putinophiles, and others, not really by Ukrainianists; Ukrainian studies are not part of the academic debate on the Ukrainian-Russian war. If you are not part of the debate, you cannot really influence it. An area that is particularly lacking is, of course, the use of social media, which is an important part of Putin's information war. Historians, unlike political scientists, do not really use social media. [...]

Combating provincialism, at a time when you want to escape Russia's influence and you want to join Europe, is very, very important. If you want to assist Ukraine today, then assist it in the field of political science, as you helped it in the intellectual development of history writing in Ukraine in the two decades after 1991. But on Professor Magocsi's idea for an international centre, I think it obviously is a great idea, but such a centre will probably never be established in Canada. The reason for that is, for example, if you were to find a Ukrainian oligarch or Ukrainian oligarchs to fund that, they are interested only in Washington, Brussels, and London, not in Canada. [...] The five different institutes we can debate separately, but certainly there is a need to work in a broader field than that originally envisaged for Ukrainian studies, including combating Russophilia. These are areas that I think Ukrainian studies can and should move into. ■

DISCUSSION

SERHII PLOKHII:

We are now moving into a different stage of our discussion. Our panel was announced as a round table; it has functioned so far as a panel, with presentations and a commentator, and now we will have our moment of the round table. I would ask each of the members of the panel to speak in response to what they heard, and to the comments made by Taras Kuzio.

I also would like to add one more challenge to Ukrainian studies—again, here in Canada, but in general in the world—saying that the project that was started by the founding fathers turned out to be a very successful one for a number of reasons. One of those achievements is that today, if you have a good or even a semi-good article on Ukraine, or a book on Ukraine, you can go into any publishing house, to the most prestigious journal, and publish it there. When the institutes were founded, their publishing arms were created, the journals were created, with the idea

39 Established by CIUS in 2014 as an online journal succeeding the *Journal of Ukrainian Studies* (www.ewjus.com).

that you could not publish Ukrainian research anywhere else because it was not considered respectable scholarship. It has changed now, and this kind of success story poses new questions to the institutes: where are we, what is our function, what is our publishing arm doing, what are our journals doing? Again, that is something that maybe was not mentioned here, and I really would like it to be part of the discussion, in terms of discussion here by the panel but also in questions from the audience.

Back to our round-table mode.

MANOLY LUPUL:

I think it is very significant that the community was not mentioned much or at all in what you heard. This may be because people did not understand what I was saying, or it was irrelevant, I am not sure. In any case, there it is. I would just simply remind everyone that without the community there would have been no CIUS. There are no two ways about it. The community made possible a Ukrainian member on the U of A board of governors that I mentioned. It was the P & B Club[27] in Edmonton that applied pressure, such as it was. I do not know exactly where it was, but there were people from the community in the government, or else these people in the community had worked in the Progressive Conservative Party. And the Institute, I would remind you, was absolutely a political act—in recognition of the fact that there was something called "the Ukrainian fact" in the country, in the province, and they had heard from us. It was not people from Willingdon [Alberta], where I was raised. It was right here in Edmonton, and it was the P & B organization, which had enormous respect—as P & B organizations have, whether they are of Ukrainian background or not, because that is the nature of business and the professional community. They are articulate, they are politically involved quite often, and they also hold power. And believe me, you cannot get things in Ukrainian studies without power in what you might call the mainstream of our culture and institutions.

I know it is difficult to address this when you have panellists who are—I hesitate to say this—perhaps not even Canadian citizens. Nonetheless, this is a fact that we face. People who come here, members of the community elsewhere, somewhere, they know its importance, its significance, and they are to serve it. We have one here too, in Canada as a whole. So why ignore them? You want them to buy your books? You have got to talk to them. You have to advertise it. Take up the issues of Ukraine. They are interested in the issues of Ukraine, let me assure you of that. But they also live here as a group, and they have life as a group, and they have immense problems as a group, trying to make sense of surviving as a group in a society that really marginalized them constantly. So this is all I would say off the top of my head.

PAUL ROBERT MAGOCSI:

By the way, as a citizen of Ukraine—*pardon*, as a citizen of Canada, note that Freudian slip—as a citizen of Canada I am very happy to be not in Edmonton but here in Strathcona, where I understand the University of Alberta is located, and therefore I can become not only a Canadian but also a Strathconian patriot. For those of you who even have sensitivities in that area of differentiation, which some of us really like, a few comments on the basis of what I have heard.

First of all, we were invited here from various parts of the world to a setting that, quite frankly, I do not like. Why do I not like it? From an intellectual point of view, just stop and think about this: the amount of money that has been invested to bring people literally from all over the world, to speak for fifteen minutes. I mean literally. So what can one say in fifteen minutes? One has to be very selective. Actually, in my presentation and even some of the other presentations, there was a lot of commentary about the Ukrainian community in the United States and Canada and their role in making everything possible. I mean, I do not know where this was absent in the presentation. This is a fact, and we all know this.

Also, there was a comment about how after Ukraine came into being as an independent country, that actually courses on Ukraine and interest of students in Ukraine collapsed. Now, this may be the case. It was said here, but it may be somewhat of a myopic view from the standpoint of Strathcona and Edmonton, because I can tell you that this is exactly the opposite of what occurred at the University of Toronto in the 1990s and well into the 2010s. The general course in Ukrainian history had 35 to 40 students every year, which made it one of the largest courses in Ukrainian history anywhere in North America. So much for the alleged collapse. It may be in one part but not necessarily in others, if one is aware of that. Also, interacting with the Ukrainian community: when it is possible, it is done, and it has been done. There was an allusion that Taras Kuzio made to the Chair of Ukrainian Studies and Borys Wrzesnewskyj. We work very closely with James Temerty and are heavily engaged in community affairs.

Another thing: we have been successful in drawing in non-Ukrainian foundations. One of the biggest supporters of the [U of T] Chair of Ukrainian Studies is the Jackman Foundation of Ontario, which is one of the leading philanthropists at the University of Toronto and in the arts generally. There was also a comment that Dr. Kuzio made pertaining to my fantasizing of creating five institutes, and that we should be thinking of political science. Well, this is exactly what the institute of Ukrainian statehood would be concentrating on, and allowing not only talking about the past evolution of Ukrainian statehood but also how it should function at present. This is where political science definitely could become involved.

The other thing about combating Russophilism and discussing what kind of subjects would be used—and one might say, "Why art, and why music?"—this is really the battleground of Russophilism. There is no Ukrainian art and there is no Ukrainian music in the outside world. Where was Malevich from, as one example? And who were some of the other great composers that are all described as Russian? This is literally part of the combat—to show that Ukraine is on the level of any other culture in Europe and not just interested in classic history or folklore. No one knows about this; first and foremost Ukrainians do not, and not only Ukrainians in Canada and the United States but in Ukraine. That is what I would comment in terms of my reaction to some of the things that were said. Thank you.

FRANK SYSYN:

There are many topics, and I will just name a few that I think have been central. First, the role Ukraine and Ukrainian independence played in the development of Ukrainian studies here. I would say that when the Institute of the early 1990s moved towards Ukraine, it was also moving in concert with the Ukrainian community here. It became their major interest, and certainly in terms of the endowments and monies that came in there was great interest in dealing with Ukraine. By now, we face an entirely different issue. The existing Ukrainian community, in both Edmonton and Toronto, includes a prominent fourth wave of immigration that has made a whole new community. The community has shifted in its interest, and Ukraine has played a role in it.

Then there is the issue of the fields we dealt with. One thing that we left out of the presentations—particularly for history but not only, also for most of the social sciences—was the move away from the "national." That is, when we—at least three of us here—began our careers, everyone accepted that national history was a normal field of study. Trends changed, views of nations changed; they affected the way departments are structured and how those studies go. I can give an example from Columbia: the attempt to establish a chair of Polish history has had tremendous difficulties simply because history departments do not want this kind of history anymore, and that has influenced what we have.

Then there is the issue of social sciences, as opposed to what might be called the three "traditional" fields. I think that the turn away from the "national" has also affected sociology, anthropology, and political science particularly. In many areas, when the Soviet political scientist retires at universities, he or she—usually he, it has been—the retirement is not replaced; that is, political science departments moved away from what might be called "area studies." There are exceptions, but that has been a constant problem in continuing the field and supplanting it. There is no one doing anything dealing with that bloc in many places.

One exception, for instance, is the Harriman Institute at Columbia University, which plays a very important part in the development of regional studies. There are, of course, differences between Canada and the US. While in Canada, in many universities, and particularly in the Prairie Provinces, the enrolments and the teaching have declined in numbers, that is not true of the US, and not only because of the community formation. That is, the University of Kansas began a Ukrainian program after Ukrainian independence; last year the University of Texas and the University of Illinois hired lecturers in Ukrainian language. Columbia's interest in Mark Von Hagen's work came partly because Ukraine became independent, but it has taken funding from the Ukrainian community. Not just the Harriman has put money in. I do not wish to exaggerate the increase, but the situation is somewhat better in the US than in Canada.

And finally, what do we do with our definition of Ukrainian studies when, and particularly, people in the social sciences do not tend to concentrate on a single area? Many more people are involved in the field and study Ukraine because they can go there now. You now have Pittsburgh doing anthropology in Ukraine, which you never had before. Zenon brought up the problems of our generation. I was also rejected from the exchange and could not do my thesis research in the Soviet Union. So we did face that, but now you have all these people who do their work in Ukraine, and so suddenly fields like anthropology or sociology have people studying whom they would not have had before Ukrainian independence.

ZENON KOHUT:

I will amplify what Frank has just brought up, since Taras challenged me on that—why did CIUS not develop political science somehow? There are a number of reasons. At the University of Alberta there was no one interested in that, there was no political science department, there were no area studies at all at that time, and I do not think there are even today. All the political science people were doing theories and structures that were supposed to solve problems for any nation anywhere, in a comparative way. You could not even get a discussion going about that.

At the Institute we had David Marples doing research on contemporary Ukraine, so at least we had something. The only way we could encourage political science was to give grants to various political scientists for specific projects, as we did not have the wherewithal to do anything else. I actually was engaged in discussions about perhaps getting some seed money for CIUS for a political scientist. We always had political science in mind in creating any new positions, but new positions were never really created and those discussions went nowhere.

TARAS KUZIO:

Professor Plokhii, the European perspective is actually in some ways more interesting because Britain, since the 1990s, has had three readers on contemporary Ukraine—in London, Birmingham, and Essex—funded by the British government. There was a big wave of creating new positions in areas that were not previously covered when the USSR was around. They were created around 1996–97. But the biggest concentration for the study of contemporary Ukraine is in Warsaw. There are at least ten-plus people working in two or three think tanks in Warsaw who write excellent material, very objective as well, on Ukrainian nationalism.

I would just echo one thing about teaching that Professor Magocsi said. I brought teaching on contemporary Ukraine to the University of Toronto when I arrived in Canada after 2001. I launched courses there in 2002–3. I think Professor Kohut's approach is wrong. One can do things. You do not have to create, for example, a chair or a professorship; you can create lectureships and other areas. My courses were created on the basis of getting small seed money from the Danyliw Foundation and from the Wrzesnewskyj Family Foundation. I had huge numbers of students, undergraduates and graduates, because topics such as NATO, EU, Russia, Ukraine, and the Orange Revolution were attractive, and that was also true at George Washington University, where I taught and had the same kind of numbers.

The question of political science I understand, but how does that excuse the fact that CIUS has published only one book on Ukrainian politics in twenty-five years—Professor Harasymiw's book? One book. You might not have the positions, but why can you not publish the material? And why has the CIUS journal, since 2014, completely ignored what is going on in Ukraine?

QUESTIONS

DEREK FRASER:

I am looking at this question from the point of view of a practitioner, as a former Germanist, Kremlinologist, and Ambassador to Hungary and Ukraine, among other places. I would like to add to Professor Sysyn's remarks about the decline of area studies. It seems to me there is potential for a return to area studies. We have been faced with the problem in the last few years of being made fools of by Putin, by not understanding the Middle East, and being not too sure exactly how to handle China. A good many of those problems can be attributed to the fact that the structure of area knowledge built up during the Cold War has been allowed to decline, and it seems to me that a good case can be made that centres for Ukrainian studies should consider the future requirements of the Canadian government, certainly the Department of Defence, and certainly the Department of Global Affairs. In addition, the Department of Defence used to finance regional strategic centres at various universities. Calgary was a very good example. A case can be made that the Canadian government should have an interest in supporting area studies. And it seems to me that what is required is a certain degree of dialogue between centres of area studies at various universities in Canada and the Canadian government in order to work out the needs of the Canadian government and also of other organizations, such as the press, for experts on certain areas in the world.

DAVID MARPLES:

I would like to make a comment on my own [U of A] Department of History and Classics, and since I am chair now, I have got pretty much a handle over the statistics we have. It has been a fairly pessimistic morning, to be honest, not only with the weather, so I thought maybe I would say something a little positive. We have roughly 60 graduate students, including the classics side as well. Almost one-third of our graduate students are doing MAs or PhDs on either Ukraine, Belarus, or Moldova; and Belarus and Moldova applies to one student each. In other words, just under one-third of our graduate students are working on Ukraine. Most of them are from Ukraine, but there is also a significant contingent of Canadian students. To me, if you look at the balance of the world and Ukraine's place in the world, it is actually far overrepresented among the graduate students, more than any other area. And why is that? It is partly because—with greatest respect—John-Paul Himka began this process of bringing graduate students from Ukraine to Canada. It was continued by me, although I also focus on Belarus as well as Ukraine, and it is continued now by the addition of Heather Coleman, whose recent work has also been based on Ukraine. Between the three of us, we have such an enormous load and are able to fund these students. I think this is a positive development.

BOHDAN KLID:

Just a note about the Institute over the last few years. We have activated a Contemporary Ukrainian Studies Program. Dr. Bohdan Harasymiw headed it until just recently. We held a number of events, one or two in which Dr. Kuzio participated, and of course you know this is one of our areas of priority. In addition, as of 2014 we have also instituted two post-doc fellowships focused on contemporary or modern Ukraine. We also have been working closely with Professor Yaroslav Hrytsak in Lviv on problems of modern Ukraine, and I know that through my work in HREC—the Holodomor Research and Education Consortium—we are working not only on a historical problem, that is, the Holodomor specifically, but also on topics of concern to the contemporary world, and one of them is an upcoming conference on the Holodomor and colonialism. So it is not as black as you paint it.

SERHII PLOKHII:

Maybe it is black and white, or maybe grey.

MARK VON HAGEN:

I am Mark Von Hagen, and I wear a lot of hats. One of them is half in the Political Science Department at Arizona State University—for my sins, I suppose. My other half is, strangely enough, not in history these days but in the School of International Letters and Cultures. But that is another story.

On the topic of political science, I will start with my own example. I gave a talk to my faculty seminar in political science on my own research project, which is about the creation of the Ukrainian state out of World War I and [Russian] Revolution, from 1914 to 1922. The graduate students in international relations came. One junior faculty person who does research on Eastern Europe came. No senior person in any other field, no tenured person, came to my talk. I am used to being ignored by historians because I study Ukraine, but it was even more apparent that political science was not interested in the world outside the United States, and that is part of our "Las Vegas complex" concerning Ukraine ("what happens in Ukraine stays in Ukraine"), which is of course foolish and a delusion.

I will not leave it at my example. My presumed successor, or possible successor, as director of the Melikian Center (Russian, Eurasian, and East European centre at Arizona State) is Sam Green; he currently teaches at King's College, London. He is a political scientist with a British degree from University College London and spent about eight years at the Carnegie Moscow Center studying Russian politics. He came out with a book on the protest movement. For his talk two weeks ago, I was the only person from political science of a senior rank. But for the poor junior person I just mentioned, not a single person came, even though his talk was a very creative adaptation of the field of political psychology from American political science. Arizona State has two specialists on political psychology. Not one of them showed up to his talk. It seems that if you do not do numbers, and if you do not do US politics, you do not attract much attention, and that is too bad for political science.

When I was at Harriman a couple of weeks ago for their 70th anniversary (another anniversary we can talk about), I spoke with Alex Cooley, a political scientist, who said he has given up on trying to get his colleagues in political science to care about Central and Eastern Europe, because political scientists care about numbers. They do not care about peoples, they do not care about their cultures. You are blaming the victim, I think, in some sort of way, because political science has abandoned *us*; it is not that we have abandoned political science. I started as an undergraduate at Georgetown in international relations. I read political science, or what was then called "government and politics," and international politics, and now I really find it difficult to read anything that my political science colleagues write because it is all about numbers and graphs and charts, and very little to do with the real world and real-world problems. But the situation in the social sciences is such that "Putin is not Russia": political science is not social science. Thank goodness we have anthropologists and sociologists, who were mentioned, who are doing wonderful work, who still believe in talking to people, who still believe in listening to their stories, who still believe in studying their languages and cultures—and they can be our allies until political science comes back from wherever it landed, an area of almost irrelevance. I have my own theory about this: that political scientists had a sort of economics envy and wanted to make the salaries and have the potential influence that economists had, and so they went into this rational choice for political science, in which the most important qualification is multivariate statistical analysis. That is what language means to them: numbers. If numbers have overtaken people, we cannot expect political science to come back to us soon. It is going to take a reconstruction of political science before they can come back to us.

BOHDAN HARASYMIW:

The situation in political science is not quite so bleak or black and white, because at the same time as the main body of political scientists does do the kind of inscrutable and apparently irrelevant work that Mark Von Hagen just described, there is a whole cohort of young American academics, many of whom have no genetic connection to Ukraine, who are specialists in the politics of Ukraine. I have in mind primarily people like Henry Hale from George Washington University, and they are publishing and researching and uncovering Ukraine from a political science point of view. In addition to those, there are, as Mark said, various people in anthropology and related disciplines who are doing the same thing as well. There is a cohort of scholars, but unfortunately they are Americans, and we do not have many Canadians in this field, unless we include people like Lucan Way at the University of Toronto, and maybe he should have been invited here as well.

DOMINIQUE AREL:

Well, Bohdan [Harasymiw] already said what I wanted to say, and I am going to be speaking tomorrow, but it is good that we have provocative comments. But Mark, when you say political scientists have run away from us, or kind of distanced themselves from us, well, the "us" actually includes the political scientists who study Ukraine—that is, it is internal to political science. I will provide the figures tomorrow, but just off the top of my head, in the last twelve years we probably had 60 political scientists who actually do fieldwork and generally do not publish in the inscrutable journals that you mentioned. I will provide more details tomorrow.

OLEKSANDR MELNYK:

Just a brief comment regarding the general context of Ukrainian studies and possible future direction. It seems to me that it is important to keep in mind the broader context in which this is taking place, whether it is political, cultural, or economic. And I think, from my experience this past year meeting a lot of people outside academia, I understand the economy in Canada and the United States is shifting radically. There is a generational sort of growth. Everybody in business circles talks about millennials and reaching out to them. There is also an economic change. It is not just in Ukrainian studies or the humanities: the university itself is potentially coming into a greatly diminished role in the future, because in certain types of professions you no longer require a university degree to perform the job efficiently.

The other point is about Ukraine. Related to this larger context, a lot of people in this field talk about the importance of interdisciplinary teams for solving real problems. Ukraine has a lot of problems, but Ukraine's problems are not unique to Ukraine. Many problems that Ukraine is experiencing today—whether statehood, security matters, or nation-building—apply to many places all across the world in different ways. The world is interconnected, and what happens in Ukraine, the Middle East, and Africa affects the world at large. It has consequences for the US and Europe, to an even larger degree at this moment. It seems to me that Ukraine's problems can be looked at as an opportunity for Ukrainian studies potentially to engage in this broader complex and to mobilize different constituents. To echo some of the comments that Professor Lupul has been making, these constituents are within the Ukrainian community as well as in Canadian society at large, possibly government organizations, and international structures. We can advance Ukrainian studies not only by pushing the field in different directions but also by serving the larger community.

ANSWERS AND COMMENTS

MANOLY LUPUL:

I want to follow up on what David Marples said. There has been talk here about optimism and pessimism, and it is nice to hear that there are so many students in the Department of History and Classics. I also know who brought them there—people like Drs. Marples and Himka, and there are others. How long will they last? As you know, they are either retired or about to retire. That is one comment. We do not have replacements at the present time. Now, if the replacements are going to come, since he also mentioned the fact that a good number of them are now from Ukraine, then they should follow, in my opinion, the example of our own moderator, Serhii. One certainly would not be mistaken in urging perhaps at least six months if they have an idea in mind to teach in Canada. If they are going back home, it is irrelevant.

If you are a professor raising these future scholars, I would think that if they intend to function in this country, then at least introduce them to the history of Canada, especially its political and cultural aspects. Especially introduce them to the Ukrainian problematic. They need to know that these people do have problems, and they appreciate someone talking to them about those problems. Especially, for example, at the present time, and for the last decade at least, they should have been talked to about the nature of changing university life, especially university administrative life, because it has changed radically from when I was a director. I had freedom, precious freedom. It does not exist now. Instead there is too much worry about simply picking up the money and even getting students who are not very likely to remain here. What about those who are going to remain? They should be aware of the situation in North America and especially in Canada, or they will have a very difficult time dealing with, as I said, the nuanced maze of the culture of academia when it comes to dealing with authority, where there is political and senior authority. They are cute and they are good: they know just how to fox minorities or non-mainstream interests, to make a specialty of it, because you are so marginal.

PAUL ROBERT MAGOCSI:

Very briefly, it seems that one kind of thread that has been going on in this discussion is concrete institutions that in this case happened to focus on the study of Ukraine and the rest of the world, including in Ukraine. Just because an institution is physically located in one place does not mean that it should not be concerned, as part of its mandate, with the entire world. This may come as a surprise to some people who are focused on one particular geographic area, but I mean, if I heard correctly just now, why should we be concerned with students who come here to the University of Alberta for a couple of years and then do not stay here and go back to Ukraine? Well, that is primarily what we should be concerned about. If you are interested in sharing and expanding your expertise, taking part in transforming a society that needs to be transformed in a post-Soviet world, that is part of our job as well. You know, institutions are in one place, but their concern, if they are studying a particular subject, is worldwide.

FRANK SYSYN:

To Ambassador Fraser's point—I think yes, the return to area studies is important. Where area studies institutes have been maintained, the fields have been largely protected. I pointed out Columbia and Harriman. The others would be, of course, the Munk School of Global Affairs at the University of Toronto, and the Centre for European, Russian, and Eurasian Studies. Without them, I do not think there would have been a great change. At the University of Alberta, what that largely has meant is the existence of CIUS plus the Kule Folklore Centre and the Wirth Institute for Austrian and Central European Studies. These are really what constitutes the area studies community, and that is a place they can be worked on.

Then there is a point to be made on strategies. One of the most important strategies has been post-docs. Bohdan Klid brought up the post-docs here, at the University of Alberta. By the way, the Institute has had considerable funds that Department of History and Classics students receive because they have been endowed at the Institute for carrying on such work. But we also have experience from the Jacyk post-doc at the University of Toronto: in the seven years that they have been given, five of those people have gone on to tenure-track positions. I grant you, that was remarkably fortunate. I do not say that is going to hold. That is the difficulty of academic jobs, but by giving younger people in the field at least a chance, a year or two or three, we see whether they fit into the field. There are also post-docs at Columbia and other such places. I agree that one cannot do all the fields, but the institutionalization that has been done for Ukrainian studies has helped in some ways. [...] There are more possibilities for maintaining ourselves, at least for a while, by dealing with Ukraine with these post-docs and the institutions created. In contrast, there are great problems for Polish studies at the moment (Spain was also brought up, or Romania), so our institutions do create a certain structure, you know. Whether it fulfills all needs and will fit with the teaching faculties remains a problem.

ZENON KOHUT:

I would like to reassure Professor Lupul that CIUS, at least, was and is going to continue to be very closely linked with the community. The problem is that the community has changed: the P & B[27] organizations that were so powerful then are virtually non-existent now, and we have to refocus our links with the community. For example, CIUS's pivot toward Ukraine was not only a natural outcome of Ukrainian independence but also a demand of the community. Most of the money coming for endowments was for projects that dealt with Ukraine, and not only studying Ukraine but doing work in Ukraine, such as the Kowalsky Program for the Study of Eastern Ukraine. We have established a whole number of institutions in Ukraine, and this was a demand of the community, because it was funded by the Kowalskys, who gave $2 million for this. Thus, that was also a community thing, and we have been working very hard with the community throughout the period. Then, the other pivot to Ukraine was also working with the community and government there. In the 1990s, for almost a decade we had a program for legislative reforms in Ukraine. Looking back at it, you might think this was extremely naïve at that time, but the community was also demanding that we do something there, and we obliged. We got a major CIDA[40] grant and a subsequent CIDA grant, and worked for about eight years with that. So there has always been a relationship with the community, and I think serving the community was and will continue to be a major avenue of activity for CIUS.

TARAS KUZIO:

Just on that particular final point. My friends in Boston say that one of the major differences between HURI and CIUS is that HURI does not reach out to the community in Boston. At least that is what my Boston friends said.

Professor Von Hagen, you are right about political science in America. *The Economist* did a very detailed analysis of why political science completely failed to see Trump coming or predict his success. Political scientists were writing him off all the time, and in that sense they are irrelevant to this discussion.

On the question of Bohdan Klid's conferences, I personally think those kinds of conferences are a waste of money. Why? Because they do not exert any influence in academic discussion. Unless you have people writing conference papers and then getting them published, it does not matter. Without getting them published, there is no influence. What lasting influence do you have from those conferences? I am sorry, you do not. The problem we have today is that when Ukrainian studies were founded, there was no interest in newspapers for op-eds, or blogs, or social media; that did not exist. Now it exists, and it is the battleground with Russophilia or Putinophilia, however you want to call it. It is not just in academia, and maybe people missed the number, but since 2014 nearly 300 articles have been published dealing with the Ukraine-Russia crisis, and on the Donbas

40 Canadian International Development Agency (1968–2013).

and the Crimea—three hundred! Ukrainian studies are not really part of that debate, and that's the problem we have, because Ukrainian studies are dominated by historians, not political scientists. Historians do not go on TV and radio, as Professor Sysyn did in Toronto in 2014. Historians do not write blogs or do Facebook, and they do not do op-eds. In fact, in the whole of North America there are really only four people doing op-eds on Ukraine: Karatnycky, Motyl, Marples, and Kuzio. That is it.

To give you one example of fostering influence, the rather loathsome and unpleasant British academic Richard Sakwa (whose book on the Ukraine-Russia crisis is kind of "Putin lite") published an e-book on the Euromaidan Ukraine-Russia crisis, and it has had 30,000 downloads. That is influence: 500 to 1,000 have been sold in hard copy, but 30,000 have been downloaded free of charge as e-books. We are not anywhere near that in Ukrainian studies, but that is the way we should go. I think if those conferences that Bohdan Klid talked about had been published as a special issue of the CIUS journal, I would have some sympathy, but they were not. You continue to focus exclusively on the Holodomor.

SERHII PLOKHII:

Thank you. I am really tempted to ask for one more positive comment now [laughter], but we really do not have any time. So again, let me thank the participants in the panel. And thank you, all of you, for your questions and comments.

Round Table I: Foundations.
L–r: Taras Kuzio (discussant), Zenon Kohut, Frank Sysyn, Paul Robert Magocsi, Serhii Plokhii (moderator), Manoly Lupul (at the podium).

YAROSLAV HRYTSAK
Moderator, Ukrainian Catholic University

YAROSLAV HRYTSAK is a professor of history at the Ukrainian Catholic University (Lviv) and director of the Institute for Historical Research at the Ivan Franko National University of Lviv. He has taught at Columbia University, Harvard University, and the Central European University. He is the author of numerous publications on modern Ukrainian and East European history, and has won international awards for academic achievement and public service.

Dear ladies and gentlemen, my name is Yaroslav Hrytsak. I am from Lviv, from the Ukrainian Catholic University, and have the special honour and privilege to chair this session, which in a sense will be a continuation of our morning panel, but with a slightly changed focus. We will be focusing on the challenges that scholars in Ukrainian studies are facing now. We have very distinguished scholars here, but before we proceed, let me just give my five-minute introduction as an opportunity to share with you some of my thoughts on that topic.

I do not really remember who said—unfortunately Google fails here...I believe it is in the Bible, but we do not have the bishops here anymore to check with them. [Laughter.] Somebody said, "Vision is what transforms an ethnic group into a nation. Without a vision, a nation is not a nation." As a student of nineteenth-century intellectual history, I can confirm the veracity of these words, because the vision of Ukraine as we know it now, in the twenty-first century, emerged in the minds of a group of nineteenth-century Ukrainian intellectuals. More often than not they had something to do with Ukrainian studies—but in all possible fields, in many possible ways. Bishop Borys, in his keynote speech today, reminded us that the founders of Ukrainian studies at Harvard and Alberta universities had a very broad vision that was anything but parochial. Actually, the vision was *very global*, and they put Ukraine in this global context. Professor Sysyn later reinforced this point by saying that people at Harvard and the University of Alberta set standards for scholars in other fields that were not even related, at least directly, to Ukraine. In a sense, all of us sitting in this conference hall are products of this vision, and Ukraine is the first, utmost product, which confirms that this vision has been successful and has had a very long and lasting impact.

Moreover, it was very timely, because a few years after the emergence of the Harvard Ukrainian Research Institute and the Canadian Institute of Ukrainian Studies, independent Ukraine emerged and many findings that had been made in Ukrainian North America were then implemented in independent Ukraine. As a member of the Ukrainian academic community in Ukraine, I can hardly imagine our days, our academic life, how it would look, if not for your works, books, projects, and funds that came from here—from North American institutions of Ukrainian studies, and first and foremost from CIUS. I could hardly think of a better opportunity to extend my gratitude—in my own name, and also in the names of my colleagues in Ukraine, to the CIUS people for their tremendous work, what you have done for us. Thank you so much.

> *"As a member of the Ukrainian academic community in Ukraine, I can hardly imagine our days, our academic life, how it would look, if not for your works, books, projects, and funds that came from here—from North American institutions of Ukrainian studies, and first and foremost from CIUS."*

All the more so because this vision proved to be very viable, and probably the best test of this viability was the failure of Putin's plans with regard to Ukraine in 2014, during the cold Russian Spring. That said, I do not mean to say that this vision is still viable for the future.

As a recent Nobel Prize winner keeps reminding us, the times are changing. Ukraine grows in strength, but so do the challenges; they are becoming more and more complicated and, I am sorry to say, threatening. If I may formulate this challenge in one sentence, I would quote the words of Ivan Lysiak Rudnytsky. He said on one occasion, but I believe it still sounds true, *"Perestan'te buduvaty Ukraïnu—modernizuite ïï!"*[41] Ukraine needs not building but rebuilding—or, if you wish, renovating or transforming—that will bring it into the status of a nation with what is called *sustainable growth*, which will put Ukraine on a par with European countries, North America, Asian countries, and its more successful neighbours to the west, like Poland and Slovakia. This is challenging—nearly impossible but worth doing.

In a way, we have to welcome such challenges. Let me remind you that in Chinese the word *challenge* is made up of two hieroglyphs: the first is "crisis," the second is "opportunity." We have a crisis in Ukraine, thank God! What is missing now is the vision that overcomes this crisis. I do not mean to say that we have to come up with this vision immediately, in this room, today, by the end of the session. But at least we have to give it a try, to the best of our possibilities, as people who are dealing with Ukrainian studies, which I believe is part of our job description. ■

MARTHA BOHACHEVSKY-CHOMIAK
Ukrainian Catholic University

MARTHA BOHACHEVSKY-CHOMIAK, a Phi Beta Kappa graduate of the University of Pennsylvania, received her MA, PhD, and Russian Institute Certificate from Columbia University, where she specialized in Russian intellectual history. She has taught Russian and Ukrainian history at Manhattanville College, Seton Hall University, the Catholic University of America, Harvard University, Taras Shevchenko National University of Kyiv, Kyiv-Mohyla Academy National University, and the Ukrainian Catholic University in Lviv. She directed research programs at the National Endowment for the Humanities in Washington, DC, while teaching at Johns Hopkins and George Washington Universities. At the turn of the century she developed the US Fulbright Programs in Ukraine.[20] Currently she directs the Ukrainian National Women's League Lectureship in Women's Studies at the Ukrainian Catholic University in Lviv.

41 "Stop building Ukraine—modernize it!"

Reflecting Ukrainian history: New directions in Ukrainian studies

I particularly thank you for inviting me here, because I have always seen myself as a hovering outsider to the various academic establishments dealing with Ukrainian history, since I myself was never trained in Ukrainian history. That being said, I also want to use this opportunity to thank the Canadian Institute of Ukrainian Studies, and particularly its first directors, Professor Lupul and Bohdan Krawchenko, for being brave enough and taking the risk of publishing *Feminists Despite Themselves* at the end of the 1980s. At that time, in Ukrainian studies this was a dramatic and really risky thing to do. In a sense, between CIUS and the women who organized the *"Druhyi Vinok"* conferences,[42] Edmonton could consider itself to be the cradle of modern Ukrainian women's studies, if not the Ukrainian women's movement. As a movement, the Ukrainian women's movement does not exist, but as studies, Edmonton really should take the cake. But as our Ukrainian journalists say, *"Ia ne pro tse khochu hovoryty"*—I want to talk about something else.

I want to go back a little bit to the 1960s and 1970s, and gallop through what was discussed at the last session. Certainly the 1960s and 1970s were a period of experimentation in academic fields, but people in Ukrainian studies did not experiment or take different approaches. Rather, our organizations and our scholars had other functions, as was pointed out. First of all, to legitimate the field of Ukrainian studies, which basically, in the United States and even in Europe, was non-existent. And the other area that they dealt with was to establish the canon on which Ukrainian studies were to be built. In this respect, HURI focused almost in an archaeological fashion on establishing the canon. The community, on the other hand, was involved with the *cannon* of the double "n": it was involved in spreading information on Ukraine. The two sometimes were able to work together but often did not, particularly in the late 1970s and 1980s, which marked a period of tension between society, especially in the United States, and academia.

The other point that was not raised—that complicated the work of both HURI and, to a lesser extent, of CIUS—was

42 "Second Wreath" (Edmonton and Toronto, 1985–87); the name references an early feminist almanac titled *Pershyi vinok* (First Wreath), published in Lviv in 1887.

the emergence of what I would call the academic-political schools of various organizations: the Ukrainian Historical Society, which had a particular political base, and the Lypynsky Institute. (I cannot believe I am actually saying this, but a person who is largely overlooked is Mr. Stepan Horak and his founding of nationality studies, which was initially funded by the rightmost group of the OUN.[43]) So while HURI dealt with the establishment of the canon, CIUS was in a better position to engage in outreach projects, in slight experimentation, and in really reflecting more realistically what the climate of the times was.

One of the questions that we have been asked to discuss is the relationship between Ukraine and the Ukrainian diaspora. What always struck me was the similarity between the Ukrainian diaspora organizations and the way Ukraine functions. Just multiply the Ukrainian diaspora organizations by a few million, and you have Ukraine. During the long years that I spent in Ukraine, I had a number of really major difficulties, issues that I had to deal with, and they seemed to be the same issues with which I dealt in the United States.

> *It is not necessary anymore to spread the news about Ukraine ... we really do not have to. What we need to do is to make sure that we study and reflect the reality that is Ukraine, the reality that is Ukrainian history.*

Among the many functions that I have performed in my life was administering and sort of organizing the review of various research projects funded by the American government through the National Endowment for the Humanities; among those were a few volumes of the Hrushevsky translation[13] and a couple of other publications.

The major problem I had in Ukraine was to break the resistance of people and institutions to taking risks, especially to taking risks when applying for grants, looking at alternative approaches, other sources of funding, or some other things that could be done. There is risk in engaging in open debate, risk in potential co-operation, risk in co-operating with a person with whom you may disagree, or even risk in talking to that person.

I am not even discussing the fact that in terms of grants, the first problem was that the people at the top always felt that they had to be first in receiving whatever funds there were. As a result of these failures, which I see in the diaspora also, it is very surprising how few of my American colleagues availed themselves of the possibility of at least trying for grants or co-operation. As a result of all of this, we have not engaged as we should engage in interdisciplinary co-operation, in interdisciplinary projects, and also, in looking at scholarship and history, looking at everything with a little bit of lightness, with a little bit of lightness of approach.

In Ukraine, I failed miserably. I failed miserably at getting the Ukrainian academics to establish a self-help organization for themselves, to establish an association of Ukrainian professors. What *has* happened is that every funding organization in Ukraine has established its own alumni association, and people really work at those individual alumni associations, but they have not yet decided that perhaps it would be a good idea to have only one of these associations.

The outstanding issues that I see are really: to accept the reality of Ukraine and to move on. It is not necessary anymore to spread the news about Ukraine, *shyryty pravdu pro Ukraïnu*; we really do not have to. What we need to do is to make sure that we study and reflect the reality that is Ukraine, the reality that is Ukrainian history. The unconvinced cannot be converted. We have to expand Ukrainian studies into other areas: focus not on Ukraine, focus on where Ukraine can shed light on some other issues. For instance, on the topics of Ukraine and minorities, Ukraine and modernization, etcetera.

My favourite request, of course, will not be honoured—to limit what I call the "sanctification of scholarship." Scholarship is not the be-all and end-all, and scholarship should not be viewed as the alpha and omega of faith. Faith itself is questioned, even STEM is questioned; we should equally question scholarship. We should also approach various trends a little bit more critically, especially in Ukraine. Just because the French discovered another way of looking at literature does not mean that we have to rewrite the whole study of Ukrainian literature from the postmodernist perspective.

Methodologies that are so favoured in Ukraine are actually beginning to be promoted here. Let's not lose sight of the

43 Organization of Ukrainian Nationalists (https://is.gd/ieu_oun).

fact that the methodology of garbage collection does not collect any garbage, and that really should be a lesson in Ukraine. Another: closed circles in Ukraine—not networking, but closed circles in academia. We have difficulty drawing outsiders into our midst. What we need is real outreach—to develop courses other than courses *on* Ukraine, but *with* Ukraine, and co-operate with all players. In short, I see the function of Ukrainian studies as I see the function of area, women's, or economic studies: develop the field, integrate it, make it redundant, and proceed with scholarship. ■

YAROSLAV HRYTSAK:

I want to remind you that relevant biographical information can be found in the conference program. Our second speaker does not need an introduction, but I just want to say that in a sense, his presence here highlights significant change that has occurred in Ukrainian studies during the last fifteen to twenty years: we have a new, young generation of scholars doing Ukrainian studies who are not necessarily Ukrainians, as the names testify here. Rory Finnin is the director of Ukrainian studies at Cambridge, in Britain, and he came a long way.

RORY FINNIN
University of Cambridge

RORY FINNIN is the head of the Department of Slavonic Studies at the University of Cambridge, where he also directs the Ukrainian Studies programme and chairs the Cambridge Committee for Russian and East European Studies (CamCREES). He received his PhD (with distinction) in Slavic languages and comparative literature from Columbia University. He also holds certificates from the Harriman Institute and the Institute for the Study of Human Rights at Columbia University. In 2015 Finnin won a Teaching Award for Outstanding Lecturer from the Cambridge University Students' Union.

Ukrainian studies today: War, ethics, and the importance of the humanities

First of all, I would like to thank all of the organizers of this terrific conference for their warm hospitality and Professor Kravchenko for the kind invitation. I would also like to thank the entire CIUS team, past and present, for forty years of outstanding scholarly achievement, for forty years of generous support for students and scholars around the world, for forty years of many sleepless nights rigorously annotating the letters of Volodymyr Vynnychenko or the translation of Mykhailo Hrushevsky's *Istoriia Ukraïny-Rusy*. And on behalf of the University of Cambridge, I would like to thank the Canadian Institute of Ukrainian Studies for the past eight years of your guidance and support, and for offering us very firm academic ground to stand on. I said the same things at Harvard a few months ago: it is impossible to imagine Ukrainian studies without HURI or CIUS, and I would particularly like to thank the donors who have shared this vision with generations of scholars. Thank you for your support.

This panel is entitled "New Challenges for Ukrainian Studies." I am from the Midwest of the United States, where we tend to be by nature optimistic Pollyannas, always looking for the bright side of things, and I do feel that cataloguing challenges can be more or less tantamount to shaking your fist at the sky. It tends to be counterproductive, because after all, as a number of presenters in our first session noted, our challenges are really perennial. They are familiar to us. They are largely financial, institutional, and intellectual. They nearly always relate to a familiar problem, to a failure, I think, in the academy—not in our field, actually, but outside our field—to disentangle intellectual merit from rather inert, stale perceptions of politico-cultural power. This is a logic that we are very familiar with, a logic by which might is not only right but read. This is a logic that puts us in a position of often having to state the obvious: that Ukraine—the largest country within Europe, the most geopolitically contested country in Europe—is worthy of more advanced study.

When I am speaking of challenges today, I am of the view that we need to be expanding our work in such institutes.

I really believe that, and I will raise a couple of examples from the Cambridge case to illustrate my point.

Earlier, Professor Magocsi mentioned the very helpful questions that we were furnished with to help ground our discussion and stimulate thought, and I am very grateful for them. I want to begin with a question that actually was not included, however, and that is the question of this armed conflict in our work, particularly the ethical consequences of studying a country at war. I think this is a conversation that we have not had very often. Obviously, Ukraine is a place, a country with which we have many personal and professional bonds. It is a country that is now subject to consistent political and military aggression. This raises a lot of professional questions for us that we need to tackle, and at least, by my lights, we have not done so yet. I think we can improve in that respect, because if, as Tim Snyder has suggested, "the Russian annexation of Crimea and the revolution of Ukraine have transformed the world," then I think we have to consider and take stock of the ethical implications of that transformation for our work—not only in the realm of our own research and teaching, but also in the way we reach out to the public: how we, for instance, consult with political analysts, diplomats, and in particular how we relate to journalistic media.

> *"Our challenges are really perennial.... They nearly always relate to a familiar problem, to a failure, I think, in the academy—not in our field, actually, but outside our field—to disentangle intellectual merit from rather inert, stale perceptions of politico-cultural power."*

This is a really important point that we need to take on board. Perhaps it is impossible for us in a venue like this (although it is a really welcome suggestion) to articulate a very basic, simple message about the mandate and mission of Ukrainian studies at a time of armed conflict. But I think it is certainly worthwhile to try to do so.

We simply cannot conduct business as usual. Certainly we can hope against hope for an imminent end to this conflict, but we also need to be prepared for more escalation. In 2014 we were all caught off-guard by the invasion of Crimea by Russian forces. We were thrust in front of cameras. Some of us were media-ready, some were not. Many of us were in Ukraine, some of us were farther afield. To speak about a war in real time, as events are unfolding, carries a tremendous responsibility that we need to support each other in understanding. And that is where I think a venue like this and an institute like CIUS are extremely valuable.

With this in mind, I think that very practical things like media training should be requirements for all of us. We also need to be building more public-facing online repositories of information about who we are and what we do. This was a point that Professor Kuzio made in relation to Facebook, but we all know also of the tremendous organic emergence of initiatives like the Ukraine Crisis Media Center,[44] which really filled a vacuum. There are also more local, more modest initiatives such as the website "Ukraine Scholars of North America,"[45] developed by an environmental scientist based in the United States, Motria [Poshyvanyk] Caudill. These types of initiatives point to a need for us to actually show the public who we are, to show what we do, to consolidate our commentary, and to offer ourselves a venue to share knowledge about editors and media producers.

In my experience, media coverage is really a game of arbitrary interpersonal relations. It is about an assistant to some editor somewhere who is either going to stick his or her hand into a hat of well-worn names or reach out at the last minute to a university, looking for expert commentary so they can fill a particular hit time. A lot of scholars who often represent the Kremlin's point of view (I will not name them here) are very savvy about such things. I think we can be just as savvy. Meeting together here in this type of context and occasion can perhaps offer us an opportunity to share ideas about how to do so without sacrificing what we are also here to do, which is to advance knowledge about Ukraine and conduct scholarship.

Another general challenge to Ukrainian studies that I think has been foregrounded by the Russian-Ukrainian war is something psychiatrists often refer to as *perseveration*—that is, the persistence or repetition of various narratives and frameworks despite countervailing evidence that actually

44 www.uacrisis.org.

45 See https://ukrainescholarsofnorthamerica.wordpress.com.

they are not that applicable or topical any longer. And the kinds of concepts and narratives I am thinking about are these Huntingtonian concepts of Ukraine as a cleft country. The extraordinary and tragic events of the past three years belie this thesis, or at the very least they problematize it hugely. Nonetheless, despite the fact that we see Russian-speaking Ukrainians from eastern Ukraine—whose families perhaps took pride in the Soviet legacy, the legacy of the Red Army—dying for the sovereignty and independence of Ukraine, we still see this idea sticking around. I have seen it repeatedly in keynote addresses by very well-known and very intelligent historians and political scientists who work on Eastern Europe and Eurasia, who keep speaking about the "pro-EU west" and "pro-Russian east" in Ukraine as if the cliché still matters to us, when in fact we have seen it disproven in many ways.

We also see it from the other side (and I have unfortunately encountered this with some of my students): an expression from our Ukrainian colleagues that somehow Russian is the language of the occupier. This is a tremendously dangerous concept. Russian is the language of the occupier, but it is also the language of the IDP,[46] of patriotic soldiers, of victims in this conflict. We need to get past a lot of these various narratives; we need to be thinking differently about the way we approach Ukrainian studies. I do think we need to consider approaching and persuading our colleagues outside of Ukrainian studies, not simply countering them or correcting them but really trying to reach out to them in new ways.

At a deeper level, I think a large part of this challenge relates to the way we tend to cast Ukraine as an object of knowledge. If we look at English-language scholarship on Ukraine, one might say that there is a lot of the past, so to speak, in our work, and not enough present and future. There is much focus on what rhetoricians call *constative rhetoric*, *assertive rhetoric*, rather than on *performative rhetoric*. There is much focus on *meta-narrative*, and little on *paralogy*, to use a postmodern term—that is, an instrument of knowledge that is comfortable with uncertainty and play. What I am trying to get at is that *culture* is often left out of the picture in Ukrainian studies. I was very pleased when Professor Magocsi mentioned the idea of launching new institutes for music and art; I think that is a tremendously interesting idea. Certainly in Great Britain this is a problem, and that is very clear. If one takes even just the most cursory glance at dissertations produced in the United Kingdom, you will see that the humanities are woefully under-represented. Beyond a few recent notable exceptions, Ukraine tends to be presented in British scholarship as a creature of politics, history, and economics, but not culture.

> *"This is of course why the study of Ukrainian is sine qua non for any scholar of the country. It is a matter of simple professional competence. If you do not understand Ukrainian, you simply cannot speak or understand the language of the national idea."*

Similarly, if one looks at the pages of the *Slavic Review*, the landmark journal in the field of Slavic studies, at least over the past decade, I think you will find one feature article on Ukrainian literature. It is on Gogol, of course, although I could be wrong about that; Taras Koznarsky would know better than I. But in my exploration of the *Slavic Review* of the past ten years, that was as much as I could find. In English-language scholarship there is very little work being done on probably the most successful, the most daring independent theatre in Europe, that is, Vladyslav Troitskyi's Dakh Centre of Contemporary Art, which has produced DakhaBrakha, Dakh Daughters, and the annual Gogolfest, which is a major European cultural event. There are no better ambassadors for contemporary Ukrainian culture than the practitioners at Dakh; they operate in music, in drama, clearly, and also in visual art. At least to my knowledge, they are largely outside our scholarly radar, and this is something that we need to address.

When I speak about the humanities being woefully under-represented, I suppose it is understandable, because there is certainly a crisis in the humanities more generally. There is a crisis in Slavic studies, and Ukrainian studies sits in the interstice between these two areas. Nonetheless, it is still quizzical for us in the field of Ukrainian studies. Professor Magocsi, in the first session, suggested that we launch,

46 Internally Displaced Persons.

perhaps, an institute for the study of Ukrainian statehood, also an intriguing idea. I would love to pursue it, but it is very hard for me personally to imagine a study of Ukrainian statehood that excludes culture from the picture.

In my opinion, Ukraine owes its existence to culture, to Cossack *dumy*, to folk music, to popular ethnography, and to Romantic poems written in the Ukrainian vernacular that cajoled and invited people to join the Ukrainian national project. This is of course why the study of Ukrainian is *sine qua non* for any scholar of the country. It is a matter of simple professional competence. If you do not understand Ukrainian, you simply cannot speak or understand the language of the national idea. I think, in the same way, if we do not study Russian, we do not understand one of the living, breathing languages of Ukraine as well. The same goes for Crimean Tatar, Yiddish, Polish, and many other languages. We need to create particular pathways to studying these languages for our students so that we can access cultural material that shows us something beyond black and white, something that complicates the familiar picture. I think students gravitate to this kind of fascinating material, and we need to clear the path for them.

Another thing, and this was mentioned earlier: certainly the study of Ukrainian culture, as we all know, stands in the wake of two centuries of colonial exploitation. We can stand here and perhaps debate the existence of Ukraine as a political or an economic colony, but its fate as a cultural colony of its neighbours is not in doubt. And this colonial legacy, I keep feeling, comes up in our conversations in ways we don't always understand, very implicitly; I heard it in many ways in the first session today. That is, we are constantly dealing with a kind of haunting, in which we see a provincialization of Ukrainian culture on the one hand, and on the other hand a *politicization*, or making political, of Ukrainian culture. These are practices that we might say reduce very vibrant, complex cultural figures to either zeroes or heroes, as people unworthy of study or unassailable beyond various norms. This type of thinking, this bifurcation of thinking, can stifle conception innovation.

And that is where I want to conclude, because as much as we can, let us say, enumerate these challenges, the situation today represents for us a remarkable opening. It is an opportunity for our scholarly entrepreneurism. I am personally very intrigued by something completely fantastical in the context of literary studies, and that is the application of computational criticism to a large corpus of Ukrainian literature of the nineteenth and twentieth centuries.

Many of you have perhaps heard of Franco Moretti at Stanford, who is "pushing" large texts—hundreds and thousands of texts—through various computers and seeing very formal features that are not, let us say, apparent to us reading the texts individually. And we have long been awaiting from the Shevchenko Institute of Literature the preparation and publication of the 100 volumes of the works of Ivan Franko. We are essentially waiting for something that none of us individually can ever consume or analyze in any holistic fashion—unless we are Yaroslav Hrytsak, for instance. [Laughter.] But imagine taking all these volumes, processing them through computers, and doing something like Tamara Hundorova has done really admirably in her literary scholarship: combining them with works from Moloda Muza or Volodymyr Vynnychenko, to start to see Ukrainian literary modernism in a new way. That is an extremely exciting possibility.

I just want to conclude with, again, a word of thanks and gratitude for the work of all the Ukrainianists and all the supporters of Ukrainianists out there. I think ours is a tremendous, uplifting story. We at Cambridge have seen, in the past eight years, close to two hundred undergraduates who have studied Ukrainian, of whom I think there have probably been two who have any kind of Ukrainian ethnicity in their background. So there is a lot that we can do—a lot that I look forward to doing with you and with the Canadian Institute of Ukrainian Studies. ■

YAROSLAV HRYTSAK:

Dr. Finnin testifies to one new trend, and Andrii Portnov is kind of a symbol of another new trend. Rory is not Ukrainian but is in Ukrainian studies at Cambridge. Andrii is Ukrainian, born in eastern Ukraine and raised in Ukraine. He made his career there but then moved to the West, to Berlin, and he is continuing his career very effectively, I believe. This is quite a new trend—a group of young Ukrainian scholars who are now normalizing the field in leading centres in the West.

ANDRII PORTNOV
Forum Transregionale Studien

ANDRII PORTNOV graduated from the Universities of Dnipropetrovsk (MA in history) and Warsaw (MA in cultural studies). He is a long-term fellow at the Forum Transregionale Studien Berlin and director of the Berlin-Brandenburg Ukrainian Initiative, as well as guest lecturer at Humboldt University in Berlin (since 2012). In 2006–10 he worked at the journal *Ukraïna moderna* as humanities editor-in-chief. In 2012 he co-created, and has since co-edited, the Ukrainian intellectual web portal historians.in.ua. He has lectured and conducted research at the universities of Cambridge, Helsinki, and Vilnius, as well as at the Centre for Holocaust and Genocide Studies in Amsterdam and the Centre d'études des mondes russe, caucasien et centre-européen (CERCEC) in Paris. In 2015 he was awarded the Baron Velge Prize and delivered a series of lectures as International Chair for the History of the Second World War at the Free University of Brussels, and in the spring of 2016 he was a guest professor at Sciences Po in Paris.

Some remarks on Ukrainian studies in Germany

It is my first time in Canada, so I am very happy to finally be here. But I should probably mention that many years ago, I would say between Dnipropetrovsk, Kyiv, and Lviv, I was one of those wacky young Ukrainian historians who received a CIUS fellowship. The fellowship was for the history of Soviet Ukrainian historiography, and I also remember very well that Yaroslav Hrytsak was the one who recommended me, so it really feels like coming back to the beginning of my academic writing now. I should also tell you that I have a big temptation to speak about the situation in Ukraine, but I will not do that yet, at least not now.

I will focus on the German story instead, because I think it is really interesting, and in some way it is also a challenge. And of course, in speaking briefly about this German situation, I would very much like to continue, or address, Professor Magocsi's point that there are too many Ukrainian studies centres at the university level in North America. Let us compare these points to the situation in so-called Western Europe, especially in Germany.

I would say that the biggest challenge, in the case of Germany, would definitely be an institutional one, despite our optimism. If you look at the situation of Ukrainian studies—even, broadly speaking, of East European studies—in Germany, you see that until recently it was very difficult to find any professorships in Ukrainian history, literature, politics, etcetera. If you know how the German system works, it is actually crucial to have professors, full professors appointed to some particular field. There are many people doing Russian studies, of course, some are doing Polish studies, and so on. If you apply for a project, for a grant, German or European, there is no way to do it without a professor who would at least formally support you, and that is of course very much a personal problem as well.

The second institutional challenge, related to the first one, is the situation with language teaching. If you look at Berlin, for instance, the capital of Germany, there are people potentially interested in learning Ukrainian—not just students but also journalists, political analysts, and so on. There was no possibility to have a Ukrainian language course at the university level on a regular basis until now—nothing. Interesting.

When I came to Berlin, it was actually kind of a coincidence, because I am not a specialist in Germany (maybe now a little bit). When I came there, it was in 2012, before the *Maidan*, before all the events that are, as Tim Snyder said, changing the world. I had started giving lectures on Ukraine at Humboldt University, and I should tell you that even before the *Maidan* you could see that there was a big interest in attending the lectures. I was also amazed that something like sixty people came to my first lecture. I was thinking: why? Because again, there is no Ukrainian at all in the university curriculum, at least in Berlin, and what is also interesting is that I did it and am continuing to do it, not in the history department but at the Institute of Slavic Studies. So quite often, paradoxically (I have no time to explain why), it is easier to get access (at least for me) to Slavic studies than to East European history.

What happened after the events, after the *Maidan* of this so-called "Ukrainian crisis" and all the well-publicized public debates, were some institutional changes. The most notable, of course, was the creation of a new centre in Berlin called ZOIS,[47] and it is now starting to function. The second story is that of the preservation of the professorship and the re-establishment, if you will, of the professorship in Ukrainian cultural studies in Greifswald, a city in the north (so it was formerly East Germany), north of Berlin. What is interesting is that in both cases, the new centre and this professorship—not a full professorship but a junior one, which means you should wait 5–6 years to make it real; we will see what happens in five years—both of them were financed by the German Foreign Office: not by private foundations, not by Ukraine, but by the German Foreign Office.

Maybe I should also mention another new development—at Viadrina University on the Polish-German border in Frankfurt an der Oder, where we have first of all this new series of summer schools in Ukrainian studies. You have also Ukrainian language courses for the first time, and now they are looking for someone to become a professor of Ukrainian history, but it will also be a half-position, so not a full professorship but fifty percent. You see, you already have a paradox: two professorships, but neither of them is a full one, which is very telling. But still, those three cases—Viadrina, Greifswald, and ZOIS—are long-term projects. The rest could be, in my view, described as short-term, and if you compare the amount of money given to Ukraine-related research in Germany, you will see the absolute dominance of short-term projects. There are millions of Euros given for huge conferences, the most expensive hotels in Berlin, to be held at the end of December, because you should spend the money before the end of the year, and that is it. It is also interesting that it is much easier to get huge financial support for something really short-term than to ask for something even for three years, not to speak of five or ten. So in this sense, of course, the CIUS and HURI experiences are impressive, amazing, and it is hard to believe in something like that in the German situation, especially for people like me, people without a regular position at all.

Coming back to the language issue, last year there was a meeting with the director of Humboldt University. I was there with the Ukrainian ambassador to Germany, Andriy Melnyk, who is a very good diplomat (Ukraine is lucky to have such an ambassador in Berlin, believe me). So we tried to convince the important guys in Berlin that the Ukrainian language should be introduced, and it was very positively accepted. We need financial support for at least the first five years from the Ukrainian state, some foundation, whatever, and as you could imagine, so far all attempts to find such support have failed. This means that there are no regular Ukrainian language courses at Humboldt University, although they are absolutely ready to establish them tomorrow, if you come and do it. After this five-year term, it will be paid by the university itself. So it was a very good offer, but it was not taken.

Now, very briefly, not about institutions but the intellectual landscape. I support what was said by all my colleagues, and also what was written by Mark Von Hagen many years ago in his famous article in the *Slavic Review*.[48] So, we still have very strong stereotypes—in Germany it is very visible. One of them is, of course, the idea that Russia is a continuation of the Soviet Union, which means that all the stories of the great victory over the Nazis are a Russian story, not a Soviet one. It is a trap, because we see, as Rory mentioned, that Ukrainians would say, "We have nothing to do with the Soviets," and the response would be, "Okay guys, we have nothing to do with them." All this positive stereotypical view of the Soviet Union accrues to Russia, and what are we left with? We are left with the idea that "Ukraine" actually means "ethnic nationalism." That second, very strong stereotype, apparent in public debates, in Helmut Schmidt's well-known comments and many others, is highly influential in Germany.

> *"The only way to face this challenge is to minimize the false logic of talking or writing about Ukraine only, and to expand the field as much as possible. In other words, to show how Ukrainian topics could enrich Jewish, Ottoman, Polish, and Russian studies."*

The only way to face this challenge is to minimize the (false) logic of talking or writing about Ukraine only, and

47 German acronym for the Centre for East European and International Studies (www.zois-berlin.de).

48 Von Hagen, M. "Does Ukraine have a history?," *Slavic Review*, 5, no. 3 (1995).

to expand the field as much as possible. In other words, to show how Ukrainian topics could enrich Jewish, Ottoman, Polish and, last but not least, Russian studies. That is the only way that could, at least prospectively, succeed and contribute something new.

In this respect, we could also mention a point raised by Serhii Plokhii, that Ukraine is a gateway to Europe, a key to understanding what is, or was, going on in different parts of the continent. Ukraine as a state is almost completely missing in the fight for more Ukrainian studies in Germany, and that is very bad. Compared to other post-Communist and post-Socialist countries, it is a challenge. How do you convince those people to be more engaged and motivated? Otherwise, German readiness to pay for it, to participate, is limited and based on their own perceptions and expectations. ■

YAROSLAV HRYTSAK:

To voice a tiny bit of disagreement with Rory Finnin—Rory said that there has been no Ukrainian publication in the *Slavic Review*. There has been one, and it was a forum (I am talking about [printed format]) you probably know, the Forum on Ukraine, which had an article by Tim Snyder and was followed by a discussant, Andrii Portnov.[49] The first one was initiated in the 1960s by Ivan Lysiak Rudnytsky's [article] in *Slavic Review*,[50] and the second one, the most important, by Mark Von Hagen.[48] Forums are important, because they put forward questions concerning, in our case, an agenda for Ukrainian studies, including challenges. These challenges are not only to structures, but I believe what is more important are the questions we pose, the agendas we formulate, and the paradigms we form. In this sense, all three forums had a very significant impact indeed, as they suggested new paradigms.

49 "Critical Forum on Ukraine," special thematic section with contributions by T. Snyder, M. Torodova, I. Gerasimov and M. Mogilner, A. Portnov, and Y. Hrytsak, *Slavic Review*, 74, no. 4 (2015).

50 Rudnytsky, I.L. "The role of Ukraine in modern history" and "Reply," *Slavic Review*, 22, no. 2 (1963).

MARK VON HAGEN
Arizona State University

MARK VON HAGEN teaches the history of Eastern Europe and Russia, with a focus on Ukrainian-Russian relations, at Arizona State University (ASU), after having taught for 24 years at Columbia University, where he also chaired the Department of History and directed the Harriman Institute. He was president of the International Association for Ukrainian Studies in 2002–05 and presided over its congress in Donetsk in 2005. He also served as president of the Association for Slavic, East European, and Eurasian Studies (2009). Among his recent publications are the introduction, "The Entangled Eastern Front in the First World War," in *Empire and Nationalism at War*, (2014), a volume in Slavica's series Russia's Great War and Revolution; and *The Entangled Eastern Front and the Making of the Ukrainian State: A Forgotten Peace, A Forgotten War, and Nation-Building, 1917–1918*, a forthcoming publication of the Austrian Academy of Sciences. Currently he is the interim director of the Melikian Center for Russian, Eurasian, and East European Studies at ASU; he is also chair of the international advisory board of the German-Ukrainian Historians' Commission and a member of the international advisory board for the 1917 centennial projects of the Leonid Nevzlin Center at the Hebrew University of Jerusalem.

Achievements and challenges for Ukrainian studies: A view from New York, Arizona, and Germany

Like Bishop Borys, our first speaker this morning, I am a bit intimidated, awed, and humbled by speaking in front of people who have been my teachers in Ukrainian studies, who have helped "Ukrainianize" me, who have converted me to the mission and made me a disciple. It is a bit intimidating, but I rise to the challenge as best I can.

I am also glad that Andrii [Portnov] right before me raised the German question, because that is another perspective I have something to say about. I have been dean of the Philosophy Faculty at the Ukrainian Free University for the past few years—again, thanks to a lot of you people here—and I could not have done that or taught what I am teaching there without CIUS, without HURI, without the Lypynsky Institute, everybody that you have heard from now. I owe a great personal and intellectual debt to the Ukrainian diaspora more broadly, but particularly to the institutions that you have built, which have helped translate your culture and history to non-Ukrainians, even though I have some Habsburg blood—well, Austrian, not Habsburg—but that is the closest I come to Galicia.

For me as a historian, the work of the institutes in preserving archives, in the teaching of Ukrainian language, literature, and history, and their engagement with independent Ukraine, and even pre-independent Ukraine, is something we cannot praise too much. I had a text prepared for this, but I have been rethinking things as I have been listening, so I am going to try to say what I want to say when I get there. But I want to focus on a few other things.

> *"For me, and for the field of history, Ukraine has been (and again, thanks to CIUS and HURI above all) the most important factor in what we now call the "imperial turn" in Russian and East European history. Ukraine's example has forced Russian ... and Polish historians to rethink a lot of their own history."*

First of all are the achievements, from my point of view, of CIUS and Ukrainian studies; second, the new context and the challenge it poses for us; and finally, some strategies and opportunities. Dr. Lupul spoke from the beginning about power, and power has to do with strategies—and strategies for us, as sort of marginal, small-time players in the big picture, involve building coalitions and seizing opportunities for coalition building in and outside the universities. Twenty-five years ago, the end of the Soviet Empire across Eastern Europe brought all sorts of positive moments, and I was able to take part in many of them. The biggest moment was the change from isolation and the Cold War ideological warfare of the past to something much more open and free, and exchange was collaborative. I was involved most intimately with CIUS through the Russian-Ukrainian Encounter project[51] with Frank [Sysyn], Zenon [Kohut], Andreas Kappeler in Germany, and the Humboldt Foundation, and that did get published. We had all sorts of dreams back then, not just of getting Ukrainian historians and Russian historians to talk to each other, and Ukrainians and Russians to talk to each other, but even fantasies about writing a collaborative Ukrainian-Russian history book, on the French-German model that has gone before us.

There has been a lot of progress in training a new generation of historians, anthropologists, cultural studies scholars, with a focus on expertise on Ukraine. They are now getting tenure in some of their home universities. As Andrii [Portnov] reminded us, even in Germany lately there have been some positive developments against a generally not-so-positive background, with the German-Ukrainian Historians' Commission, another institution that was funded by the German Foreign Office—again, not a university and not a private foundation, but the German Foreign Office in the wake of Russia's war with Ukraine—and the position at Viadrina University that Andrii also mentioned, in Frankfurt an der Oder.

But there is the problem of replacement. There is no one in a position at German-speaking universities, and that includes Switzerland and Austria, to replace Andreas Kappeler—neither in Vienna nor in Köln or Berlin. But before we get on to the challenges, I want to say that for me, and for the field of history, Ukraine has been (and again, thanks to CIUS and HURI above all) the most important factor in what we now call the "imperial turn" in Russian and East European history. Ukraine's example has forced Russian historians (the most important audience for some of us) and Polish historians to rethink a lot of their own history—at least they had to do so for a while. And again, the Russian-Ukrainian Encounter was part of a moment of opportunity which is very lamentably lost since 2014, if not before. So I think you all have to give yourself more credit for the "imperial turn." We do not think of Russia anymore as a nation-state as much as we think of it as an empire, and that includes Communist Russia, the Communist Soviet Union, and Putin's Russia as well. It is still parting

51 Four sessions held alternately at Columbia University and Cologne/Köln University from June 1994 to September 1995, co-organized by the Seminar for East European History at Cologne, the Harriman Institute at Columbia, and CIUS. The proceedings of the first three and fourth sessions, respectively, were published in: *Culture, Nation and Identity: The Ukrainian-Russian Encounter (1600–1945)*, edited by Andreas Kappeler et al. (2003), and *Peoples, Nations, Identities: The Russian-Ukrainian Encounter*, a special issue of *The Harriman Review*, vol. 9, nos. 1–2 (Spring 1996). An earlier, thematically related book from CIUS Press is *Ukraine and Russia in Their Historical Encounter*, edited by Peter Potichnyj et al. (1992; out of print, but downloadable at www.cius-archives.ca).

very painfully with its imperial legacy; whether it will ever do so is another question. I want to leave that achievement as the most important one for me and for historians and, by extension, for those who read history.

Most Americans and Europeans now have some sense of Ukraine but still have trouble distinguishing it from Russia, and that is the problem that I am going to focus on a bit more. Most ominously, it is the shadow of Russia and its war with Ukraine, and I am glad Rory [Finnin] brought it up, because I think that the ethical challenges we face now in area studies and history—teaching about Russia, teaching about Ukraine—are something that we need to talk about more and share experiences. This is indeed one of the most important challenges we are facing, and it is not going to go away anytime soon.

The shadow of Russia and its war with Ukraine is a constant challenge, indeed to the very survival not just of Ukrainian studies but of the Ukrainian state, or at least one with the borders of 1991. *"Shche ne vmerla Ukraïna"*[52] has taken on a new urgency and poignancy in the face of this new existential threat. But as one colleague recently noted, one of the positive things to come out of the war, if you can find a silver lining, is Ukrainians' definitive divorce from Russian identities and loyalties, perhaps inevitable though still very painful. Last year, here in Edmonton, I compared Austria's long co-dependency on Germany, the Anschluss complex—even Nazi Germany, when Austrians thought that they had to live with a powerful Germany because they did not have enough faith in Austria to survive as an independent country. And I think the war of the last two years has helped Ukraine get over its Anschluss complex, and wars do have ways of shaping and creating nations and national identity. We know that from Charles Tilly, if not a few other people.

After my first trip to Israel, I think Israel may be a possible model for Ukraine's future as a militarized democracy. That is my latest thing: [...] if Ukraine is going to survive as a democracy, it is going to be a militarized democracy, because Russia is not going to go away soon, just as the Arab nations around Israel are not going to go away soon, and war is not going to be something that we can forget about.

Another consequence of the war has been the prospect of long-term non-access to Russian archives and to exchanges with Russian scholars, given the important role of Russia in Ukraine's history. In my own case, I have been working on Pavlo Khrystiuk and on Oleksander Shulhyn, from the first Ukrainian government a hundred years ago—another important anniversary that we need to think about—and considering how we can best make use of raising Ukraine's role in 1917, in what we still call the "Russian Revolution." But Oleksander Shulhyn and Khrystiuk's archives were in Prague and then ended up not just in Kyiv but in Moscow, so we are not going to get to see those archives anytime soon. And that is just one example of many cases of disruption.

At the same time, historical narratives and identities, as we heard also, starting with Bishop Borys this morning, are themselves becoming in some sense weaponized, and I am going to try to make a case that Russia is currently waging civilizational conflict against Ukraine and the West, up to and including denial of the Ukrainian nation, and with it the denial of the legitimacy of any independent Ukrainian state. Again, this is something we have known: Patricia [Kennedy] Grimsted's work on the trophies of war and empire, the archives of the Museum of Ukraine's Struggle for Independence [in Prague]—all these things are not new to us, but they are back in our lap. Another challenge we have heard from the beginning is the changing political economy of contemporary higher education in the West, in the United States, and in Ukraine itself. This means the nearly across-the-board decline of funding for the humanities, both in the West and in Ukraine, and together with the humanities, area-studies centres that focus on international relations and foreign cultures and societies. In Ukraine, the recent austerity measures introduced in the National Academy of Sciences have also produced similar declines in humanities education, in the reform of higher

> *"We do not think of Russia anymore as a nation-state as much as we think of it as an empire, and that includes Communist Russia, the Communist Soviet Union, and Putin's Russia."*

52 National anthem lyrics: lit. "Ukraine has not yet perished."

education there. The humanities are being made less and less attractive, as is the teaching profession in general, all the way down to the primary-school level, and this crisis is bigger than just Ukraine but is particularly hard-hitting in Ukraine.

It is hard to keep straight my several hats that I have been wearing lately. My immediate context is that I am the interim director of the Melikian Center for Russian, Eurasian, and East European Studies at Arizona State University, and there we face many of the same challenges, I think, that the University of Alberta has faced and all public universities face. And I think Arizona and Alberta probably at some point shared an unenviable place in how much public education had been cut and privatized, together with the social net, by neo-conservative politicians. I have long contended that we did not need Communism to destroy the free world. We had, in our case, the Republican Party, or neo-conservative party, which starved public education and would very likely starve it further. Unfortunately, they have been abetted (only sometimes resisted) by university presidents, provosts, and deans who have pursued short-term solutions for constantly expanding not only their missions but also their administrative staffs. And again, the biggest victim of this sort of corporate—neo-corporate, whatever you want to call it—new political economy of universities is the humanities. This applies even to the more humanistic sides of some of the social sciences, like political science, which we discussed earlier.

> *"We face many of the same challenges, I think, that the University of Alberta has faced ... Arizona and Alberta probably at some point shared an unenviable place in how much public education had been cut and privatized, together with the social net, by neo-conservative politicians."*

Just as we did not need Putin to destroy Ukrainian studies—we probably did not—because we had the neo-conservatives destroying the humanities more generally, that leaves us with a very *presentist* focus in the American case, very provincial in its America-centrism. I mentioned the Las Vegas complex—I do not know what the Canadian equivalent of a Las Vegas complex is, but the idea that we [in the USA] do not need to know what happens around the world is reflected in the miserable coverage of the world in American media. Whether it is MSNBC, Fox News, or anything, you can hardly find news these days about anything but the horrible [US presidential] election campaign that we are enduring.

A final challenge to the survival of Ukrainian studies is the continuing crisis of the Ukrainian political system and its culture, and its half-heartedness in overcoming decades of corruption, abuse of power, and repression. [...] Along these lines, the brain drain from Ukraine is another one of the symptoms of that, not just at the younger level. The students we teach at the Ukrainian Free University are those who decided that Ukraine does not offer them an attractive future, and they want to see if they can enhance their chances by getting a German degree. But Ukrainian studies centres in the West will face more and more requests from scholars from displaced institutions, as in Donetsk and Luhansk—not just the ones from displaced institutions but also those with failing finances, or we face losing a whole generation of post-Soviet scholarship.

Now to where I think we have some opportunities in all this bleakness. The function and mission of area studies and Ukrainian studies is a wonderful exemplar that has been above all about helping our fellow citizens and one another to better understand the cultures and societies of foreign countries, but also to help educate our fellow citizens about the diasporas connected to, and broken off from, those countries and civilizations. It has also been about translating our own cultures, and someone mentioned American studies or Canadian studies as something we should all probably think more seriously about, too. Helping students and scholars from our part of the world to understand our own culture, wherever possible in the language of our guests, we have helped our international colleagues to navigate their way through our bureaucratic Byzantine universities and communities in the first place, and in our nations more broadly. That mission is more than ever vital for universities, given the mobility (for some, a forced mobility) of our colleagues in the regions that we study.

Another area of opportunity—and again, this is thanks to "Comrade Putin"; as I say, he has made our cause a bit more visible than it had been for a long time—I am helping to plan a new online Master's degree in global security, where the Russian war with Ukraine, unfortunately and tragically, is at the centre of this new MA. I work together with an international humanitarian lawyer and a lawyer-engineer colleague named Brad Allenby, who is responsible for my use of the phrase "civilizational conflict." We have heard about "hybrid war," as NATO calls it—the Russians call it "new generational warfare," the Chinese call it "unrestricted warfare"—and this is how my colleague defines this phrase: "All dimensions of a civilization in the process of long-term intentional coordinated conflict, one aspect of which may or may not be conventional combat." Narratives and identities are at the centre of this kind of civilizational conflict, and who does narratives and identities if not those involved in the humanities, above all? Again—literature, history, anthropology, the arts—what we are talking about in this sort of civilizational conflict is "the creation of belief systems that can be maintained within a much larger, chaotic information system by adroit manipulation of culture, psychology, beliefs, ideologies, perceptions, opinions, and religions of subgroups using appropriate levers such as comment boards, blogs, websites, and yes, even traditional print and broadcast media."

[...] So this sort of civilizational conflict is competition across economics, social media, propaganda, disinformation, cyber-war, and again, only occasionally resorting to conventional military confrontation; usually those are special operations disguised as humanitarian missions, as we have seen more recently. But it is above all about narratives and identities, which brings us back to the humanities and area studies and Ukrainian studies. This image of weaponizing narratives and identities sounds too militaristic and, for me, too geopolitically focused.

I want to leave you at least with a more upbeat mission of the humanities and Ukrainian studies, not in my own words but some other person's words, in a recent article in the *Chronicle of Higher Education*:

> For humanity doesn't just exist; it has to be created, over and over again. If our violent history shows anything, it is that we are not born with an innate sympathy for, or understanding of, all humankind; and without those, "humanity" is just a word. So humanity has to be built, and the only way to build it is to show young people already rooted in their own birth culture that they can move beyond that culture without abandoning it—that what is foreign to that culture can remain foreign and still be worthy of thought and respect.
>
> Humanists thus build humanity, one work of art at a time. In this function, the humanities are useful to individuals, to be sure, but indirectly: Rather than helping an individual to a more interesting and prosperous life, they first build a shared and—let's call it "humane"—world, in which such lives can subsequently find a place. It follows that cultures which do not teach the humanities to as many people as possible (or who adopt, for example, a narrowly nationalistic view of them) are inviting serious trouble; for continuation of the current dystopia is not the worst possibility before us.[53]

This is the kind of argument our university presidents, provosts, and deans can and should make to their governments, corporate sponsors, and other private funders, not to mention their legislatures and governors. The humanities and Ukrainian studies, with a strong humanities core, are a *national security priority*, if only we expand our overly militarized understanding of what makes our nations, societies, and the world secure. ■

YAROSLAV HRYTSAK:

Mark mentioned the "imperial turn" in Russian studies. Among those who have contributed to helping people to rethink what is Russian and Soviet in Ukrainian studies, I would put Serhy Yekelchyk at the top. His works on 19th-century Ukrainian history, and most importantly his book on the Second World War and the representations of that war, have been important for rebuilding and rethinking Russian history. They have also contributed to the field of Russian history rethinking Ukrainian history a lot.

53 McCumber, J. "How humanities can help fix the world," *Chronicle of Higher Education*, 63, no. 6 (7 Oct. 2016).

SERHY YEKELCHYK
University of Victoria

SERHY YEKELCHYK is a professor of history and Slavic studies at the University of Victoria and current president of the Canadian Association for Ukrainian Studies. Born and educated in Ukraine, he received his PhD from the University of Alberta in 2000 and taught at the University of Michigan (Ann Arbor). Professor Yekelchyk is the author of six books on Ukrainian history and Ukrainian-Russian relations, including *Ukraine: Birth of a Modern Nation* (2007), which has been translated into five languages. His monograph *Stalin's Citizens: Everyday Politics in the Wake of Total War* (2014) received the "Best Book" award from the American Association for Ukrainian Studies. Dr. Yekelchyk's most recent book is *The Conflict in Ukraine: What Everyone Needs to Know* (2015). He is currently completing a history of the Ukrainian Revolution of 1917–20.

A global-minded approach to teaching about Ukraine

I am going to start by making an introductory comment about something positive, which the chair of the previous panel was asking for several times, and I thought I would finally answer with a positive starting point—namely, that I represent here a program that is brand new and actually is being built rather than being in decline or undergoing difficulties. But the challenge of being part of a small university—not really so small anymore, but one in which Ukrainian studies will always probably be a part of some wider curriculum—presents us with a number of interesting opportunities. One of them is: if you have a university with two people in Ukrainian studies, neither of whom was in fact hired as a Ukrainian specialist, then that is essentially a bonus to the university. But how do you take advantage of this bonus if you ended up there as a Russianist and then your spouse was hired as well, basically as a Slavist, and both of you want to introduce Ukrainian courses? Well, we did, teaching Ukrainian language at the beginner's level and teaching a Ukrainian history class as well (which is rather well subscribed, with usually between thirty and forty students). In order to systematize my ideas about our approach to establishing and developing Ukrainian studies at the University of Victoria, I thought I would engage the rather tired metaphor of "one world"—which sounds like a commercial slogan for an airline or the banking industry, or something like that, the overused and tired language of globalization—but I thought I would try to work with it and see if it can actually apply in this particular case.

From this point of view, let us start by saying that in Victoria we are not actually building a full-fledged Ukrainian program that would take a student all the way from the beginner's level to the 400-level and graduate school, although we are in fact hoping to have graduate students [specializing in Ukrainian studies]. I thought that the starting point would be to come up with a concept of what exactly we want to do. Our take on this was to establish Ukrainian studies as an acknowledged and important component of a wider curriculum, as something that touches upon and is possibly part and parcel of well-established, recognized programs and disciplines. This, of course, means that you need to make an argument about the value of Ukrainian studies, so you would seem to be back in the same trap. But it does sound different when one argues for Ukrainian studies not as a stand-alone discipline but as a crucial component of European history and Slavic studies, as an important component of becoming globally minded. It is also a different, more inclusive notion of Ukrainian studies that is used here. When we say that Ukrainian studies can contribute to our better understanding of the world, it is not just the language and literature that we have in mind. Today we can make the argument that one cannot really understand the world and its crises, or the politics of our own government and others, without some command of the situation in Ukraine. That, as Mark has just said, still involves dealing with issues of identity and culture, now seen in a new light.

One of the possible approaches we ended up using was studying present-day Ukraine through the lens of the post-imperial condition, which applies in a great many places in the world, but perhaps nowhere so prominently as on the Russian-Ukrainian border these days. There is also the issue of hybrid identities, which tends to be connected to the post-imperial condition in much of scholarship, and in real life in Ukraine as well: when you have a conflict that is ostensibly about the Russian language, and yet you have people speaking Russian on both sides; when you have a conflict that is ostensibly about monuments to Lenin, but Putin is not a member of the Communist Party. With hybrid identities and proxy identities in which you encounter stand-ins, one symbol standing for something else, these are rather interesting things for today's students to consider. This way, one can recruit students with no Ukrainian heritage.

Moreover, Ukraine is a wonderful example of how new social media get involved in social mobilization and revolution just by virtue of two Ukrainian revolutions, the Orange Revolution of 2004–05 and the Euromaidan Revolution of 2013–14, which were started essentially by social media. The more recent one was started by the famous invitation from the Ukrainian journalist Mustafa Nayyem (of Afghani descent) to come for a stroll on the central square in Kyiv, and people did show up. Now if we think through these notions, they would actually help enormously in undermining the traditional narratives that the disciplines very often try to protect, and yet at the same time they do acknowledge that "interdisciplinarity" and a transnational approach are important. Ukraine happens to fit into these categories rather nicely.

This also means, moving now to the second part of my argument, that "one world" should also be a serious component of the subject matter of Ukrainian studies, because it is not enough, of course, to call on others to understand the importance of your field. It also imposes an obligation on the form and content of your delivery, and your open engagement with the wider world of the humanities and social studies. For instance, we need to keep up to date as a discipline and get engaged not only with the most recent theoretical developments but also with practical things, which students tend to appreciate. Among the most recent ones are travel and field schools, which students in Canada, at my university at least, just love, and those of them who end up going to the Kyiv-Mohyla Academy for summer school come back transformed—they come back essentially wearing Ukrainian dress, embroidered shirts and all, even though the majority of our students taking Ukrainian classes have nothing to do with Ukraine, really. They are not of Ukrainian background, just a typical cross-section of British Columbia's youth.

The very modern trend of studying literature together with film, along with some history and notions of social mobilization in a single package, also works very well with them. Making guest appearances in other courses, which seemingly are not necessarily relevant to Ukrainian studies, is also very rewarding, because once you show up there, you are required to find some explanation of why exactly you are standing before that audience. And actually you do come up with something, persuading them to enrol in your courses while in the process formulating for them and for yourself the importance of Ukrainian materials for challenging accepted truths and disciplinary boundaries.

Going beyond that, an important component that I would like to highlight here, given the occasion of this conference, is the actual "one world of travel," which does involve airlines but also social communication and the Internet. This is an important function of CIUS: to create a global space of Ukrainian studies, and a great many scholars from Ukraine—like myself, who underwent schooling here at the University of Alberta—have held scholarships and have been research assistants here at CIUS.

The Institute played an important role after Ukraine became independent. It was a time for Ukraine to discover Canada, and Canada to discover Ukraine by way of direct contact, and this meant a unique opportunity for the previous generation of Canadian scholars to influence the way humanities and social studies would be taught and researched in Ukraine. This in fact happened, and now it is very common to have festschrifts published in Ukraine for Canadian scholars, to have significant numbers of authors from Ukraine in any given collection—edited collections and such. CIUS played a major role in fostering such connections, making it a global world of scholarship about Ukraine.

> *"Today we can make the argument that one cannot really understand the world and its crises, or the politics of our own government and others, without some command of the situation in Ukraine."*

One of the last points on this list of how you implement this new world of global academy is to connect modern Canadian identity to developments in Ukraine and to position

Ukrainian studies as part of the Canadian heritage, which tends to resonate very well with students. In fact, I am very happy to see that Orest Martynowych's book about the early stages of Ukrainian settlement in Canada was distributed to the participants of this conference. I actually assign one of the chapters from this book in my class, and it tends to be by far the most popular reading. Perhaps only reading about the hairstyle of Yulia Tymoshenko competes with this one in popularity. [Laughter.] The chapter I assign explains why the Ukrainian settlers accepted inferior land, and what their journey was like. This material is quite stunning for Canadian undergraduates, and I put it on exams too, regularly.

> *"Ukraine is a wonderful example of how new social media get involved in social mobilization and revolution just by virtue of two Ukrainian revolutions, the Orange Revolution of 2004–05 and the Euromaidan Revolution of 2013–14, which were started essentially by social media."*

But now we have to move to the actual content of what we study, and what kind of issues you take from Ukrainian history and culture in order to present meaningful, interesting puzzles for Canadian students. I want to give you a few examples here, emphasizing that we have to address the issue of content as well. We need to watch the new disciplinary trends and seek the Ukrainian reflections of global social and cultural developments if we want to claim a place for ourselves in the global world of learning. For instance, there is the challenge of the ongoing war and how this can be connected to larger global trends, and actually to the Soviet past as well. It is rather engaging for students when you can tell them that the Ukrainian state is still struggling to find an appropriate form of commemorating the soldiers fallen in the new war with Russia and Russian-supported separatists, and that one of the proposals supported, at least temporarily, by the presidential administration was to create a new Unknown Soldier and bury this unknown soldier in the Park of Eternal Glory—a very Soviet and very large memorial complex from 1957, one of the first such memorial parks in the former Soviet Union—and in this way to add the current war to the existing Soviet cult of the "Great Patriotic War." But of course this is not the way to imagine the recent conflict, because the Russian side is using precisely the metaphor of an "ongoing Great Patriotic War" to such a great advantage among its citizens. Then you could ask *them* what kind of remembrance politics would be appropriate—"How would you, a Canadian student, suggest going about commemorating and mourning the victims and celebrating those who saved lives?"—and you would hear a lot of very interesting responses informed by our Canadian experience, by memorial practices connected to the Holocaust and other Western forms of commemoration. Also, the students would suddenly feel a connection with Ukraine.

Another example that I greatly enjoy giving to students is that of a society claiming public space, which was very visible in recent commemorations of the Euromaidan Revolution, when Ukrainian dignitaries needed to go to pay their respects to the Heavenly Hundred—but the space was very public because of the very nature of the Euromaidan. A protective barrier was built, not allowing the public into this space, which of course was precisely what the revolution was all about—*removing* the physical and symbolic barriers in that very same space. So now, the new authorities have installed a barrier as well, and it took them quite a considerable time to realize that they need to find a more appropriate form of involving this new "civil society," which now has a voice, which claims certain symbolic spaces as its own. This unfolded around the same time that the Kyiv municipal authorities decided to allow cars on Khreshchatyk Street—which had been a pedestrian zone on weekends—and suddenly those who had participated in the revolution came up with a protest against that, because they now felt themselves masters of this public space. The Ukrainian public took on an important role in controlling the urban environment. This beautiful example also resonated very well with Canadian students, who share global environmental concerns and know that the issue of urban space can start social action. They know about the Occupy movement and the Gezi Park revolution in Turkey as well.

The last thing I am going to mention underscores the

importance of true interdisciplinarity, and it so happens that true interdisciplinarity can be rewarded by student interest. I have never taught any subject more popular with Canadian students than "The Art of the *Maidan*," which somehow speaks to their own culture, to their own understanding of how you express protest, how you create a community, how you initiate social action, how you risk something in your life—and produce new culture, new meaning. This resonates enormously, and I am so grateful to colleagues of mine in various fields who now publish on the art of the *Maidan*, and especially online articles and exhibits. ■

DAVID MARPLES

Discussant, University of Alberta

DAVID R. MARPLES is Distinguished University Professor of Russian and East European History and current chair of the Department of History and Classics, University of Alberta. He is the author of fourteen single-authored books, including *Our Glorious Past: Lukashenka's Belarus and the Great Patriotic War* (2014) and *Heroes and Villains: Creating National History in Contemporary Ukraine* (2008). He has over 100 articles in peer-reviewed journals. He has also edited three books on nuclear power and security in the former Soviet Union, on contemporary Belarus, and, most recently, *Ukraine's Euromaidan: Analyses of a Civil Revolution* (2015).

On the integration of Ukrainian studies into the humanities

I have been a discussant on many panels, but I do not think I have ever been a discussant on one that covered such a broad area. I feel a little bit like that [British] MP discussed by Winston Churchill, who said, "When the honourable member gets up to speak, he has no idea what he is going to say, and when the honourable member speaks, he has no clue what it is he is saying, and when he sits down again, he has no idea what it is that he just said." [Laughter.]

However, I think that we did cover a lot of ground in a number of different areas. We heard, for example, from Marta [Martha Bohachevsky-Chomiak] about the need for taking risks in the Ukrainian scholarly community. We heard from Rory [Finnin] about the fact that culture is often left out of the picture, and the need to focus more, even to the extent of computerizing twentieth-century Ukrainian texts; from Andrii [Portnov] about the situation in Germany, where the focus is really on short-term projects, so it is very hard to get anything more permanent in place; and then, on a more difficult level, from Mark [Von Hagen], about both the attack on the humanities and what he described as a civilizational conflict. Then we heard from Serhy [Yekelchyk], who focused on a number of issues to do with teaching Ukrainian studies at the University of Victoria. He looked at the matter of social media and the need to bring into Ukrainian studies the fact of the conflict in Ukraine, the meaning of this conflict, and perhaps the need for a transnational interdisciplinary approach as a way to go forward for the future.

I have been in Ukrainian studies for some time. Although Manoly [Lupul] suggested this morning that I am about ready to retire, in fact that is far from the truth: I have at least three years to go as chair, and then they give me a year off for free, and then I have to come back and teach another year, so it will be a little while before I can retire.

Now, I would like to focus first on the problems for the humanities, and here I may be speaking not as a Ukrainianist but as the chair of a large department. It is an ongoing concern, how to come up with ways to defend the humanities in light of what might be called the *corporatization of universities*: the focus on engineering, mathematics, and business in particular. We have, for example, at the University of Alberta (and probably some outsiders do not know this) [some thousands of] students from China, the vast majority of whom tried to get into business. Those who cannot get into business, which is the majority, have to go into economics, and those who do not make the grade in economics might come into history. In fact, we have actually increased our majors this year for the first time in ten years because of the Chinese students. But the Chinese students cannot speak English. More to the point, they cannot write in English, so they create a new problem altogether. Nevertheless, I am inclined to think that overall, this is a good thing rather than a bad thing.

We are constantly defending our turf. [U of A Dean of Arts] Lesley Cormack made a very good comment, I think, in one of the chairs' councils recently, when she said, "We should stop defending the humanities because there is no need to defend the humanities." I think the same is true of Ukrainian studies. We should not have to defend the fact that we are studying Ukraine.

More emphasis, I believe, should be put on social media. Social media is really the way forward right now. For example, the governments of Russia and of Ukraine both have spokespersons for their ministries filing daily reports on Facebook, on Twitter, and other media. If we do not go there, we miss out on 90 percent of the issues that are being discussed on a daily basis. So I think that is essential, the use of social media. I do not want to make it sound as if I am always optimistic, because I am not, but I am kind of encouraged by the fact that twenty years ago (well, let us say forty years ago, but certainly twenty years ago) you would not have had positive stories about Ukraine in the *New York Times* or *Foreign Affairs*—even for that matter, as was mentioned, I think by Manoly, the *Globe and Mail*. But today that situation is quite different. Most of the stories in those major media of North America are quite positive about Ukraine—and rather negative, I would say, about Russia, and obviously for some good reasons. So there are steps being made forward. The really difficult thing is to say, after forty years of CIUS, where should one go from here?

> *"Dean Cormack made a very good comment, I think, in one of the chairs' councils recently, when she said, "We should stop defending the humanities because there is no need to defend the humanities." I think the same is true of Ukrainian studies. We should not have to defend the fact that we are studying Ukraine."*

There are possible ways to approach this. Professor Lupul focused on the local community. We have to start with the community, the fact that there have been more than six generations of Ukrainians in Canada now, but more importantly, to communicate to the Canadian government the sheer importance of Ukraine for Canada. Bob Magocsi was talking over lunch, saying, "How much influence do the Canadian and American governments have on the government of Ukraine?" It was more or less a rhetorical question, because I think he expected the answer to be "none." I think in the case of Canada that the answer *is* "none," I will say that. But it could be more—because of influential Ukrainian Canadians and the fact that we have, for example, centres for the study of Ukraine not merely in Edmonton and Toronto but also in Ottawa and Winnipeg. And Saskatchewan also has important centres for the study of Ukraine. We have a major Ukrainian historian, however he started, at the University of Victoria. Ukrainian studies are represented now across Canada, not just in individual centres. Beginnings have been made, and the way forward will be difficult.

Professor Lupul also mentioned a question this morning that I would dispute in a way, when he talked about the fact that we have masses of endowments at CIUS. In fact that is true, but many of the endowments are so specific that we cannot simply take an endowment and do something with it. If we have an endowment that specifies, for example, a million dollars for the study of Ukrainian poets in Lviv—not that there is anything wrong, Rory, by the way, with studying Ukrainian poets in Lviv—but if you want to use that for something else, say you want to use it for contemporary Ukraine, you simply cannot do it. Usually the terms of the endowment are so specific that they limit the future of Ukrainian studies. What is needed, I think—whether or not you can build an institute as Professor Magocsi suggests—is, say, an endowment for "Contemporary Ukraine," or for "Transnational Studies in Ukraine." Something as broad as that, rather than specific, because the development office, and also the endowment centre in the Faculty of Arts, will not even consider endowments in certain areas. But endowments are very important for the future of Ukrainian studies.

In terms of Ukrainian studies in the classroom, I agree completely with most of the comments. Ukrainian studies can be integrated with the studies of other areas, with those of Russia, of Poland. We already have a massive institute on campus for the study of Habsburg Austria—the Wirth Institute—which actually focuses on Ukraine as well, because Ukraine was part of the old Habsburg Empire. That is a very good example of something on a very broad level.

Lastly, to talk about the continuing conflict with Russia,

and this is something I touched on last night. Ironically—since I just said that social media is of great importance—I think also that social media can be very divisive. There have been a lot of problems with this war polarizing not only specialists of Ukraine from specialists of Russia, but between Ukrainian specialists as well. There are now many people who study Ukraine who are not of Ukrainian background. I was not the first; in fact, John Armstrong started back in the 1950s, and he was probably not the first, either. But it is an increasing factor, and many of us do not always see things naturally from one perspective or another, but I do not think there should be any reason for critiques of that. I think there are reasons why we could have broader approaches. ■

DISCUSSION

MARTHA BOHACHEVSKY-CHOMIAK:

Well, I was very impressed by my fellow panellists and all the work that is being done in the field of Ukrainian studies, especially as far as the most recent generation is concerned. I am just wondering if there are enough specialists, or if there are enough people interested in Ukrainian studies. The problem I saw in the United States is—Rory [Finnin], you are right—a very slight presence of Ukrainian topics in general publications, even within the Slavic field. For some reason I think the things that make us strong as a Ukrainian society are the things that also tend to undermine our effectiveness; that is, the amount of time that one has to spend on internal Ukrainian issues, social issues, or other issues limits the time and the interest that we have available for general issues. When I was running the program on translations, one of the things that was very difficult to explain to scholars who were requesting funds—for instance, to translate the basic documents of the Iranian culture—was to convince them that they should explain why precisely this document, why precisely this thing, why is it important? How can you explain it to the American congressman who is going to say that the money is needed for other issues? And I think that is also the problem that all of you have stressed: the need to position Ukrainian studies within a general context but also to explain why it is particularly important. Now, as far as the crisis of individual centres, I was not aware that CIUS is in any crisis, given the amount of material that comes out of it. It is certainly the most productive of the centres of Ukrainian studies. This reminds me of the problems of the 1960s that the individual small colleges had when facing competition from the larger state universities or from the larger, better-funded institutions. And simply, the argument is that small is better, and in the case of Ukraine perhaps that is also an effective argument.

RORY FINNIN:

I do think it is a great privilege, particularly for me, to be sitting up here with everyone, with scholars whom I greatly admire and respect. I think all I would like to say at the moment is that we need to be clear about the presentation of Ukraine as both a centre and an interstice, that is, a kind of nexus. I worry that sometimes, when we talk about, say, transnationality and comparative work with Ukraine, we mean that we are going to be diluting, essentially, our focus, in a disciplinary fashion, on Ukraine and Ukrainian-language material itself. I think we need to do both. We need to be thinking about how, for a prospective literary scholar, one can work on the once-banned political pamphlets of Mykola Khvylovyi in Ukrainian, or the early prose of Olha Kobylianska in German, or the *samvydav* (or *samizdat*) of Boris Chichibabin from Kharkiv, in Russian, or the novels of Shamil Aladin in Crimean Tatar—and never leave the Ukrainian context at all. That is a really exciting prospect for any scholar of literature, but of course we still have to be equipping our students and cultivating our field with expertise in the variety of texts that simply are not being studied any longer. We need to be looking more deeply into other areas beyond, say, canonical literary figures, into texts that were very widely read but rarely studied. The recent inroads into studying Volodymyr Vynnychenko are really important—one of the great, best-selling writers of the first half of the twentieth century, who slipped through the cracks. So I suppose all I would like to say is that I think it is terrific for us to be thinking about all the ways we can incorporate Ukrainian material into Russian material, Polish material, etcetera. I seek to do that.

At the same time, I always wish to ensure that we work on the canon and that we do try to make central our focus on Ukrainian material. I suppose there is only one thing that I would mention before passing the baton to fellow panellists: to a degree, it seems to me that for decades in

Ukrainian studies there has been, let us say, a lack of emphasis on undergraduate education. We have been very good at funding, equipping, and training postgraduates, and that has been terrific. The issue is that I think sometimes we have students who come through their undergraduate career having worked in Russian or Polish, and so by the time they get to their postgraduate career, they come to Ukraine as kind of a second destination. I really believe in teaching undergraduates, equipping them with the kind of theoretical, methodological tools to handle complex Ukrainian historical, cultural material, so that by the time they get to their MA program, their PhD program, they are already used to fending off the very familiar Russocentric historiographical narratives. They are already accustomed to a variety of things that I think we need to be seeing from scholars of this region. So an emphasis on undergraduate education is something I think we can really promote going forward.

ANDRII PORTNOV:

I would add to make a kind of provocative comment, if I may. First of all, we should keep in mind and always remember the enormous economic differences and inequality between those of us who work, averagely speaking, in Ukraine, and those who are do not. You probably know how much people receive as professors or associate professors in Ukraine. I could give you the numbers; they are, you know, incredible, lower than the lowest fellowship for students in Germany. I have heard this many times from my students, because they have stopped their academic career in Ukraine just to go to Germany as students, to start from the beginning. It makes more economic sense, and let us not pretend that it is not a problem. It is a huge problem—especially, for instance, if you do not have your own apartment in Kyiv or Lviv. The university will not pay for you, and you cannot pay for it if you are merely a scholar; this was my problem also, for years. So we should really keep it in mind. Generally speaking, we are in the company of well-established people who have no such problems, but I really know what I am talking about. That is first.

Second, there is another inequality, no less important: it is a kind of generational inequality, if you wish. I am talking about the difference between people who started their real academic careers in Ukraine in the early 1990s or late 1980s; those who started, like me, in the twenty-first century; and those who are starting now. Again, that is a very different context, and even a fellowship from CIUS differed significantly in the 1990s and when I got it, in 2006 or 2007. So let us face this issue seriously and not just pretend that it is a kind of abstract topic, because it is not an abstract topic at all.

And another point, a different one: I very much support Rory's point about culture because it is also a significant problem in Germany and in France. Last spring I was giving lectures in Paris, and it was the same problem, you know. A very practical suggestion, if I may, in this respect: if you would like to give a student a good book, Ukrainian literature, to read in English, in German, in French, there would be a huge problem because we have pretty much translations only of recent, present-day literature. Everyone says too much, sometimes, but there are absolutely no translations of authors like Valerian Pidmohylny, Viktor Petrov ("V. Domontovych"), those who could actually give a very positive, very modern view of Ukraine. I was also giving lectures on Ukrainian literature in Berlin, and I found that there was no chance that you could give a lecture about Oles Honchar's novels. But Honchar was a socialist realist, and Pidmohylny was not, and that is a huge problem. I would hope that at some point the best translators will not just translate our young writers—we know their names—but translate Pidmohylny, Domontovych, and authors like them. It is very important—a real task for all of us—and it could influence our teaching of Ukrainian literature and culture outside Ukraine.

MARK VON HAGEN:

I would like to come back again to the present war, and what it has exposed in the field, and the divisions that have been alluded to a bit before, and the risks that we need to keep in mind all the time. Remember, the Soviet Union was an economy that was not supposed to fail and a party system that was never supposed to lose an election, so risk is a much bigger problem than even what scholars are facing. But coming back to Germany, at Humboldt University in Berlin, which was mentioned by Andrii a couple of times, two of my colleagues who are known as Russianists primarily (or at least were once known primarily as Russianists), Andreas Kappeler and Karl Schlögel (especially Schlögel), have been leading the media and sort of educational *prosvita* activities to counter the Russian narrative. And most recently, Karl Schlögel wrote a book called *Entscheidung in Kiew*, in which he says that the destiny of Ukraine is being decided in Kyiv. That is a German-language thing, and scholars who had a different relationship to Russia have now had some sort of epiphany since 2014 that we need to help them with, because history is becoming a topic of war right now. The story of Crimea—whether it is Chersonesus and Volodymyr, *Vladimir*, or whether it is the Crimean War of 1853–56—is being waged by historians, pseudo-historians, and would-be historians.

And again, in the American case [...] I bring to this example a book called *Brothers Armed: Military Aspects of the Crisis in Ukraine*. It came out in Moscow in 2015. It is in English, a translation. I think Ambassador Fraser mentioned Ruslan Pukhov—he is involved in this thing. The foreword is by David Glantz, and the reason I brought the *New York Times* is that David Glantz is cited as an expert on Soviet and Russian uses of *maskirovka*[54] and other unconventional forms of asymmetrical warfare. Glantz, one of the preeminent historians of the Soviet Army and World War II, has written endless volumes. He knows the field, and I just want to give you something from his foreword:

> If the world is to contend with many new and often irrational challenges, it would be better served if instead of brothers armed, the armed forces of the Russian Federation and Ukraine, together with those of the United States and other nations, become brothers *in* arms.

And in an earlier sentence, he writes:

> The geopolitical realities in today's world confront the Russian Federation, the US, and, to a lesser extent, Ukraine, with common challenges, whose importance far outweighs the fate of Crimea or the eastern provinces of Ukraine.

Again, the concluding statement is by another general, Peter Zwack, and he writes:

> I myself, as an old Balkan hand, have seen tangible albeit itchy US-NATO co-operation with SFOR,[55] at a time few said it could have been possible, have always had a predisposition toward finding a way to work with the Russian military on the multitude of next-generation threats facing us both. We have much in common and need to focus on areas of potential co-operation. In closing, I must emphasize how much I admire and care for the Russian people and Russia's rich culture, and respect the members of the Russian military. Needless to say, the current difficult state of affairs with Ukraine and Russia must be resolved beyond force of arms.

What I wanted to emphasize with this is that even in the American military there is a kind of Russian hegemony that continues and is expressed in these American versions of brotherhood of peoples, the older brother, the friendship of peoples. In all this, General Zwack's statement, there is not a word about Ukraine or his respect or love or admiration for Ukrainians, who are also dying in this war (and he is an American, of some kind of ethnic East European background), but the Russian hold on our discourse is very strong. And again, Comrade Putin is making very good use of this, whether it is Trump (who has been mentioned a few times) or General Zwack and General Glantz, who are experts on the Russian army but seem to forget that there are other countries involved in these conflicts. That is, again, a challenge. I am working on Khrystiuk and Shulhyn back in 1917, 1918. Dismantling the Russian narrative is something we cannot *not* do anymore. Serhii Plokhii's book *Unmaking Imperial Russia*—I mean, that is what we have to do, and Ukraine is the best example. This is the best time to do it, and we should not squander our opportunities.

SERHY YEKELCHYK:

So, two brief comments: one on the use of social media, which David [Marples] picked up on, and the other on the Ukrainian communities. On social media, I think there is actually quite a bit of pressure from university administrators to get involved in it, but in a way that is fundamentally misleading, because they encourage professors and graduate students to go online and tweet endlessly and put pages on Facebook. Then you realize that, say, fifteen people saw this page, and you know all of those fifteen people, and you could have talked to them in the classroom instead, right? [Laughter.]

But of course there is a different approach to that—letting students run free and then come back with what they really like. Because once you ask them what they find new and exciting on social media related to Eastern Europe, you realize that there is an entire different world you have no idea about. And then, of course, there would be a challenge: all this stuff that they should *not* in fact read, or should read with a very critical eye, and finding the stuff that they find

54 Russian word for military deception (lit. "masking").

55 Stabilization Force in Bosnia and Herzegovina (1996–2004).

"cool" and you find interesting in terms of critical analysis.

And the community. I am very privileged actually to be working with a small but strong Ukrainian community in Victoria—many of them are retirees from Edmonton, actually, escaping the snow—and the position is nice. It is funded by Ukrainian[-Canadians'] money, and what they are doing is something very important long-term—they are working to create scholarships, not necessarily very large ones. But what I realized is that strategically, over the long run, if you create five to ten Ukrainian scholarships, it means that when I retire and it is my turn to serve "perogies" at the Ukrainian Cultural Centre, they are actually going to hire another Ukrainian specialist in the so-called Russianist European position because they would want to spend all this money on the scholarships. Also, as I mentioned, I am really grateful for the presence of the perogies (which should not be called "perogies," of course) on the Victoria scene, because everybody knows where the Ukrainian Centre is. So many people line up around it for Friday night Ukrainian dinners, and it is an easy way for students to go and actually take a look and chat with our distinguished retirees serving these dishes. It is what universities talk about a lot but rarely do—community-based learning. So, as I keep saying all the time, I am getting ready for the period when I am retired, and I am ready to serve perogies, and then, you know, a new generation will show up. [Laughter.] I will know what to say to students when I hand them their plate.

DAVID MARPLES:

To comment on what I would call "populism," including on social media, it has kind of descended into manipulation of facts, manipulation of the truth. It applies not only to Russia today, it also applies in some ways to Donald Trump. If you listen, with Donald Trump it does not really matter what actually happened; it is just a matter of the perception of what happened. And I think Russian "media"—I would say "quote unquote" because it is not really media—has kind of taken off in this regard. It has forged new paths in deception and pure lies. But also, at the same time—someone mentioned it this morning—it has used the Second World War as kind of the basis for the existence of the present Russian state, which is somewhat ironic when you consider how many nationalities took part in that war, and proportionally how many Russians died in that war compared to some of the other republics, like Belarus and Ukraine. But nevertheless that has taken place, and then the question is, how should one respond to that? How does Ukraine, for example, or how do people in Ukrainian studies respond to such lies, which have impact? Obviously they have impact, because there are so many scholars today who have supported, by and large, the Russian version of why Russia is waging war in Ukraine, or in fact, as it sometimes says, "not waging war in Ukraine," although recently Putin has decided that he is waging war in Ukraine and did actually invade Ukraine. And this brings up the question of history, questions of the past—something CIUS tried to do back in the 1980s, where it was really providing an alternative voice on Ukraine and Ukrainian studies. And I think World War II is probably the biggest single dilemma for Ukraine today: it simply does not know what to do about the Second World War. Recently I was in Ukraine, I visited the Museum of the Great Patriotic War—in which, when you first enter, you find Russian tanks that were taken in the Donbas and brought back to Ukraine, just to show that Russians were in fact in Ukraine—but when you actually get inside it, it is almost exactly the same as it was in the Soviet period, word for word, with one exception. The exception is that now it also covers 1939 to 1941, so there is a room devoted to 1939–41, whereas in the past, Russia kind of denied that the war even began in 1939. Some time ago, in Kharkiv one could actually find in the museum of history an exhibit of the Holodomor, and on the second floor the Soviet liberation of Kharkiv from the Nazis! That kind of paradox really has to be eliminated, and I do not really think the way the Ukrainians have gone about it, particularly the Institute of National Remembrance, is the best way forward. That is, more or less, to replace old heroes, if Lenin was an old hero—old heroes with new heroes. We have our heroes. I think a broader, more sophisticated approach is necessary, and I think that is something where Ukrainian studies in the West could play an important role.

[...]

RORY FINNIN:

I just want to point out that we have said quite a lot this afternoon, and we said a lot this morning, but there are two things that really stand out to me.

First, a lot of the challenges, and prescriptions for overcoming these challenges, speak to the need for institutions like the Canadian Institute of Ukrainian Studies. Number two, a lot of the ways in which we are talking about how we can package Ukrainian studies, reinvigorate Ukrainian studies going forward, speak to our capacity to build a market for more students—students who, let us say, are coming from unexpected quarters. So in the first session, we talked about the problem of supply and demand, particularly with respect to academic jobs, a hugely important topic that we need to take very seriously. Presuming a steady state with respect to the size of the market, I think we could absolutely grow that, for all the reasons that we have mentioned. And I do want to agree very vocally with what Andrii [Portnov] said earlier about our colleagues in Ukraine, the state of salaries being abysmal. You have seen a number already, I am sure, of pieces in *Politico* about academic corruption in Ukraine, written from an individual perspective. This is something we need to keep addressing and pressing.

For my part, I think I have failed in Britain even to convince authorities that I have been in contact with in the Border Agency and the Foreign Office for quite some time, to at least reduce the cost of an academic visa to go to the UK. I mean, it is something on the order of a hundred pounds, which is much more than a month's salary for an academic in Ukraine. And the way I often explain it to colleagues in Cambridge and political officials is to say, "Well, can you imagine spending something like £3,500 for a visa to travel to Ukraine, for instance, because that is the equivalent of a month's salary for an academic in the United States, or the UK, for that matter." So this is a really important issue that we can only address successfully if we work together on it. If it is just a few of us here and there in separate contexts, we are not going to have the desired effect. But we need these types of venues, these types of networks and institutions, for us to do this more effectively. I just want to make that point a bit more clear.

YAROSLAV HRYTSAK:

I just realized that I am the only scholar here from Ukraine. So if I may, in the few minutes that are left, I would like to provide some kind of Ukrainian perspective, which also extends to my personal perspective. But this is also a perspective being discussed very much in Ukrainian academia.

I believe there are two kinds of challenges. One is structural: we have discussed a number of institutes we should create, money to raise salaries, books to translate—which is perfectly fine, because this is the bread and wine of Ukrainian studies. It is called "hardware," and you cannot function without it. But in Ukraine the "software," the *agenda*, is much more important. If you are creating an institution, to what purpose? Do we continue the work that we have done so far, good or bad—I believe good—but still, does it suffice?

There are three scholars living in Ukraine, none of them of Ukrainian origin, who do not really know one another well but came to the same conclusion, and it relates to what Marta [Martha Bohachevsky-Chomiak] was saying: that postmodernism has ended, and it ended in Ukraine on the *Maidan*. None of them is Tim Snyder, even though one of them is his wife, Marci Shore, who reached this kind of conclusion. Another is Vic Pomerantsev, Jr., who wrote a brilliant book on Russian propaganda, how it functions. He says, what is Russia now? It is not sufficient to say anymore that it is a kind of imperial regime. Rather, he says that it is a *perfect postmodern state*. And the third is Ilya Gerasimov, probably the most brilliant Russian historian, who now has to find shelter in the US because he was accused of being a Western agent back in Russia. So what is important here is that there are three scholars who came to the same conclusion. They believe that Ukraine stands in the forefront of the processes that are going on in the world and that also have some effect on academia.

Lilia Shevtsova, a name that I believe is familiar to you—she is one of the fiercest critics of Putin, a liberal author who was the director of the Carnegie Fund in Moscow and had to move to Washington, for obvious reasons. By the way, she was born in Lviv. She made a point once during a discussion: what is the intellectual problem with Ukraine in crisis? It is not just that we have to withstand the challenge from Russia; it is that we do not have any book, not even the hint of a book that we could grab to get explanations about what is going on in Russia. We do not even have a vocabulary to describe this conflict. New concepts are emerging, like "hybrid war." Who ever heard of hybrid war before? This is the first thing. Or new terms—there have been many during the *Maidan* that I do not believe were present in any kind of Ukrainian studies before—"precariat," for example. A key aspect, I believe, of why the *Maidan* happened in Ukraine is generational.

Another is, why the social energy in Ukraine?—and most important, why is this energy not limited to Kyiv or Lviv only but also found in Odesa, Kharkiv, Dnipro? So what I am saying here is my impression. But again, it is shared by my colleagues in Ukraine, because for us it is a very urgent issue. It is that we have not yet begun to formulate and pose new questions, right questions, that can help find a right answer, so to say. We are still dealing with identity, with language—which is necessary, I am not denying the importance of this issue—but they do not explain really what is going on in Ukraine.

Just to give you one example, for months and months the most important issue in Ukraine—the status of the Russian language—was getting zero attention in the media. Nobody cares nowadays in Ukraine, but look at what our scholars are writing, say, in the United States (I will not name names, but you can probably guess): that Ukraine is suffering from *language schizophrenia*, that something has to be done! But once we stop dealing with it, then we can refocus our attention on the most important issues, like corruption. So I believe that we are still very much stuck in the old agenda. It sounds renovated, refurbished, but still it is very much about national identity, or identity per se—which is important, no way to deny it, and it is necessary. But it is not sufficient: you cannot get a real understanding of what is going in Ukraine if you just focus on this idea. I have many examples, but I will not exceed my allotted time.

Just a final point. There is no doubt that we have to fight Putin on the front of identities and narratives; without a doubt, that is a must. But if we fight only on this front, we cannot win, because it is *his* playground. He has many more resources, and we simply cannot withstand them. [...] He is stuck with a Huntingtonian agenda. I know for sure that Putin believes Huntington,[56] and I know people who say that actually he treats Huntington very seriously. You probably know that Putin is very fond of conservative thinkers, Huntington included. I would say that he really believed the divided-country idea [concerning Ukraine], and his plan for dividing Ukraine, for the Russian Spring, was based on reading Huntington. But I am afraid that many Ukrainian scholars read Ukraine the same way. And so—Huntington, the importance of the Russian language—if we deal with these kinds of issues, we have no chance to win the war on Putin's playground, because *we* still believe that national identity, nationalism, those kinds of things, and historical memory are very important. Representation is very much a part of this postmodernist agenda. But I would say that there are much more important, more real things to discuss. I am afraid that we are not covering them, and my experience comes from working in think-tanks in Ukraine. There are several think-tanks, both state and civic ones, which are trying to come up with a new strategy for developing Ukraine and some kind of vision—and believe me, there are no academic scholars in the think-tanks. They have nothing to say when it comes to these things.

It took me a long time to find an economist in Ukraine who could provide me with statistics on the share of the so-called service economy in Ukraine, which I believe is probably one of the most important phenomena. During these Euromaidan years, there has been a transformation: the industrial sector has ceased to be the main source of GDP in Ukraine. Now the main part belongs to the service sector, but again, you could not find such data. I believe that to a certain extent it is a result of our agenda, because we still follow the old agenda—which is fine, it matters—but we do not discuss the challenges. You have to come up with a set of ideas, suggestions to help this country fight the historical legacy (not with historical memory per se). I believe that corruption is a part of this legacy. Who will write the history of corruption in Ukraine? Who will explain why corruption is so persistent? Why is it so different, say, from other countries of the former Soviet Union? That said, I believe that Ukrainian scholars have a unique opportunity to formulate a new agenda for Ukrainian studies. That might be a new field of study for the humanities—exactly what Gerasimov is saying. About post-colonialism. Because Ukraine and Ukrainian scholars—I am talking about Ukrainian scholars *in* Ukraine, definitely—have to start speaking in their own voice, which requires formulating a new agenda, and I believe we still greatly lack discussion along these lines.

QUESTIONS AND ANSWERS

BOHDAN MEDWIDSKY:

I have a minor question. There used to be in Germany a Ukrainian Free University. Is it dead now?

56 *The Clash of Civilizations and the Remaking of World Order* by Samuel P. Huntington (1996).

MARK VON HAGEN:

As dean of the philosophy faculty of the Ukrainian Free University, I do not think it is dead. It is not in its golden age, I would say that, and it is facing many of the same problems that we have been talking about, the flight from the humanities. And *ukraïnistyka*, one of the faculties at the Ukrainian Free University, is one of the least subscribed to because all the Ukrainian students in Germany—well, not all of them, but many of them—are looking for more practical and profit-making opportunities, including business and law and administration. So *ukraïnistyka*, even at the Ukrainian Free University, is not in good shape right now.

Since 1991 the Ukrainian Free University has not received German government support because of Ukraine's independence, so it has relied entirely on diaspora fundraising efforts. And it is taking in not only students who decided for one reason or another that their future was not in Ukraine, but also a lot of faculty from Ukraine who are teaching on a regular basis, every year. Political science, history, literature, language. So it is going on, but it faces many challenges, not so different from the ones that Alberta and Arizona and other places are also facing.

BOHDAN MEDWIDSKY:

The *Mizhnarodna asotsiiatsiia ukraïnistiv*,[57] is that dead, too? Because they should be doing the work.

YAROSLAV HRYTSAK:

If I may answer very briefly, it is more dead than alive. [Laughter.] Hopeless, believe me. Very much like academia in Ukraine.

FRANK SYSYN:

I am not sure that Professor [Michael] Moser would agree with you about that, so it is interesting. But that brings up Vienna. Just one comment on what Yaroslav said at the end: I think it is an antidote to say that maybe too much attention is paid to language. But it is not just scholars abroad. It is the Kyiv Patriarchate, for example, as each time it takes over a parish, it talks about the right to pray in Ukrainian. The radio controversy about Ukrainian songs did not come from scholars abroad, either, so there are still tendencies in Ukraine where we see language and cultural production there. Somewhere between what Yaroslav said and what Rory said, which were the opposite sides of this thing, we do indeed want culture and language paid attention to.

On the general discussion, one thing that strikes me out of all this is that Ukrainian studies have developed differently, but always because of an ability to take opportunities when they come up. I thought specifically of Cambridge—we heard the story, and I want everyone to remember it: two hundred students in the past eight years taking Ukrainian at Cambridge University. Right? I would have said before, phenomenal! It took a number of things; one of them was that the Department of Slavic Studies *wanted* to do Ukrainian. Many years ago, Simon Franklin approached Ihor Ševčenko and said, "Can you find a Ukrainian donor in North American who has three and a half million quid, who could hand it over to us for Ukrainian studies?" But they did want to do it.

The second thing is that they have an academic spine in Cambridge to defend academic traditions, to not go along with whatever the last bureaucracy or dean says: redo all the studies, abolish this department, stick it there [...] They kept Slavic studies, they knew how to develop it, and they have done it. And then it always takes a person who can do it, and Ukrainian studies can develop if we take hold of these opportunities—if we are able to provide support, which in some cases the Ukrainian studies community has done. The very different situation we have heard about in Germany is that of a much more bureaucratized government in a top-down society—but no one in Germany planned that Andreas Kappeler would get interested in Ukraine. Right? Kappeler had a chair, decided he was interested in Ukraine, and then within a decade, German scholarship on Ukrainian history in the West jumped tremendously. With one generation of his students, we had eight or nine or ten basic monographs, and you could argue that a graduate student in North America specializing in Ukraine who does not read German is no longer abreast of his discipline.

I think of that as another of these opportunities. What I fear is that it also tells us that we get wedded to whatever structure we have. We are doing forty years of this institute, Harvard will do its anniversaries. You get a model, it goes for a while, but it is not always going to work, and we have got to be ready to go on and change rapidly. And you have to bet on specific people. If Giovanna Brogi had not been in

57 MAU, Ukrainian acronym for the International Association for Ukrainian Studies (www.mau-nau.org.ua).

Italy, had she not done all she did at that time, Italy would not have become a leading force for the study of baroque literature, of Ukrainian literature, for generations. It may not continue now. We will see if she has a good student who is taking over, but each of these were opportunities for the field. Every time I have dealt with my European colleagues, they have said, "Oh, well, it is not like North America, where you have a Ukrainian diaspora that can create a community and go on and do it."

RAYMOND PALLARD:

There was mention earlier about Cambridge University's great tilt toward the East, Central Slavic studies, and how Ukraine has benefited from it. If I might pose a question: is that some sort of atonement for Cambridge University's production of all the Kim Philbys and the others from the 1930s—the "House of Traitors" from England? [Laughter.]

RORY FINNIN:

It must be an atonement for Kim Philby. There is a lot to atone for with Kim Philby. I would like to say that one of the proudest moments I have had at Cambridge actually is pointing to another alumnus named Gareth Jones. We all know him as the one journalist who put his name on the story of the Holodomor, and paid for that quite dearly. Coming from a North American Ukrainian studies context, we are aware of the name, and I had gone to Cambridge thinking that everyone would know Gareth Jones there too. He was not known at all, even at his alma mater, Trinity College, where he performed with first-class results in Russian and was invited to a lot of secret societies that people like Kim Philby joined. He always declined because he was worried about this kind of monolithic ideological thinking that secret societies invite. And we displayed his diaries that were put together during 1933 in particular, when he crossed the border into Soviet Ukraine and wandered around *Kharkivshchyna*,[58] seeing the situation in the countryside.

So now, instead of Kim Philby, you will often hear Gareth Jones's name spoken about. However, when I bring this up, I also have to point out that guess where Walter Duranty went to university? [Laughter.] So Cambridge has a lot to be proud of, a lot to atone for. But of course all universities do, and one with 800-plus years has got a lot in the rear view.

58 Kharkiv region.

OLEKSANDR MELNYK:

I will ask maybe a slightly provocative question. Since we are at a Ukrainian studies conference, there is a little bit of temptation for each of us to engage in some kind of self-serving agenda here. That is normal, we all have our interests. Suppose we abstract ourselves from the field of Ukrainian studies itself and try to project toward the real world that we study, to which we contribute in different ways. What if I were to ask each one of you: what do you see as the most important problem confronting Ukraine today, or the home societies in which we live? And the second question is: given your competencies and interests, what could you possibly see yourself doing to sort of elevate the problem in that particular domain?

RORY FINNIN:

I suppose, really, I am perplexed by the epistemological problem that the study of Ukraine presents. Why are we in this position? As Marta [Martha Bohachevsky-Chomiak] was saying earlier about defending Ukrainian studies (I am not sure who actually brought up this question), it is absolutely right that we should not have to defend Ukrainian studies. But why is it that certain areas of study, from African studies to Balkan studies to Ukrainian studies, why is it that they are considered niche areas? I mean, when we abstract ourselves, as you put it earlier, from this issue, we try to think about our various individual intellectual journeys to our field of study. In the end, it is a massive territory, highly complex, geopolitically significant. The fact that actually we are in some ways marginal still baffles me, and I suppose that is the one problem that I cannot quite get my mind around.

Even during this war, we still encounter this problem, and, as Slavko [Yaroslav Hrytsak] just put it, these problems keep sneaking around. And we are not yet, with our colleagues, particularly those in Russian studies, able to break free of these old methodological, intellectual fetters. We need to be thinking in radically new ways about a Ukrainian national identity, which I would say is probably the most powerful and yet underestimated force in modern European history. All the most renowned historians in this room taught me very clearly that Ukraine was composed of three different imperial peripheries that were themselves civilizational peripheries in the eyes of the West, yet somehow they created a new centre for themselves in Kyiv. That is not supposed to happen—that is defiance of geopolitical gravity. It's fascinating. Why do we keep revisiting these topics? Why can we not get past them? I suppose that is the problem I find myself scratching my head about, whether it is Ukraine or other contexts.

MARK VON HAGEN:

I would like to pick up on Rory's challenge but also come back to Slavko's question about Putin and civilization and Huntington. And I agree with you that Putin does have a very—well, not so simple-minded reading of Huntington, and when I talk about civilizational conflict, as with Eurasia, it is anti-Huntingtonian. And I did come from Columbia, where [Edward] Said was one of the leading critics of Huntington on Islam. And recently, for my sins, I went back and reread Huntington because I wanted to make sure that when I talked about civilizational conflict, it was on some firm ground. Huntington did not even mention Sunni and Shia when he talked about Islamic civilization, which is kind of the most important civilization for him in that book. But even when he talks about Orthodox/Slavic civilization, he assumes a kind of monolithic unchanging essentialist unity, which Putin would like to believe too. Putin talks about the "Russian World" and about Russian values and decadent Western values, all that good stuff.

It is a kind of paradox in that this self-righteous wonderful Russian identity of Orthodox/Slavic morality is, on the one hand, so "superior" to us but, on the other, it is so "weak and fragile" that we [Russia] have to shut down alternative newspapers, we have to shut down alternative media, we have to fight against *Gay-ropa*[59] on all kinds of social media. So it is at once powerful but very vulnerable and subject to contamination by these strange "civilizational" things. So when you go back and read Huntington on Orthodox/Slavic civilization, how does he explain Orthodox Russia fighting against an Orthodox patriarch in Constantinople and Crete, with Serbs and Bulgarians, and against Ukrainians and others? [...] You know, for the first time in—I don't know, a thousand years?—it was an attempt to reunify Orthodox civilization that failed this summer. So where was this uncontested Orthodox monolithic civilization? Not to be seen. And then you have Orthodox Russia attacking Orthodox Georgia. You have Orthodox Russia attacking Orthodox Ukraine, ostensibly over a Muslim Crimea. So does this mean, if anything, that this war and Putin have exposed how simple-minded and how wrong Huntington was? And what was he wrong about? He was wrong in believing that these civilizations are watertight, hermetically sealed, unchanging, and monolithic, and the only way they can exist is in a permanent clash, and that we, the West, have to keep all those other civilizations at bay.

Instead, what we all believe, I think, and I tried this with Eurasia a long time ago, I did not do anything but provoke a lot of controversy. Civilizations, cultures, societies are not one thing, but they are mixtures, they are migrations, they are boundary crossings. And thank you, Rory, for reminding us that Ukraine was at three imperial intersections, interstices, so it is a civilization that is, again, hybrid, not watertight, not completely separate from others. I mean, even Orthodox civilization lived with Jewish civilization, and Islamic civilization, and Protestant and Catholic Christian civilization, so this idea that there is some sort of hermetically sealed, perfect Orthodox civilization is bunk. So we need to convince those people who believe it, including Huntington and Putin, that it is not reality but a wished-for kind of reality. One other opportunity that I raised earlier that we have not come back to is the hundredth anniversary of 1917, the first Ukrainian state. How is Russia going to mark that? Putin is obviously not going to like February, because that is democratic. Even October is Lenin, and Lenin was guilty of all kinds of crimes, like giving away eastern Ukraine. So Lenin is not good, October 1917 is not good, so what is left? The White Russian counter-revolution. Again, if you look at his favourite authors from that period—Anton Denikin, Ivan Ilyin—the only thing that Russia is going to celebrate, if anything, is the White Russian reaction and counter-revolution.

Ukraine, by contrast, has the opportunity to celebrate the most democratic revolution it ever had. It failed, but why did it fail? Because the Bolsheviks did not play by the rules. The Ukrainians were playing by the rules, they had a majority of the vote, and they were willing to accommodate the Jews and Poles and Russians in a unique experiment of national autonomy (that did not last long), but Ukraine was the only country that did it on its own. And I do not think this revolution is known by Ukrainian citizens. It is

59 Anti-*Maidan* homophobic slur against Europe (*Yevropa*).

certainly not known in the West, and that revolution is something that is worth—I do not know about celebrating, but at least having a more positive intervention in the study of revolution. And that is why I mentioned that I went to Israel for the first time. And why did I go to Israel? Because of the Ukrainian Revolution of 1917—because Israel is planning a whole bunch of events next year to reconsider, revise, and revisit what happened in 1917 and its impact to this day, and I was invited because I work on the Ukrainian Revolution of 1917. And if that is not an opportunity for us, I do not know what is.

MARTHA BOHACHEVSKY-CHOMIAK:

I would love to continue this discussion on a very high plane of what would be the great issues, what issues Ukraine should be facing, and how to do that. But I think that is one of the major problems Ukraine has had. Maybe it is the end of the Soviet reliance on Kant and the need always to have an ideological justification. But from my long travels over Ukraine, I have come to the conclusion that basically Ukrainian society is a quintessentially bourgeois society that really wants a good, decent life, and forcing people to come to a decision of what *Weltanschauung*, or world view, they all have to accept is generally not top on people's agendas.

I think it is necessary for us scholars to understand that we should write the books we want to write. I would personally urge Ukrainian scholars and Ukrainian journalists to write something readable and try to publish what other recent émigrés from the former Soviet Union are now publishing in the *New Yorker*. We do not! Ukrainians do not publish there; we publish in *our* journals [...] But when it comes to practical issues, when it comes to what Ukraine needs, Ukrainian scholars—and we all—need to realize that we will always have an eternity of issues, and we will always keep trying to resolve this generational conflict, this marginalization. We personally will always be on the margins. All this reminds me of the earliest sessions of the feminist movement—trying to define yourself. For God's sake, you cannot define yourself without defining your whole community. What I think the Ukrainians should do is solve those issues that can be solved, in whatever way they need to be solved, and let their children deal with the rest.

SERHY YEKELCHYK:

Just two very quick comments. One on language, culture, and society, which is something I have been thinking about as well. I would argue that it is becoming increasingly difficult to separate these issues now, because in the course of revolutionary events, I think the Ukrainian language and culture acquired the status of a symbolic marker—which is attached to the concept of true democracy, anti-neo-Stalinism, against Putin, against the Russian agenda—and it is now kind of difficult to artificially, analytically separate them. If a person demonstrates respect for them—not necessarily when practicing the Ukrainian language and culture—that alone positions this person politically, I think, in a very important way.

Also, I would argue that the core values of the recent revolutions were in fact civic and political. So this is the new identity that Ukraine is building, but language and culture are still markers. Secondly, I thought that it would be important also to kind of issue a warning against walking into Putin's trap, which is what I see in present-day Ukraine quite a bit, especially in connection with the far right, which tends to get rejuvenated every time elections are nearing. And somehow they are not at the front, yet somehow they are right in front of the parliament, and on Khreshchatyk,[60] being funded from some rather obscure sources. These may in fact be connected to Russian television, which is benefiting from the picture of these people demonstrating in the centre of the Ukrainian capital with various emblems and symbols that look very much neo-Nazi. So that is playing right into the hands of Putinist propaganda, and there is, I feel, a bit of a temptation in Ukraine, and also among the younger public, to identify with the most extreme opposite of Putin's Russia. It is as if the depiction of Bandera becomes acceptable on the *Maidan* because for Putin's Russia, Bandera is construed as its diametrical opposite, not because people on the *Maidan* have read a lot of Bandera's work, so they join the organization and things like that, because this is what Putin hates most. But this is the symbolic function, and there is always a danger that beyond that there would be an acceptance of political practices, which would only play into Russia's hands.

YAROSLAV HRYTSAK:

If I may, [...] I would just tell you a story. Two years ago, I met a young professor in the Warsaw airport. He was re-

60 Main street in the centre of Kyiv.

turning from Moscow, he was working there, and he had a presentation at the so-called *Vyshka*,[61] probably the best university in Russia nowadays [...] in the humanities. He said to me, "Can you imagine what the world is coming to? I, an American professor of Jewish origin, had to defend Bandera against the accusations of a Russian professor and students." He himself is very much disliked (to put it mildly) in Poland for bringing up the Jedwabne issue.[62] So that is why I am saying this here. What a complicated story we live in, and Ukrainian things do belong to this story, Bandera included.

The British ambassador to Kyiv put it in a very nice metaphor that I like very much. He says that Ukraine confirms the paradox of the bumblebee. According to all laws of aerodynamics, bumblebees should not fly, but they do. According to all the theories, Ukraine should not exist as a viable state, but still it does. So this is the beauty of Ukraine, because it defies gravity, and we are still following this law of gravity because we believe it is important. But this exactly is something that we have to explain—in what way is Ukraine defying this kind of paradigm, these kinds of laws? This is what I see as probably the main challenge for Ukrainian studies, because I believe it is a Ukrainian riddle, a Ukrainian paradox, but also, I believe, a paradox of today's world, which is becoming more and more "Ukrainian" in that way.

And, talking about myself, I am also caught by the transformation, by political events in Ukraine. It is quite a different perspective from being here...and I believe it would be very selfish to continue with my academic career by writing a new book, six hundred pages, that probably only fifteen people would read. So what am I doing? I am blogging. I consider blogging a very important part of the academic agenda nowadays. You should offer some ideas to a large audience, especially to this new young middle class, and your blog must be very short. It is a challenge, for nobody reads more than two pages. If their attention is not caught by the first two paragraphs, forget it, they will not read your third paragraph. So along this line, my ambition is to write a very short history of Ukraine, but a global one, based on the bumblebee paradox. And not according to Hrushevsky—which I believe is important; many people have written about Hrushevsky, and Hrushevsky himself wrote [histories]—no one could do that better than Hrushevsky. But my book would deal with countries such as Ukraine in order to explain their corruption and authoritarianism. Douglass North and Ronald Inglehart, who are not historians but political or social scientists, have written global histories of this kind, and this is exactly what I believe Ukraine now needs, because it provides a new perspective and helps to better explain what is going on.

ANDRII PORTNOV:

To answer Oleksandr Melnyk's question: for me, at least at the moment, maybe the most interesting aspect of what could be said about Ukraine is the question of the origins and nature of violence. I am trying to write something about it, actually using your paper as well, and it is incredibly helpful and interesting in this already mentioned transnational context, because you could perfectly use the story of ex-Yugoslavia and also some parts of northern Africa to compare it critically.

As you also know, we are doing intellectual projects on Ukraine all the time, at historians.in.ua—actually, one of our contributors is also here, Oleksandr Pankieiev, one more function of his—and I should also tell you that it is done almost entirely without money. I could tell you the annual budget: nobody believes me, especially when I talk to Russian or Polish colleagues who are doing comparable projects. Their budgets are hundreds of thousands of euros; ours is a couple of thousand euros. It is not just that I am sitting in Berlin and trying to learn German; I am also trying to be very active in Ukraine, maybe even too active, and it also interferes considerably with my attempts to find a position in Germany. And I am very sorry for the other colleagues waiting here to speak, but I would still insist on the importance of inequality, for I wish to give you two more practical suggestions.

First, Ukraine desperately needs—but of course I do not see it as realistic in the nearest future—something like a higher school of economics, already mentioned by Yaroslav [Hrytsak], or even, if you wish, Nazarbayev University in Kazakhstan. Russians and Kazakhs, as well as Americans, can go back to their countries and work and teach and be well paid. Not so in Ukraine, and that is why almost nobody goes back. Everybody tries to stay in Poland, Germany,

61 Higher School of Economics National Research University (www.hse.ru).

62 Local Polish involvement in an infamous Nazi pogrom in 1941.

or Canada, anywhere. If you go back, you go back to the situation described by Rory [Finnin]. You have no money to pay even for a British visa, which was also my case a couple of years ago.

The second thing is a kind of abstract vision. Maybe we need a program to translate the very good books produced and published in Ukrainian, in Ukraine, into English. Such programs exist in Lithuania, Poland, and some other countries. I can identify some very good books in Ukrainian by Valerii Vasyliev on communism, Hennadii Yefimenko on Soviet politics in the early years, and Volodymyr Masliichuk on eastern Ukraine. Unfortunately, they could not write those books in English, and if we are thinking of integrating Ukrainian-based and Ukrainian-language scholarship into international debate, maybe we need a program to do something real, not just talk about beautiful concepts.

PAUL ROBERT MAGOCSI:

There are two points that I would like to share with you, since we are in the discussion mode. First, we should always keep in mind that we are already today, and in general, in a very luxurious mood—that is, we have the luxury to discuss a success story. We are really talking about the price of success. Ukraine has been an enormously successful "project," to use the modern term. A hundred and fifty years ago there were no Ukrainians. No one in the world knew about Ukrainians as a separate people, as a distinct people, as a distinct language. Since 1991 an independent country, against all odds, has now existed for twenty-five years. Now, whether one wants to use the metaphor of the bumblebee or not, really we are talking about the problems of success, the challenges of success.

The other thing is the direction of this panel. I am a bit confused. We started this panel—in the context of this entire conference—to discuss the past and present challenges of the academic enterprise of Ukrainianists, primarily in the West. What this panel was starting to do—and maybe what many of us get drawn off in—was asserting that Ukraine has a problem right now: its greatest enemy is Putin, and what should we, as academics, be doing to counter the activity of Putin in Russia. Well, excuse me, that is not our job. Our job is as academics, and we should not be mixing up academic goals, scholarly goals, or pedagogical goals and activity with work as propagandists or political activists vis-à-vis an enemy state. That is for somebody else to do. And Yaroslav mentioned that for him personally, what is the point of writing academic books anymore, for him or for you, at this particular moment in your life? You feel it is more important to do your two-minute blogs. Fine, but you said that is what academics should be doing. I do not think so—that is for public intellectuals. So if you want to move from the status of an academic concerned with larger matters, long-term matters—if you want to be a public intellectual and go out on the barricades against the enemy, that is fine too. This is what I mean by "I am confused" here, because I think it is very dangerous to move along that slippery slope of being concerned first and foremost with scholarly, pedagogical, and academic matters, and then becoming—as if we suddenly have a responsibility to be fighting against Putin. That is not our job.

DAVID MARPLES:

I think what Professor Magocsi said is very pertinent, that academics should not become politicized, but I do not necessarily think there is a real contradiction between someone using a blog and being an academic, if the goal is to simply disseminate more widely among an audience. Obviously it is not a scholarly contribution. I would also say that one of the stipulations that seems to be emanating from the office of our president [David Turpin at the U of A] is that we have to become public intellectuals. He said that directly. You know, basically, then, for someone like Professor Magocsi to stand up and say, "Well, we cannot be public intellectuals and objective academics," does not seem to me to make a lot of sense. I think that one can be both. Obviously the line can be crossed at times, and there are academics who have become political activists (I could name ten off the top of my head, but I would not do it here). The goal, though, should be to avoid falling into that category, but I do not think that one necessarily negates the other.

I was going to make a comment earlier about Putin and about Russia, because I think the emphasis on Putin is overdone. I realize that if you are sitting in eastern Ukraine or somewhere like Dnipropetrovsk, there is a very real threat of conflict in your area. At the same time, to demonize Putin makes him much more powerful than he actually is, and I would ask people at least to take into consideration a couple of not exactly statistics, but just information. The GDP of the European Union is seven times larger than the GDP of Russia—not the West, but the European Union alone. The European Union is more than three times larger than Russia, whose population has been declining for the last twenty years. When you talk about Russia, you are talking about many autonomous regions that would, in fact, like more power ceded from the centre and have been deprived of power for the last ten years. In other words, Russia is not a monolithic entity run from Moscow under one man, Putin. Putin is not even the most extreme of Russians by a long shot. There are people far more right-wing, "fascist," than Putin. So I think we give him too much credit, quite honestly, and I think the focus on Putin is really overdone when it comes to Ukraine.

In fact, if you look at the summer of 2014 and the forces fighting among the separatists, Putin simply abandoned them, completely abandoned them and left them to their own fate. And it was not Putin's idea that they would suddenly move from Sloviansk to Donetsk; he did not plan that. He simply gave up because the concept of New Russia, or *Russkii Mir*, had clearly failed, mainly because most people in Ukraine refused to go along with it and were not interested in being annexed or invaded by Russian forces. I think Russian leaders have actually seen that, and this is one reason why they do not know what to do with Donetsk or Luhansk today. So I think we can take that into consideration when looking at the future of Ukraine.

I do not think the future of Ukraine is in any doubt. It is really a matter of looking perhaps more at regions than simply at one particular entity—just as, if you look at the Canadian state, you could also say the same thing: it is divided into very distinct regions. What do we here, for example, really have in common with the Maritimes? Not a great deal; they are farther away from us than, say, London is from Moscow. So I think that more emphasis on the regions of Ukraine is important, and even—this is something Volodymyr [Kravchenko] talks a lot about—border issues as well, because there are certain commonalities between border regions of Russia and Ukraine, just as between Ukraine and Belarus, just as between Ukraine and Poland.

YAROSLAV HRYTSAK:

As I understand, the question from Professor Magocsi was addressed personally to me. So let me continue, because "public intellectual Hrytsak" was mentioned, correct? [Laughter.] I am sorry if I gave the wrong impression that I would force you to write blogs. God forbid. You are doing your work brilliantly.

I have two points. First of all, the challenges depend on conjuncture, what you stand for, where you come from, what the issues are where you live in your society—and I believe that therefore our perspectives are very different. There is one take if you live in Ukraine, and your colleagues are going to the front, and if you feel endangered, so it is quite a different pressure and probably one that is not as luxurious as you said. That is okay. It does not mean that one is better and the other worse, just different.

Secondly, I do not believe there is anything wrong with being a public intellectual. I believe it is very good. It is rather an issue of quality, whether you are a good public intellectual or a bad public intellectual. For sometimes, the less public you are, the less intellectual you are—this is really the danger, and good public intellectuals are aware of this danger. So just let me provide you with a list of very famous historians who have been public intellectuals—in my estimation, very good public intellectuals. Mykhailo Hrushevsky was the first. I am talking about professional historians, because Ivan Franko was also—but Mykhailo Hrushevsky was the first. Ivan Lysiak Rudnytsky was a public intellectual. Mykhailo Drahomanov, it was also discussed, was a public intellectual. [...] A. J. P. Taylor was an intellectual, a public intellectual. Ernest Gellner was a public intellectual; he wrote a lot of pieces, short pieces in *The Guardian* on academic-related issues. Tony Judt, who in many ways is my idol, also wrote extensively. And Tim Snyder—this is the same ethos—he is a public intellectual. In the Russian case, there was Dmitrii Furman, who I believe was one of the historians with the best understanding of the difference between Ukraine and Russia. He was a very good historian, and he was a public intellectual. Do read the two-part essay by Perry Anderson in his review of books on Dmitrii Furman, because it says that he was both a brilliant historian and a very good public intellectual.

Final point: a book that is very much discussed nowadays, the *History Manifesto*, written by the chair of history at Harvard.[63] His main point is that there is an impression that the world is going in the wrong direction. Why is it

63 *The History Manifesto* by David Armitage and Jo Guldi (2014).

important? Because we have lost our bearings; because many of the issues that we are now facing are not short-term issues, not snapshots. They have long-term causes, and to find and explain them you need a long-term perspective, which means a historian's perspective. Who will do it—economists, political scientists, politicians? No, this is something that historians have to do. Therefore, the *History Manifesto* ends up saying that historians should stand up and fight. I am not saying that everybody has to be a historian and teach public history, although probably it is not a bad idea to have a public history. But at a certain point, for certain people, being public intellectuals does not necessarily mean bad things.

Round Table II: New Challenges for Ukrainian Studies. L–r: Rory Finnin, David Marples (discussant), Mark Von Hagen, Martha Bohachevsky-Chomiak, Serhy Yekelchyk, Yaroslav Hrytsak (moderator), Andrii Portnov.

JARS BALAN
Moderator, CIUS

JARS BALAN is the administrative coordinator of the Peter and Doris Kule Ukrainian Canadian Studies Centre at the Canadian Institute of Ukrainian Studies (CIUS), University of Alberta. He has authored numerous scholarly and popular articles on Ukrainian-Canadian history, literature, and theatre, and an illustrated history of Ukrainians in Canada. A lifelong activist in the Ukrainian community, he is the initiator and curator of the Kalyna Country Ecomuseum. Jars has been involved with CIUS, in one capacity or another, for most of its existence.

I would just say by way of introduction that you should all be aware that intellectual interest in and the study of Ukrainians in Canada began long before the creation of the Canadian Institute of Ukrainian Studies—in different areas, in terms of literature, sociology, history, the arts, folk and fine arts. The study of Ukrainians in Canada exists and has evolved outside the Canadian Institute of Ukrainian Studies. I am very pleased that our panellists reflect that this morning.

We have Natalia Khanenko-Friesen speaking first. She is with the Prairie Centre for Ukrainian Heritage at the University of Saskatchewan. We have Lubomyr Luciuk, who is with the Royal Military College of Canada but was at the University of Alberta and involved in the Institute in its early years. Andrij Makuch is my partner in the Ukrainian-Canadian program at CIUS; he is at the University of Toronto. Roman Yereniuk is with the Centre for Ukrainian Canadian Studies at the University of Manitoba; he chaired it for years, and he is with St. Andrew's College. We also have Natalie Kononenko from the Kule Folklore Centre, so we will bring a range of perspectives to this whole question of Ukrainian-Canadian studies, which of course is an area that straddles Ukrainian studies, Canadian studies, diaspora studies, and forms a separate area unto itself. The panellists will have fifteen minutes each to make their presentations. Afterwards we will have a discussion involving the members of the round table, and then we will open it to the floor. ■

NATALIA KHANENKO-FRIESEN
St. Thomas More College, University of Saskatchewan

NATALIA KHANENKO-FRIESEN is a professor of cultural anthropology at St. Thomas More College, University of Saskatchewan. Among her publications are three essay collections, most recently *Reclaiming the Personal: Oral History in Post-Socialist Scholarship* (2015), and two monographs, *Ukrainian Otherlands: Diaspora, Homeland, and Folk Imagination in the 20th Century* (2015) and *The Other World or Ethnicity in Action: Canadian Ukrainianness at the End of the 20th Century* (2011). Dr. Khanenko-Friesen is the founding director of the Oral History Program at the Prairie Centre for Ukrainian Heritage at the University of Saskatchewan and an inaugural editor of *Engaged Scholar Journal: Community-Engaged Research, Teaching, and Learning*, a Canadian scholarly journal on community-university collaborative scholarship.

Ukrainian-Canadian studies are an exploration of the Ukrainian-Canadian "legacy" from a given disciplinary perspective

[SUBMITTED TEXT]

In the field of Ukrainian-Canadian studies, it is often a challenge to figure out who is our audience and who are the "consumers" of our research. I would like to address this presentation to the students who are considering an academic or professional career with a focus on Ukrainian-Canadian studies, and to the Ukrainian Canadian community that supports this research in the first place and is its primary focus. I will first present my general understanding of the field of Ukrainian-Canadian studies. Then I will discuss the challenges and dimensions of the field, and finally I will focus on the pursuit of Ukrainian-Canadian studies in Ukraine, given the presence of experts in the field there.

Parameters of the field

As an anthropologist, I cannot escape my own disciplinary lenses as I consider Ukrainian-Canadian studies. To me it is a unique cultural phenomenon, a social field with its internal dynamics and agents. A short definition can be offered here: Ukrainian-Canadian studies are an exploration of the Ukrainian-Canadian "legacy" from a given disciplinary perspective. This legacy can be defined differently, narrowly or broadly. We can follow up on at least two possibilities here. We can speak about Ukrainian studies or the Ukrainian legacy, culture, history *in* Canada, and that is often the pursuit of so many of us. But we can also think of the Ukrainian-Canadian legacy in broader terms and operate with the adjective "Ukrainian-Canadian" *through* the hyphen, as applied to Ukrainian-Canadian ethnicity, culture, heritage, history, and society.

In my opinion, this second perspective opens new opportunities for us that involve comparative analysis and dialogue with other areas, such as regional studies, diaspora studies, ethnic studies, and so on.

An important point is that Ukrainian-Canadian studies is always a *multidisciplinary* pursuit, unfolding within various scholarly domains, such as history, folklore, geography, arts, sociology, anthropology, political studies, and so on. In addition to the list, which is more extensive than presented here, we work at intersections of such fields as *public history* and *local history*, and that brings a lot of uniqueness into what we do, especially when it comes down to dialoguing and conversing about what we do with colleagues outside our field.

We can continue working on the most suitable definition of our field, but all in all, Ukrainian-Canadian studies are about Ukrainian-Canadian content and an interdisciplinary approach, angle, methods, and perspective used in the analysis of such content.

This positions us as scholars in a unique way, because oftentimes as discipline-bound scholars we have responsibilities and obligations lying outside specifically Ukrainian-Canadian study areas. When considered in the context of university-based academic studies, I dare say that Ukrainian-Canadian studies are actually on the margins of both: on the margins of Ukrainian studies and of the disciplines in which we pursue our research. I do not foresee in the near future in my university, for example, a program focusing singularly on Ukrainian-Canadian content as such. When we have resources on campuses, we build Ukrainian studies first, and within Ukrainian studies we work on other topics housed under the umbrella of Ukrainian studies in general. This structural marginality presents various challenges to scholars engaged in the pursuit of Ukrainian-Canadian studies. Not to sound too pessimistic, I would like to add that being on the margin also presents opportunities.

At the same time, in spite of this marginal status in our academic settings, in public universities, this field of scholarship is extremely important to the Ukrainian-Canadian community, which financially supports this area of studies and is interested in its continuity and outcomes. That ultimately defines what we do, how we do it, and how we also navigate the two domains, the university and the "community."

This brings me to an important point. This field, Ukrainian-Canadian studies, is an excellent example of what scholars nowadays call *community-engaged scholarship*. Community-engaged scholarship is being actively pursued these days in the established academia, especially in the social sciences and humanities. It is a broad and multidisciplinary area of exploration and a growing field. Over the last two or three decades it has grown to become a recognized field, with a mandate to pursue scholarship and research in partnership and collaboration with communities. Ukrainian-Canadian studies grew precisely out of this agenda, therefore our field can be considered a precursor of this "novel" direction in contemporary scholarship. We, as scholars of Ukrainian-Canadian studies, are in the avant-garde of such scholarly pursuits in Canada. This has not yet been discussed in the fullest sense in the field of community-engaged scholarship—something for us to do.

Ukrainian-Canadian studies are shaped at the intersection of both academia and community, not only in terms of who orders the music and who plays it, but rather in a complex synergetic relationship between these two fields. It is academy-based scholarship on the one hand, and on the other hand it is community-based scholarship. We understand that we pursue our scholarship very much in collaboration with and dialogue between these two fields. Oftentimes it is very hard to draw a line between them, something that puzzles our university administrations from campus to campus. And sometimes we actually manage to enlighten our administrations, especially when they also embrace this rich formula of scholarly pursuit referred to as "community-engaged scholarship."

At the University of Saskatchewan, we also teach in the

field of Ukrainian-Canadian studies, perhaps more than on some other campuses in Canada where Ukrainian studies are being pursued. It is in teaching that we recognize the importance of the bridge between community-based and academy-based scholarship. Not only do we benefit from the community because we research it and bring students into it, but we realize that what we do and whom we teach at the university can be of benefit to the museums, archival institutions, and local cultural Ukrainian-Canadian organizations.

Where are we, geographically?

We speak of Ukrainian-Canadian studies predominantly as unfolding in Canada, but they are also pursued elsewhere. Interestingly, we have a burgeoning field of Ukrainian-Canadian studies, though maybe not conceived exactly in those terms, in Ukraine as well. I will return to this point later.

In Canada, when it comes to research topics, we also see a certain divide between western and central/eastern Canada. When I talk to my students, I often begin exploring complex ideas with the question, "What comes to mind when you hear such-and-such a concept or notion?" So, what answers might come to our minds when the same type of question is asked with respect to the phrase "Ukrainian-Canadian studies"? For Ukrainians in western Canada, the answer might focus on the "founders" or early Ukrainian settlers, the so-called "pioneers." Their history is predominantly what has been intriguing people in western Canada and Ukraine. But the Ukrainian-Canadian legacy is larger than that. Whenever I travel to the eastern parts of Canada and have an opportunity to present my own understanding of what Ukrainian-Canadian studies are, I get to hear how oftentimes what is pursued in Canada's west excludes the experiences and reflections on what it means to be Ukrainian-Canadian in the east. This divide needs to be dealt with.

Our audiences

Another important question for us to ask is, "Who are our audiences"? Obviously, we work to fulfill the needs of certain categories of people out there. Students come to mind first, at least in my world, and the Ukrainian-Canadian community is next. Different approaches are required to communicate the complexities of the field to one group, such as students, and the findings and products of our work to Ukrainian-Canadian community audiences. Then there are other scholars outside and inside Canada. We should remember that we also reach out to other audiences outside the Ukrainian-Canadian context. Our audiences are global these days, thanks to the electronic distribution of our research findings.

I recently had an opportunity to present a couple of my projects on Ukrainian-Canadian topics in Lisbon, Portugal, and I was surprised how much interest was generated by what I had to say at the University of Lisbon to the faculty and students at the Institute of Geography and Area Studies (IGOT), the people who research and explore diasporic/ethnic culture situations similar to the Ukrainian-Canadian one anywhere else in the world. As specialists in Ukrainian-Canadian studies, we have a lot to share cross-culturally, and we probably should be doing more in this regard.

> *"The dialogue needs to continue with the community, as much scholarship takes place in non-academic settings. And we should recognize the validity of community-based scholarship as well. The dialogue also needs to continue between eastern Canadian and western Canadian visions of what the Ukrainian-Canadian legacy is about."*

Challenges

We have challenges, of course. I have already mentioned the first challenge that we are dealing with—the marginality of our field in the academy. The second challenge is related to our job responsibilities. Some of us are full-time Ukrainian-Canadianists, but others, because of work obligations, are only part-time scholars of Ukrainian-Canadian studies, myself included. The Ukrainian-Canadian focus in my work is just one of several agendas I pursue as a scholar. How much time can someone like me devote to the pursuit of Ukrainian-Canadian topics? The third challenge has to do with the multidisciplinary nature of Ukrainian studies. Because we work in different disciplines, we face a certain dispersal of our scholarly outcomes. Someone in history may miss reading a sociological study, and someone in religious studies may not come upon work published in a folklore journal. The fourth challenge is the diversity of audiences I have already mentioned. We gear our work toward a particular audience, and this may affect an outcome message and its availability to those interested. We have the fifth challenge of record-keeping. It is easier to track works that focus exclusively on Ukrainian-Canadian topics. Comparative scholarship sometimes escapes our bibliographies and is not easily profiled in reviews and surveys of our field. The sixth challenge would be dealing with the ebb-and-flow nature of our self-reflection. Opportunities for shared conceptualization and joint reflection on what constitutes the field come rarely. It is at conferences like this—thank you, CIUS—that we have an opportunity to reassert our own identity as a field.

Next decade

So, what are the primary foci of Ukrainian studies in the next decade? The production of scholarly knowledge should continue in dialogue with various constituencies, institutions, and cultural groups. We should continue working in dialogue with Indigenous peoples and other ethnic cultures in Canada. We have heard from the director of CIUS that the Institute neighbours with Indigenous studies. Is there an opportunity to explore potential collaborative work between these two Canadian fields of study to reflect on ethnic/Indigenous relationships in Canada? For example, a comparative perspective is effectively embraced by the Holodomor Research and Education Consortium (HREC). Within the field of Ukrainian-Canadian studies we should also be more open to comparative analysis and research.

The dialogue needs to continue with the community, as much scholarship takes place in non-academic settings. And we should recognize the validity of community-based scholarship as well. The dialogue also needs to continue between eastern Canadian and western Canadian visions of what the Ukrainian-Canadian legacy is about.

In addition, we need to be better at networking and capacity building. It is often challenging to maintain and sustain viable scholarly associations, but networking among research institutions engaged in Ukrainian-Canadian studies is important. An international Ukrainian-Canadian studies network with an active online presence would be very good to establish.

I believe we also need to continue attracting not just Ukrainian-Canadian students, who often gravitate to us because of their innate interest in what we do, but also students from elsewhere in order to promote comparative research. Such work has already taken place. What comes to mind is the thesis defended at the U of A some time ago by Aya Fujiwara, who compared, I believe, [Scots], Japanese, and Ukrainians—an excellent piece of scholarship. We also had examples of comparative scholarship in the folklore program at the U of A, to which Korean, Bulgarian, and other students came from far away to explore Ukrainian-Canadian culture. This is a good practice that helps us to improve our capabilities.

In terms of knowledge production, we need to continue digging into all still accessible layers of Ukrainian-Canadian culture via folklore studies, ethnic history, public history, local history, oral history, and so on. We need to embrace the digital humanities in earnest, not only as a tool for the digitization of our archival sources but also as a method of scholarly research that can be supported by various grants outside Ukrainian-Canadian sources. The digital humanities also offer unique opportunities to mine and explore data, as is done in literary studies. More research on the post-1991 Ukrainian immigration and its social mobilization would also be useful. Wsevolod Isajiw's work was done some time ago, and this immigrant wave continues to grow. Recent events in Ukraine triggered significant mobilization within the latest wave of immigration, and this should also be explored and documented.

In terms of knowledge dissemination and field popularization, we need to publish not only in peer-reviewed printed and not generally accessible periodicals but also in open-access periodicals. Such periodicals are growing, and they allow us to disseminate our knowledge in the most effective way because it is easily accessible. Many of us habitually publish in scholarly venues that do not allow free access to our publications and texts. As a result, the field of Ukrainian-Canadian studies suffers from lack of access.

Ukrainian-Canadian studies in Ukraine

Though traditionally Ukrainian-Canadian studies have been unfolding in Canada, a lot is happening in Ukraine as well. A number of institutions in Ukraine are pursuing scholarship with a focus on Ukrainian-Canadian studies in one way or another.

For the purpose of our conversation today, I have gathered some information on the state of Ukrainian-Canadian studies in Ukraine. With the help of my colleague in Ukraine Tetiana Voropaieva and my graduate student Iryna Kozina, we mined the institutional and various online library resources to assemble and analyze scholarly works on Ukrainian-Canadian topics published in post-1991 Ukraine.

To understand the dynamics of Ukrainian-Canadian studies in Ukraine, it is useful to look at candidate and doctoral dissertations. Dissertation production in Ukraine is sui generis, and we can speculate that the quality of these works varies. Most dissertations may be expected to utilize secondary rather than primary sources. Of the forty theses produced in the last twenty-five years (1991–2016), two were doctoral, and the rest candidate-level.

Another way to evaluate the field would be to look at the production of monographs. What we have gathered so far, about twenty publications, includes not only scholarly monographs but other books as well. We see works on Ukrainian-Canadian topics appearing in periodicals. Some of this work is collaborative between Canadian and Ukrainian scholars. What is important is that all this writing is accessible to other local researchers. Works produced in Canada are commonly published in English, and work done in Ukraine is produced in Ukrainian. The distribution is probably very straightforward, but you also see the growth of the field and increasing interest in Ukrainian-Canadian studies outside traditional centres such as Lviv, Chernivtsi, and Kyiv. Ukrainian-Canadian topics are also explored in such places as Zaporizhia, Sumy, Kharkiv, and possibly others.

In addition to monographs and dissertations published in Ukraine that focus on Ukrainian-Canadian topics, a large number of articles, nearly three hundred, have appeared in various conference proceedings, periodicals, and collections. Every year brings a greater number of such articles.

All in all, Ukrainian-Canadian studies in Ukraine are very dynamic, involving many individuals. Some incorporate Canadian scholarship and collaborate with colleagues in Canada, but others rely solely on secondary sources.

In conclusion

Ukrainian-Canadian studies have been unfolding in Canada for a long time. This has proved to be one of the early forms of community-university engaged forms of scholarship. In the next decade, Ukrainian-Canadian studies should focus on comparative and collaborative forms of research involving other cultural groups in Canada and elsewhere. They should focus more on the latest wave of immigration and embrace digital humanities as a new research tool. Over the last 25 years or so, Ukrainian-Canadian studies have also grown as a field in Ukraine.

In the next decade and beyond let us continue what we do, but in dialogue with many other constituencies, in order to better promote and disseminate our scholarship and build a stronger position for ourselves in the humanities and social sciences. ■

LUBOMYR LUCIUK
Royal Military College of Canada

LUBOMYR LUCIUK is a professor of political geography in the Department of Political Science at the Royal Military College of Canada in Kingston, Ontario, as well as a fellow of the Chair of Ukrainian Studies at the University of Toronto. Dr. Luciuk has served as a Governor-in-Council appointee to the Immigration and Refugee Board of Canada and the Parole Board of Canada. Active with the Ukrainian Canadian Civil Liberties Association, Luciuk played a key role as spokesman and director of research for the Ukrainian community during the controversy over alleged Nazi war criminals in Canada and in spearheading the national campaign for recognition and symbolic redress for Canada's first national internment operations of 1914–20.

Reflections on the interdisciplinary nature of Ukrainian studies in Canada

I remember, thirty-two years ago this November, being in the building next door, the Jubilee Auditorium, where Chancellor Peter Savaryn handed me my PhD, and that sent me off on the course of an academic career—or a career as a public intellectual, if you prefer—that has been very different, I suspect, from the careers of many of you in this room.

I am not a Ukrainian-Canadian studies specialist, and

I am not a Ukrainianist. I am somewhere in between, because for all my academic life, I have taught in mainstream departments: in the Department of Geography at the University of Toronto, the Department of Geography at Queen's, the Department of History at the University of British Columbia, and finally, for the last twenty-five, thirty years, in the Department of Politics and Economics at the Royal Military College of Canada. So my career has been in the mainstream, but as I think most of you know, I have taken an active, vigorous, and sometimes controversial role in promoting the interests of Ukraine and Ukrainian-Canadian issues. I want to share with you the course of that career and speak a little bit to some of the themes that I have heard raised in the past day about the future of Ukrainian and Ukrainian-Canadian studies, and where we need to go and how we need to get there.

"I discovered, for example, that despite the apparent tranquility of our community, the first Ukrainian hall in Kingston was actually established by the Ukrainian Labour-Farmer Temple Association on James Street, which I had never been told about."

As many of you know, I was born in Kingston, Ontario, a small community in eastern Ontario—a very Anglo-Celtic, Protestant society when I was born there, and still pretty much the same. The very name Kingston, the "King's town," should suggest to you the nature of the community, as well as the university I went to—Queen's, very British. By and large, most of the people I grew up among, my neighbours, my school chums, and the people I went to high school and university with, were people who were indifferent, or ignorant, or on occasion hostile to the very nature of someone identifying themselves as Ukrainian. I do not want to belabour the point (I am not going to play the victim card here), but there were incidents of discrimination and incidents throughout high school. For example, people told me that the stories I had heard at home from my parents, who had come after the Second World War as so-called displaced persons, were lies, were anti-Soviet propaganda, and that my godmother, who told me about surviving the Holodomor, was a liar or perhaps confused. As I grew up, I had some connection to the Canadian-Ukrainian experience through SUM[64] summer camps. The Ukrainian-Canadian community in Kingston was very small, so we lived quite co-operatively, quite quietly.

When I got to Queen's, I went in as a biologist. I was going to be a herpetologist, studying reptiles and amphibians, a bio-geographer, perhaps. But as it turned out, for reasons I will not go into today, I eventually moved into human geography under the tutelage of Professor Peter Goheen, who has since become a lifelong friend. I was instructed, disciplined, and told that my ideas about what I would like to do for an MA thesis were wrong and I should instead do a historical geography of Ukrainians in Kingston. I hated the thought: perish the idea that I should study the community I came from! I thought that was a boring subject, but I had very little choice, so I began doing oral history. That was under the influence of Dr. Richard Pierce, who would establish the Limestone Press and actually publish several works of mine and of my colleague Bohdan Kordan, in due course.

Geography is about exploration, saying, "Look what I found, look at the patterns. Look at how I got here, where I come from, and how I get back to where I started." And as I began exploring my community, I began finding out things that I had never realized about my own hometown. I discovered, for example, that despite the apparent tranquility of our community, the first Ukrainian hall in Kingston was actually established by the Ukrainian Labour-Farmer Temple Association[65] on James Street, which I had never been told about. I found out by interviewing interwar immigrants that there were Ukrainians in Kingston *before* them. I remember it was the 14th of February, 1978, Valentine's Day, because my girlfriend was very upset that I left her and went to Toronto to interview Nick Sakaliuk. It turned out that he was one of the people interned at Fort Henry during this country's first national internment operations,[66] so I learned about that. I learned

64 Ukrainian Youth Association, est. 1946 (www.cym.org).

65 A nationwide pro-Communist organization of Ukrainians in Canada, founded in 1918. Banned in 1940, it was replaced by the Association of United Ukrainian Canadians (www.auuc.ca).

66 Against "enemy aliens," including civilian Ukrainians with Austrian citizenship, during the years 1914–20 (see www.internmentcanada.ca).

from Mrs. Charitoniuk, whose husband had fought in the Second World War in the Canadian Armed Forces, about the careers of Bohdan Panchuk and Stanley Frolick, the men and women who established the London-based Ukrainian Canadian Servicemen's Association and went on to create the Central Ukrainian Relief Bureau (CURB), which brought so many of those DPs,[67] members of the *Dyviziia*,[68] UPA,[69] OUN,[43] Holodomor survivors, and so on to Canada in the postwar "third wave" of immigration. I learned about the emergent nature of ethnicity, how it was shaped by and responded to and recreated by the socio-economic and political environment that wave after wave of Ukrainians encountered when they came here. And as I was doing all this, I always wanted to remain, as it were, in the mainstream. So when I took up an offer of a doctoral studies position, my first choice was the University of Chicago, where I was accepted. But instead, as a result of a fateful encounter with Professor Leszek Kosinski of the University of Alberta, I chose the U of A.

Again, I came here to go into the mainstream Department of Geography. I was interested more in how Canada—or, more broadly, the Anglo-American world—had dealt with the displaced persons of my parents' immigration, about the role played by Canadians of Ukrainian heritage who facilitated the third wave, about the consequences of their encounter, and so on. I was interested in those issues, newcomers versus old-timers. When I brought that as a dissertation topic to the University of Alberta in 1979, I encountered pushback in the department. I was supposed to be studying the Arctic, and the head of the department was concerned about my topic. In fact—as a result of the ensuing tensions between what the head of the department wanted me to do (the founder of the department, the late Bill Wonders) and my own supervisor—when my comps came I was failed by one person, Dr. Wonders. So there was prejudice at that time, and I remember very clearly—this would have been about 1980—that I drifted over to CIUS and met Manoly Lupul for the first time. Dr. Lupul offered me support and, in time, engaged me in the oral history project that the Institute was then promoting, giving me the opportunity to travel across western Canada and interview many of the people who played a definitive role in the creation of the Ukrainian-Canadian community.

Eventually, of course, as I mentioned, I completed my PhD thirty-two years ago, granted next door by Dr. Savaryn. I left to do a post-doc in the Department of Geography at the University of Toronto, where I would spend approximately the next three years. I was already associated with the Chair of Ukrainian Studies through Professor Magocsi, and I walked right into one of the biggest controversies our community faced in the last century. In April 1984, some of you may recall, the government of Canada established the Commission of Inquiry on War Criminals, headed by Mr. Justice Jules Deschênes. When I arrived in Toronto, I found myself "volunteered" to join the Civil Liberties Commission, an ad hoc group headed by the late John Gregorovich (who passed away only a week or so ago). This group was established by the Ukrainian Canadian Committee,[5] in conjunction with other East European communities, to address the bogus allegations that had been circulated about the alleged presence of thousands of Nazi war criminals in our midst.

This precipitated a choice: I had come from a good university, I had my PhD, I was in the Department of Geography, no one was questioning my interest in refugees. It would have been a perfect career just to stay in what I was doing. But I was faced with a choice: do I become engaged in advocating for our community, or do I step aside? There was a bit of a discussion yesterday between Professor Marples and Professor Magocsi about whether you can be a public intellectual and a scholar at the same time. I must say I smile to think about that, because both of them *are both* but like to pretend that they are not. I remember, as an undergraduate, reading someone who said that "philosophers have only interpreted the world in various ways. The point is, however, to change it" (I think it was Karl somebody). So I remember thinking to myself that I have been trained to think and to act. So I took on the role of a public intellectual even as I continued in the role of a fellow of the Chair of Ukrainian Studies at the University of Toronto, eventually coming back to Queen's on another post-doc until 1990, when I transferred to the Royal Military College, where I remain to this day.

I want to talk about two of those issues that came out of 1984. One was, as I suggested to you, the war-crimes issue,

67 Displaced Persons (postwar refugees).

68 First Ukrainian Division of the Ukrainian National Army (initially the *Division Galizien*, one of several foreign formations in the German armed forces).

69 Ukrainian acronym for the Ukrainian Insurgent Army.

where I think I earned my spurs in the public domain. I remember, with the help of Myroslav Yurkevich, drafting an editorial that was published in the *Globe and Mail* in March 1985, called "Ukraine's Wartime Unit Never Linked to War Crimes"; this was about the Ukrainian *Dyviziia Halychyna*. I remember the encounters—and this was a very contentious, frankly, and troubling and difficult period of several years—in the very public debate about Nazis in Canada. The miasma still continues, but now, from the viewpoint of several decades later, it is very clear that much of that controversy was stoked by the Soviets. We now know without a shadow of a doubt that there were NKVD veterans who were actually informers for the Deschênes Commission. That only came out many years later. The commission issued its final report in 1987, with the same position that the Ukrainian-Canadian community had taken—namely, that all war criminals found in Canada should be brought to justice under Canadian criminal law. This was adopted as the "made-in-Canada solution" by the government of Canada.

The issue still, as I say, lingers to this day, but we dealt with it as an effective, organized community, largely centred in Toronto but also with support from across the country. In that very period, the Civil Liberties Commission under Gregorovich (for reasons we need not go into today) was pushed away from the UCC[5] and became the Ukrainian Canadian Civil Liberties Association.[70] We took it upon ourselves, in 1987 and 1988 and for several decades after that, to raise the issue of Canada's first national internment operations. You may remember that around that time the Japanese-Canadian community, the Miki brothers and so on, had concluded a very successful campaign to get the government of Canada to acknowledge what had happened during the internment operations in the Second World War. So, with my colleague Bohdan Kordan, I wrote a piece, also published in the *Globe and Mail*, that called upon the government not to apologize but rather to recognize what had happened and provide historical markers, symbolic redress, and a trust fund. That indeed is what happened, some twenty-five years later, in 2008, when the government of Canada signed a settlement agreement, an accord that offered $10 million in symbolic restitution to the community (through the Shevchenko Foundation,[71] in perpetuity) and an inclusive endowment council to commemorate the First World War internment operations—a rather historic and major achievement.

I have to say, in fairness, that CIUS, which had given me support when I was here, was not particularly engaged in the war-crimes issue and was not particularly helpful or engaged with the redress campaign, despite the fact that they had done some very good research (Frances Swyripa and John Herd Thompson, for example, in *Loyalties in Conflict*, their book on World War I). Why? Well, some of it was a preoccupation with pioneer settlement as an experience. Some of it was a certain left-wing bias against the DPs and whom they represented. But the point is, CIUS did not really act as well as it could have—although again, acknowledging Peter Savaryn here, I do recall his efforts on the Deschênes Commission.

As I came to Alberta, CIUS had just started. As I was leaving, we had other centres being established—the Chair of Ukrainian Studies in Toronto in 1980, the Centre for Ukrainian Canadian Studies in Manitoba in 1981, the University of Ottawa position in 1993, the Prairie Centre in 1998—a period of almost twenty-two years of institute-building. Roughly twenty more years have gone by since then, and I have to ask: what has been achieved? On one level, a great deal. We have talked about the books, the publications, the conferences; that is all true. But I wonder whether those who funded much of this, i.e., the *hromada* (community), are really happy with what they got. This raises another issue—are we here to please the *hromada*? Are we here *for* the community? Manoly Lupul provoked an interesting discussion yesterday on that. Or are we, as academics, possessed of academic freedom to study whatever we want? Thinking about this, I would like to propose a few remedies, and in fact this was already suggested to some degree by the previous speaker.

Certainly we need much greater interdisciplinary, collaborative efforts, both nationally and internationally. This is very clear to me as someone who has been on the margins of Ukrainian and Ukrainian-Canadian studies, as someone in the mainstream of academic life, teaching courses on the former Soviet Union—where I always include a lecture or

70 UCCLA (www.uccla.ca).

71 Ukrainian Canadian Foundation of Taras Shevchenko (www.shevchenkofoundation.com).

two on Ukraine and Ukrainian issues—and teaching courses on political geography, where I also plug that in. I have been able to teach about Ukrainian and Ukrainian-Canadian themes, but in some forty years of watching these institutes and centres, I have noticed that in all that period there has never been one single annual or biennial conference that brings all these people together. There has been very little direct sharing of knowledge or results. Instead there has been a kind of competition, which you saw somewhat suddenly played out yesterday; I think some of you were noticing. Very little coordination or co-operation, and in fact, sometimes there has been a barely concealed hostility. I think that has disappointed our *hromada*. There is a little bit of donor burnout, of indifference. Of the 1.3 million Canadians of Ukrainian heritage, I suspect the vast, vast majority of them have never heard of CIUS or the [U of T] Chair of Ukrainian Studies, the Prairie Centre, the Ukrainian Canadian Studies Centre in Manitoba, and so on. They donate, that is true; the endowments are large, that is true, but the question is: so what? How do we move forward?

I think we obviously all agree that the desire should be to continue the study of Ukraine. We all came to this because of the Ukrainian cause, however you want to define it. But where are we with regard to the next generation? How are we funding them? Yes, we have these graduate student posters: I had a chance to look at them and would encourage all of you to do so as well. There is some very interesting work being done by the next generation. But we have come together, and we have spent time looking back, by and large. Looking forward, how do we reinvigorate the donor base? How do we reach out to the people, wherever they may live in Canada? How do we combine the interest in homeland issues, that abiding interest in Ukraine, with where we are today?

Hopefully I have given you some things to consider. I want to end with the words of a man who was very formative in my life, a person who many years ago, as a teacher, volunteered to serve with the Canadian Forces overseas in the Second World War—Bohdan Panchuk. When he was asked to explain himself, why he did what he did as a teacher, as an RCAF officer, as a warrior, and as a community activist, he said simply this: "I have a gospel. What is my gospel? *Roby shchos'*—do something." And that's what I hope we will do, coming out of this conference. ■

ANDRIJ MAKUCH
CIUS

ANDRIJ MAKUCH is the research coordinator at CIUS's Peter and Doris Kule Ukrainian Canadian Studies Centre, as well as associate director of research for the Holodomor Research and Education Consortium at CIUS. He has taught on the Ukrainian experience in Canada at the University of Saskatchewan and conducted research for the Ukrainian Cultural Heritage Village near Edmonton. He is the co-compiler of *Ukrainian Canadian Content in the Newspaper Svoboda, 1893–1904*, compiler of *Encyclopedia of Ukraine: Index and Errata* (2001), co-editor of *Contextualizing the Holodomor: The Impact of Thirty Years of Ukrainian Famine Studies* (2015), and guest editor of *Ukrainians in Canada between the Great War and the Cold War*, a special issue of the *Journal of Ukrainian Studies* (Winter 2003).

Features and future needs of Ukrainian-Canadian historiography

My focus will be on the field of Ukrainian-Canadian studies per se, not issues of co-operation between institutions and the like. [...] Ukrainian-Canadian studies are focused largely on history, sociology, and, more recently, ethnography and, to a small but growing extent, political science; religion also enters the picture, as does literature.

The sociological studies of an earlier era of research on Ukrainian Canadians were written predominantly from an Anglo-Canadian perspective, centring on the question of immigrant adjustment. Some examples are J.S. Woodsworth's "Ukrainian Rural Communities" (1917) or Charles Young's *Ukrainian Canadians: A Study of Assimilation* (1931). A crossover work was Vera Lysenko's *Men in Sheepskin Coats* (1947), written by a Ukrainian Canadian who was not concerned about assimilation per se, as compared to integration, but rather about the manner in which it was conducted and achieved.

After the Second World War, sociological studies were more likely to examine Ukrainian Canadians in their own right. I will use, for example, the volume edited by Roman Petryshyn, *Changing Realities: Social Trends among Ukrainian Canadians*, which came out in 1980, as well as the recent work by Wsevolod Isajiw et al. on the fourth wave of immigration to Canada, which was never published in full.

The earliest historical studies of Ukrainian Canadians tended to be recollections of the pioneering period, for example, Vasyl Chumer's *Spomyny*. Subsequently they started looking more closely at the development of Ukrainian Canadians both geographically and organizationally. The majority of these works were in Ukrainian, often descriptive, and prone to a certain amount of filiopietism and attempts at group legitimization. All the same, they established the contours of Ukrainian life in Canada.

I just want to add that as they wrote their memoirs, Ukrainian Canadians had [...] a strong sense of their critical role in the settling of the Canadian Prairie Provinces, and with it a sense of accomplishment, that they had achieved something special. This is something you will not find among Ukrainian communities in the United States in the same way. So, in comparison, they had a perception of territoriality, if you want to call it that, over broad expanses of land.

The 1970s saw the evolution of the field to include works by trained professionals utilizing primary sources and/or field research. One can point to authors such as John Lehr, Frances Swyripa, and Orest Martynowych, among others, in this regard. CIUS played a vital role in helping to move this process forward, with conferences on Ukrainian-Canadian themes, research funding, scholarships, publishing, and making resource materials available, notably a large project to microfilm Ukrainian-Canadian newspapers and serial titles published before 1970. This was undertaken very early in the history of the Institute. I will not deal here with ethnography or other disciplines.

> *One cannot really divorce Ukrainian-Canadian studies from Ukrainian studies. If you are dealing with Ukrainian-Canadian studies, you really do have to know about developments in Ukraine, because there is an interplay between them.*

One of the questions posed to us was: "Should the emphasis be on organized Ukrainian community life in Canada or more broadly on Canadians of Ukrainian descent regardless of their organizational or community involvement?" In other words, the question is whether to study an organized, elite-led Ukrainian community or general social history. I strongly believe that an initial or immediate emphasis on historical writing about Ukrainians in Canada after the pioneer period needs a strong focus on organized, institutional Ukrainian life, as well as a full picture of socio-economic circumstances, in order to establish the framework in which a broader cultural community functioned. We now have this, certainly, for the period up to the Second World War, thanks to the volumes prepared for the Institute by Orest Martynowych: for the earlier period, we have *Ukrainians in Canada: The Formative Period*, which you received with your packages, and the recently released follow-up volume, which goes up to the Second World War. Basically, we have a general framework for additional research in Ukrainian-Canadian studies.

Before getting to this matter, we need to recognize that pioneer studies have been undertaken extensively, although not exhaustively. The Martynowych volume that I mentioned, which covers the period from 1891 to 1924, required extensive primary research, notwithstanding the fact that a lot of work had already been done on the Ukrainian pioneer period. Still, it had one notable gap—the immigration of Ukrainians from Russian-ruled Ukraine. This was filled by a subsequent monograph by Vadim Kukushkin, *From Peasants to Labourers*. The history of the interwar period and the Second World War could still use research, and even the pioneer period is certainly not exhausted.

Meanwhile, a fair amount has been written about Ukrainian life since the Second World War, mainly as articles, although a fuller historical account is much needed. For practical considerations, a periodization might go from about 1945–46 until about 1967 to 1971—that is, the postwar period up to the period in which multiculturalism was proclaimed—and then the subsequent period, 1971 to 1991, and finally post-1991. Since it is now twenty-five years since the centenary of Ukrainian settlement in Canada and the proclamation of Ukrainian independence, we can certainly view this from a certain historical perspective, but I think the earlier periods would need to be covered first. The immediate post–Second World War period certainly stands out as requiring study. In the short term, actually, I do not think we have exhausted the study of Ukrainians during the First World War, particularly in view of the fact that the Ukrainian community was really under attack by nativist Canadians at that time. The question of internment is one matter, but it is part of a larger picture.

The relationship between Ukrainian settlers and their descendants and the First Nations is also a topic that requires further study. Some recent academic works have appeared in this regard, including a research report by Robert Klymasz for [the 2010 issue of] the *Winnipeg Papers*,[72] put out by the Centre for Ukrainian Canadian Studies, cheekily named "Cossacks and Indians: Encounters, Abductions, Guilt-Ballads, and Empathy," as well as some articles by Lindy Ledohowski. A proper social history of the interwar period, both urban and rural, would be much desired.

The relationship between Ukrainian and Ukrainian-Canadian studies—what do they have in common? [...] It is not an overly complicated matter. Ukrainian-Canadian studies, by definition, do have to take into recognition the role played by Old Country attitudes and experiences in the development of Ukrainian life in Canada. You can use the term "cultural baggage" or you can refer to Louis Hartz's *Founding of New Societies* (1964). People come to a country with certain preconceptions or a cultural history, and then they interact with circumstances in the New World. Also, it is important to look at the ongoing interplay between the Old Country and the New World, as immigrants or their descendants can sometimes be influenced by events in their ancestral homeland.

I will use a prime example. Ukrainian community development in the early years in Alberta was spurred by a gathering in 1909—a *narodne viche* (popular assembly) that very much had as its point of departure the *Prosvitno-ekonomichnyi kongres*[73] held earlier that year in Lviv. So one cannot really divorce Ukrainian-Canadian studies from Ukrainian studies. If you are dealing with Ukrainian-Canadian studies, you really do have to know about developments in Ukraine, because there is an interplay between them.

Let me move on to some specific items that I think should be undertaken to further Ukrainian-Canadian studies. Certainly I think we will require a major conference dealing with the immediate post–Second World War period in Canada, about 1945–55. This could be either a major public conference or a closed dedicated think-tank with papers distributed in advance.

Next, we are in dire need of a study on the fourth wave of Ukrainian immigration to Canada, and then there is always the question of the 1980s immigration from Poland and the former Yugoslavia, which still remains generally unstudied. In fact, that period of immigration is not even established as a period. Is it a pre-fourth wave or is it a fourth wave? And is what we call the fourth wave actually a fifth wave? That is an issue which will have to be resolved in the future.

I think there is a need for a statistical study of Ukrainian Canadians today—basically a snapshot of the current status of the Ukrainian community in Canada. The *Statistical Compendium on the Ukrainians in Canada, 1891–1976* was a landmark work. It was updated in certain categories by Bohdan Kordan's *Ukrainian Canadians and the Canadian Census, 1891–1996*, but time has moved on, and I think we would benefit from a major study of just what the statistics tell us about the present state of Ukrainian Canadians. And I think there is a need for more interdisciplinary and micro-local histories. John Lehr's work of 2011 on the Stuartburn[74] colony, *Community and Frontier*, is a good example. By the same token, I think there is ample room for urban histories—to look closely at major centres of Ukrainian settlement, such as Edmonton, Saskatoon, Winnipeg, Montreal, and Toronto. ■

JARS BALAN:

Our next presenter was actually supposed to be a discussant. We asked him to step up as a presenter because the person who was supposed to be here, Matthias Kaltenbrunner from the University of Vienna, was not able to make it. That is unfortunate, because he would have brought an international perspective, but I thank Roman for stepping up.

72 University of Manitoba (est. 1981).

73 First National Ukrainian Educational and Economic Congress, organized by the Prosvita Society (1909).

74 Rural municipality in Manitoba, now a Historic Site.

ROMAN YERENIUK
St. Andrew's College, University of Manitoba

ROMAN YERENIUK is an associate professor of church history at St. Andrew's College in Winnipeg and a sessional instructor in Eastern Christianity at the Centre for Ukrainian Canadian Studies and Dept. of Religion, University of Manitoba. He has also been a long-time administrator with both units of the university. Roman has written two volumes, published some 50 studies/articles, and has organized and participated in numerous conferences/symposia in Ukraine and Canada on the theme of the Ukrainian-Canadian diaspora. In addition, he has done extensive research and publishing on Ukrainian Orthodoxy, including the Ukrainian Orthodox Church in Canada, and is the editor of the journal *Faith and Culture* at St. Andrew's College.

Ukrainian-Canadian studies as integral to the study of Canadian history

I want to begin my remarks by providing a bit of background to the Centre for Ukrainian Canadian Studies (CUCS) at the University of Manitoba to put into perspective the road it has travelled, especially in the last thirty-five years. At the same time I would like to reflect on some of the questions sent out to the panellists in advance and to complement some of the things that have been said, and perhaps add some new ideas to previous discussion.

The Centre for Ukrainian Canadian Studies is housed in St. Andrew's College (SAC), and thus the college and the Centre share a common background. In 1946 in north-end Winnipeg, the Faculty of Theology for St. Andrew's College was established, and in that early program there was a component known as Ukrainian studies. In fact, some of the scholars who came over in the émigré experience after World War II, such as Professor Dmytro Doroshenko, Professor Yurii Mulyk-Lutsyk, and Metropolitan Ilarion (Ivan Ohienko [Ohiienko]), taught those courses. [...] In 1962 St. Andrew's College moved to the campus of the University of Manitoba and built a remarkable building, with tremendous support from the Ukrainian Orthodox community, that opened for the 1964–65 academic year. There was no arts or science component, just basically the theology program and Ukrainian studies, but without the university's accreditation of the latter. The U of M meanwhile had an established Slavic studies program, including Ukrainian language and literature, for fifteen years. Thus Ukrainian studies were already part and parcel of the university setting. As a result, in the agreements between the university and SAC, the college was initially acknowledged only as an associate college, with the idea that within a decade it should move into fully affiliated college status, with an arts program of one kind or another. So how did the university move to establish formal arts and science courses, or specializations as such?

This process began in 1972, 1973, when the first two SAC courses in Ukrainian studies were accredited and St. Andrew's College became an approved teaching centre of the university. Over eight years, some twenty-one courses were introduced and given from the departments of history, political studies, geography, religion, economics, fine art, and Ukrainian studies, with both Ukraine-oriented and Ukrainian-Canadian topic profiles.

Over the next decade, with a series of banquets and fundraising activities, CUCS raised significant dollars for its own university endowment to assist with the university budget line. This fundraising has continued to the present. According to the Centre's mission statement, "The Centre (CUCS) exists to create, preserve, and communicate knowledge relating to the Ukrainian Canadians through teaching, research, and outreach."

The CUCS courses provide for a program of studies as a major and minor in Ukrainian-Canadian Heritage Studies. Also, all university students can enrol in CUCS courses in the various departments and faculties of the U of M. In teaching, the Centre promotes 8 to 11 courses on an annual basis from its cohort of 21. The teaching staff at CUCS have been university and SAC professors, on overload or as their teaching complement, as well as sessional instructors. In the last few years a number of post-doc and sessional full-time positions have been created, usually shared with Ukrainian Studies (Department of German and Slavic Studies).

In research, the Centre has hired a number of part-time research staff members as funding and grants allow. Over the years these have included Dr. Alexandra Pawlowsky (Ukrainian-Canadian literature), Dr. Robert Bohdan Klymasz

(Ukrainian-Canadian folklore), and Orest Martynowych (Ukrainian-Canadian history). The Centre has published two volumes, some nine research papers, and a series of occasional articles.

CUCS has worked collaboratively with many university and community institutions, such as the departments of German and Slavic Studies, History and Religion, Archive of the Ukrainian-Canadian Experience, and St. Andrew's College, as well as the Oseredok Ukrainian Cultural and Educational Centre[75] and UVAN.[16] We have also partnered with CIUS and its Kule Ukrainian Canadian Studies Centre. Together we have held nine successful symposiums or conferences with academics and community members. The last such conference we supported, "Contested Ground," took place on the theme of Ukrainians during World War II.[76]

"Ukrainian-Canadian studies cannot be separated from Canadian studies but are an integral part of such studies. There are some other subfields, such as immigration studies, ethnic studies, and diaspora studies, in which we also should be involved."

The Centre sponsors the biennial Michael and Iraida Tarnawecky Distinguished Lectureship, which brings a prominent Ukrainian-Canadian scholar to speak on an important research topic. This lectureship has been very popular with the general community.

Several members of the staff of the Centre have travelled to Ukraine on research projects and have worked with prominent diaspora centres. This includes lectures, conferencing, symposia, as well as program review work. The staff have worked with universities in Nizhyn, Kyiv (Kyiv-Mohyla Academy), Chernivtsi, Lviv (Ivan Franko National University and the Lviv Polytechnic National University), Lutsk, Chernihiv, Ivano-Frankivsk, and others.

The Centre has participated actively with the Learned Societies of Canada, especially CAS and CAUS,[7] including its sessions on Ukrainian-Canadian studies. These meetings have become a sort of meeting place where we can compare notes with scholars working in the field.

The work of the Centre in outreach has been limited mostly to the province of Manitoba, including the city of Winnipeg. Community lectures, travel tours, presentations, book launches, and other events have been held in many towns and cities.

In Winnipeg we have worked collaboratively with Oseredok and UCC-Manitoba on themes of the Ukrainian Internment, the Holodomor, and the 125th anniversary of Ukrainian settlement in Canada. The Centre has also supported many local institutions, especially the Ukrainian bilingual school program. It has provided many media interviews, as well as newspaper, radio, and television commentary.

In discussing the needs and further work of Ukrainian-Canadian studies, I would like to make several points and observations. First of all, I would like to suggest that we need to improve sharing and communications between Ukrainian-Canadian programs across Canada. Maybe we could set up a formal or even informal council that would provide ideas, priorities, and direction, and become a clearing house for our field. We all have our corporate institutional individuality, but also we need a form of unity. This could also assist with some of the perceived duplication in our field.

Secondly, we need more intensive relationships with the general field of Canadian studies across Canada. Ukrainian-Canadian studies cannot be separated from Canadian studies but are an integral part of such studies. There are some other subfields such as immigration studies, ethnic studies, and diaspora studies, in which we also should be involved. Thirdly, I would like to support some previous speakers in talking about strengthening our teaching role and especially in becoming more involved in online courses/studies and the use of technology in spreading knowledge in our field.

Fourthly, I believe we should be doing a better job of assisting students, especially with summer projects/jobs and government projects to do research in the field. In Manitoba, Dr. Stella Hryniuk and I have worked with a unique church architecture project in the province of Manitoba (very similar and parallel to the Sanctuary Project in Alberta). This past summer we employed four students who worked

75 www.oseredok.ca.

76 Hosted by CIUS in Edmonton on 23–24 October 2015, in partnership with the Center for US-Ukrainian Relations (CUSUR, www.usukrainianrelations.org).

throughout Manitoba and completed basic archival work on thirty churches. There are many other such projects that could be undertaken, such as oral history, family documentation, material culture, etcetera. For some this could lead to jobs, maybe even careers, in archives and museology.

Still another area of co-operation that is strongly needed is with our university archival centres as well as with Ukrainian community archival centres. We are very lucky at the U of M that the Archive of the Ukrainian-Canadian Experience was recently established. This is already a leading institution in Manitoba. We can add our community archival centres, many of which could use volunteer and professional assistance.

Lastly, I would like to go on record and support Andrij Makuch, who spoke on the need to improve our work in urban history. This sub-area needs our respect, since rural history already has its champions. In addition, I would like to advocate for more work on the religious history of Ukrainians in Canada. This field is slowly declining and also needs its specialists. ■

NATALIE KONONENKO
Discussant, University of Alberta

NATALIE KONONENKO is a professor of the Kule Chair in Ukrainian Ethnography at the University of Alberta. She holds a BA from Radcliffe College (Slavic Languages and Literatures) and an MA and PhD from Harvard University (Slavic and Near Eastern Folklore). Kononenko has conducted folklore and ethnographic fieldwork in Canada, Ukraine, Russia, Kazakhstan, and Turkey. She served as editor of *Folklorica*, the journal of the Slavic and East European Folklore Association, and is the author of *Slavic Folklore: A Handbook*, the award-winning *Ukrainian Minstrels: And the Blind Shall Sing*, and other books and articles. Kononenko is an award-winning teacher and researcher, and her interests extend beyond folklore into the realm of digital technologies, an area for which she has received support from the Canadian government's Social Sciences and Humanities Research Council (SSHRC).

Desiderata for the future of Ukrainian-Canadian studies

Thank you, everyone. It was a very interesting panel, lots of good ideas, and I am going to do a little bit of a summary and then head on into a discussion with some observations and desiderata of my own.

It was kind of interesting that we had two schematic talks and two very personal talks. Natalia Khanenko-Friesen talked about defining the field, about comparative analysis. She suggested that we do community outreach, and I should point out that she is the editor of the *Engaged Scholar*, which means that she does what she preaches and actually works on a publication that works with the community, and also puts the material out. She also stressed working with Ukraine, as did other speakers. I believe Lubomyr Luciuk pointed out that our ties with Ukraine and the things that happen in Ukraine do impact us, and not just us but the entire community.

The other schematic presentation was done by Andrij Makuch. He talked about the history of the field—very nice if you can get his presentation notes, where he has a lot of things listed. Then he talked about desiderata in terms of history and areas to investigate, including the urban environment. Then we had Lubomyr Luciuk and Roman Yereniuk, who gave us much more of a personal experience.

I was really quite pleased to see how important were Lubomyr Luciuk's personal experiences and the interviews that he did, because I am a professional interviewer and I know that other people in this room have been with us on interview projects. This was really something that made a difference in his life as an academic and as a human being. Roman Yereniuk told us about St. Andrew's College and the work that it has done—again, a lot of the things that he himself and his group experienced, and how they impacted his research and hopes for the future. From all this I can draw a number of desiderata that fortunately very much coincide with my own. Obviously if you or our panellists do not agree with my desiderata, you can add and correct as we go along.

Andrij Makuch pointed out the importance of doing interviews with the immigration that came after the Second World War. It is an elderly group—if we are going to interview, we must interview them now. I know that Bohdan Kordan has worked on the refugee experience. One of the things that I would like to add, from what I see—and I know the work of a lot of these people, although it may not have come out as much—is that we do actually reach out to others and well beyond the Ukrainian community, and our work does impact other fields. Natalia Khanenko-Friesen (and I believe others also) was talking about the diversity of Ukrainian-Canadian studies—if you are going to call it that. It is ethnography and history and geography and many fields. But one of the things going on now is the refugee experience. I would love to have a big study of the Ukrainian refugee experience. I think that what we know from the kind of work we do with Ukrainians, including Ukrainians in Canada, is that first-person interviews provide extremely rich source material. I was absolutely delighted when I was offered this job as a professor in Edmonton because it allowed me to do fieldwork, which I love.

With things like that we can impact other fields, global scholarship, Canadian society, and of course Ukrainian society. One of the points that came up a number of times is that we should work together, perhaps having a conference of all the centres. It is a wonderful idea, and I would very much endorse it.

Another thing I should point out is that we do work together already in many ways. I would like to thank my colleagues. I work on the Sanctuary Project, which is the documentation of sacral heritage, primarily in Saskatchewan and Alberta, and lo and behold, we have worked with Natalia [Khanenko-Friesen] and her students. I know that we also parallel work done by Roman Yereniuk in Manitoba.

That sort of co-operation between centres exists and should very definitely be taken further, not just with the Sanctuary Project but with other projects as well. I know that Roman mentioned archiving at the University of Manitoba. Yesterday many people talked about the digital world. Speaking of sharing, linking our various databases is kind of a natural process. I will tell you that from Sanctuary, we have a photo database of about 200,000 images—that is the part now functioning. It is not open, as I was telling Bishop David, for reasons of security: we do not want to let everybody and his uncle know where the hundred-year-old gorgeous tomes or gorgeous *ievanheliia*[77] are. To date, we also have about 150 hours of sound digitized, and that database should be open shortly. I know Natalia has letters that she has been collecting and processing. So there is great potential to link the kind of material we have to what Natalia has. And Roman has very interesting documentation of sacral heritage that they have done in Manitoba in the past and are also planning to do in the future.

Speaking of the Sanctuary Project, I must bring up the names of my two dear colleagues, without whom I could have never done this, John-Paul Himka and Frances Swyripa. I bring them up also for another reason, and that is to encourage, again, collaboration. It so happens that John-Paul, Frances, and I are very different people, with very different interests. And the fact that we are very different is exactly the reason for our success. Frances does archives: we could never survive without her. John-Paul is interested in iconography and photography, and I am the interviewer. If we did not do different things, we would not be able to do a project of this scope—to work together on doing different things in different areas.

> *"I would like to add ... that we do actually reach out to others and well beyond the Ukrainian community, and our work does impact other fields."*

The idea of working with other communities, not just the Ukrainian community, came up in various ways yesterday. I was doing interviews in Falher, which is in northern Alberta, and I was interviewing an elderly Ukrainian lady. She needed some help from her daughter, and the daughter was married to a very nice Frenchman who said something that I will never forget. He said, "You know, the Ukrainians did not exist in isolation." We would never have survived had it not been for the French, the Danes, the Norwegians, and whatever other communities we interacted with. I was about to say, I know that in Manitoba the 125th anniversary was done in conjunction with First Nations. With the kind of work that we do, I would urge collaborative research. And as people have said, ethnic studies, immigrant studies, etcetera are also areas where we could work with other groups.

77 Evangelion (Book of the Gospels).

But you know, my desire has always been not just to work with other groups, not just to do community research. I am a folklorist—I want to work with the *folk*, with the regular people. Be it in the realm of technology or investigating diasporas or interacting with the home country, sharing knowledge, sharing data—I want us to do something *so cool* that it will get people from all sorts of ethnicities wanting to do Ukrainian studies. I teach 130 students, and believe me, they are not all Ukrainian but something interests them—a cool methodology, a cool approach—and they learn about Ukrainian studies. I also learn about *their* culture, we exchange information. My call on various levels is for co-operation and sharing. ■

DISCUSSION

JARS BALAN:

One thing about Ukrainian-Canadian studies that motivates me is the realization that the work we do in studying the Ukrainian community in Canada, I think, is going to be a game changer in certain discussions of Canadian studies.

I will give you one personal example. Over the years I have been chipping away, compiling a chronology of Ukrainian theatrical performances in the country from 1900 to the 1950s, 1960s. And so far I have literally thousands of entries of Ukrainian performances from Nova Scotia to Vancouver Island. What is interesting is not just the sheer volume and longevity of this theatrical activity but the fact that there is a distinct Canadian component. There are plays that were written by authors in Canada, some on Canadian themes, some on Ukrainian themes. Years ago an article was published in the *Canadian Theatre Review* on the history of Canadian theatre. Basically, the article said that Canadian theatre starts with British theatre being imported into Canada and American touring companies coming to Canada in the earlier years, but it does not really start until 1960 in Toronto with *Spring Thaw*, and then you have this whole explosion of indigenous theatrical literature.

I remember talking with my mother about this, and when she read it she said, "That's outrageous! We lived on the same street as Semen Kowbel. He wrote, like, I don't know, twenty-one plays…" People she knew personally wrote plays that were performed on the Canadian stage—well, they are in Ukrainian, but they are not known. I have spoken on this subject at a number of conferences of the Association of Canadian Theatre Research, and those people are all just riveted, fascinated.

I think another area where we are game-changing is the whole question of World War I and the discussion around it. The UCCLA[70] has raised the internment issue among Canadian scholars: it was not even on their radar before, and now it is part of the discussion of the First World War. There are a host of other areas that I think that we have an impact on, Canadian studies in particular.

NATALIA KHANENKO-FRIESEN:

A few themes I have seen recurring. One is engagement, or rather, working with the community through accessing information via interviews, via world histories.

I would like to be more specific this time and point out that this work seems to be overwhelming and resource-needing. But at the same time it is actually quite possible to accomplish a lot on the ground if one is a bit creative. The Prairie Centre for the Study of Ukrainian Heritage at the University of Saskatchewan—and we will have a presenter later, Professor Kordan, who will point out a few more pursuits we do in the centre—has undertaken several initiatives with respect to Ukrainian-Canadian studies.

Our annual budget is about $50,000 or a bit more per year, and that is not enough. One can think, if one is ambitious, of pursuing several projects. Over the course of the last ten or fifteen years we have produced collections—speaking of digital humanities—on the outcomes of our research. It is not enough just to conduct the work and write up academic articles and get brownie points. We need to present our work in different formats for other consumers out there. I am talking about oral history and other archival collections that we are trying to digitize and make publicly available. One of these projects concerns the Ukrainian-Canadian experience of socio-cultural change in the second half of the twentieth century. We have about a hundred and twenty interviews collected, digitized, and partially transcribed. They are fully available through the library system to whomever wants to research them. Creatively, with the students, we have ventured into urban history (speaking of other themes that I found important) and pursued the oral history of 20th Street, the main locale where Ukrainian-Canadian urban history evolved in Saskatoon. Granted, it is an ambitious project and granted, one cannot take a specifically Ukrainian perspective in carrying it out. While teaching the course in oral history, I have involved all kinds of students who are not Ukrainians at all. These students represent the entire community, which is multi-ethnic, multicultural, differentiated economically, and so on. This kind of work gave us an opportunity to focus on the Ukrainian-Canadian dimension of that very research and its next stage.

My emphasis here is to think creatively about the product of our work. Speaking of co-operation—which we all commented on, and obviously this comment came up—I could not help but think that we actually have a lot to learn from our colleagues in Ukraine. What I mean by that—and I always admire Ukrainian colleagues working for different research institutions who have traditionally gotten involved in these mega-meta-projects—is an annual pursuit, or several years spent on one large focused project in which members of the department or members of the PCUH would be involved. Eventually they would produce sizable collections reflecting the history of, say, the Ukrainian peasantry. That is what comes to mind from the Institute of History, for example. The meta-projects that Natalie [Kononenko] referred to, such as the Sanctuary Project, give us an opportunity for networking, and we probably should be seeking out opportunities to engage in such meta-projects that we can pursue independently. They are much like the format that has been described, where each researcher has his own interest and his own passion. Conferences would also be nice to have, where we can gather and think through what we can do with the resources we have, because resources are always limited.

LUBOMYR LUCIUK:

Concerning the question of doing oral history with the displaced persons, the political refugees who came in the so-called third wave, I think that opportunity is essentially now gone. There are still opportunities, and they should certainly be taken. I can say, and I mentioned this in my talk, that Dr. Lupul, with his oral-history project, engaged both Zenko Zwarycz in Toronto and myself here in the west, and many of the people we interviewed were of the generation that helped the DPs, people such as Bohdan Panchuk, Stanley Frolick, Anthony Yaremovych, and people who were political refugees themselves. That pool of oral-history information has recently been digitized, thanks in part to the work of Jars Balan and the Ukrainian Canadian Civil Liberties Foundation. We provided the funding to digitize that collection here, and the collection that was done at the Multicultural History Society of Toronto, and exchanged those collections. So they should all now be digitally available from both ends of the country. But more work could certainly be done.

Secondly, in terms of working with other communities, one of the founding principles of the endowment council of the First World War Internment Recognition Fund, established in 2008, was that we would always include the other communities affected by Canada's first national internment operations. For example, today we have had Hungarian, Serbian, Alevi Kurd, Polish, Turkish, and Croatian representatives on the council who have taken an active role in articulating the council's mandate and assigning funds from that $10 million endowment for various commemorative and educational projects across Canada. I have to give recognition to my colleague and good friend Bohdan Kordan, who has just written what probably will be the go-to book on Canada's first national internment operations, published by McGill-Queen's Press. But we also have Peter Melnycky here, who has had grants from them; my own daughter, Kassandra Luciuk; others such as Mark Minenko, who are being funded; and Ryan Boyko, who has come out with a great series of short vignettes called *The Camps* and is now doing a film called *Enemy Aliens*. All these are intended to be inclusive, multicultural, and reach out to a larger constituency. Indeed, it is such public-space projects that I think that we as researchers in Ukrainian and Ukrainian-Canadian studies can do a lot of good work with.

For those who do not know this, on April 8th of next year, so within a few months, a major new memorial to the Great War will be unveiled in France by Lens, near Vimy Ridge. And the central pathway, thanks to some generous donors, is going to be named after Corporal Filip Konowal, who won his Victoria Cross there at the Battle of Hill 70. A major war memorial in France, visited by approximately 750,000 people per year, will be named and posted trilingually, honouring Corporal Filip Konowal. That is the kind of profile our community needs to develop.

Finally, in terms of collaboration, which everybody touched on. As I mentioned, in my forty years or so of watching centres come and go and do their projects, there has been some co-operation, there is no doubt of that. Books have been shared, colleagues have met at conferences. But there is a need to have one annual or biennial meeting where they all get together and discuss an agenda—they can go their separate ways after that—to discuss collaboration and opportunities, graduate students, funding, scholarships, promoting the new generation. If we want to continue Ukrainian and Ukrainian-Canadian studies, I do think we actually have to provide a venue for cultivating that next generation.

Where I disagree with my good friend Bob Magocsi is that I do not think we can possibly oversaturate the market. I think we need *more* people interested in Ukrainian or Ukrainian-Canadian themes. Many of them may not get jobs in the academy; that could very well happen. We all know about tightening economic circumstances, and all that was discussed yesterday. But they will go out trained as people interested in things Ukrainian or Ukrainian-Canadian, and they will carry that with them, and that will diffuse. I think that is very important.

In terms of collaboration, comments were made about sacred space and the effort here in Western Canada, but just as an example, a very good one, is Saskatchewan co-operating with Alberta. But who is doing the Maritime churches? Who is doing the churches in northern Ontario and northern Quebec? Those have been ignored, largely because there is an east/west divide that was mentioned. We need to make sure that we are actually working together and covering the country coast to coast. There is a vibrant community of Ukrainians in Sydney, Nova Scotia, based on the coal mines. Some of whom were interned, one of whom, a man by the name of Harry Kowal, is now principal of the Royal Military College. A former brigadier-general, he was a Ukrainian called Kowalchuk, is now Kowal—or as he likes to say, "Coal," and I say, "No, that is what your father mined; your name is Kowal." [Laughter.] This is the kind of person we need to engage, but we do not engage him by studying Prairie churches. We have to study *his* church, right?

ANDRIJ MAKUCH:

As Lubomyr mentioned, starting an interview project with the post–World War II generation would have been more feasible twenty years ago than now. In terms of co-operation, I think baby steps might be one good way to start before you talk about mega-projects. Agreeing to have a clearinghouse or one place where you can share information just between the various institutes and players involved would be a great idea. I will just use a concrete example. Recently a book came out about Ukrainian churches in Saskatchewan, and if this were, let us say, posted on a Facebook page—for people to know that this is where you go to learn about things that come out—then I would not be writing emails saying, "Did you know that this book came out?" etcetera.

Also, I wanted to pick upon Natalie [Kononenko's] comment on doing something so cool that everyone would sit up and pay attention. In terms of Ukrainian-Canadian studies, two things that really are exceptional and, presented in a certain way, would be incredibly cool. One is just the fact of the bilingual, bicultural world in which Ukrainians lived in the Prairie provinces, in the aspen parkland. Manoly Lupul's memoirs mention that he grew up in—as he called it—a bilingual, bicultural world. This is really something extraordinary in terms of the North American landscape, where you have a large stretch of land with large areas that have a totally distinct culture. The other area to which we can also pay more attention—it has faded and in some cases has almost disappeared—is recognition of the role played by Ukrainian Canadians in establishing multiculturalism. In a world with growing nativist tendencies, Canada really does stand out as a beacon of tolerance, and a large part of that is the establishment of the multiculturalism policy and its general acceptance by many Canadians, although the Reform Party was strongly against the cultural heritage aspect of it.

ROMAN YERENIUK:

I believe very strongly that we have done a lot of work in oral interviews and oral history and elsewhere, but we need some form of collaboration, of putting it all together, of indexing it and doing it this way. I will tell you my story. A couple of years ago I decided to do a little bit of research on people like my mother, who came as an *Ostarbeiter* to Edmonton and settled here, worked here, and I could not find any material. And all of a sudden it popped up on the computer screen—the Ukrainian Canadian Research and Documentation Centre at St. Vladimir Institute [in Toronto], an institution that is not affiliated with the university in a formal sense. They had a whole volume of *Ostarbeiter* stories that I could glean and learn more about the history of what my mother went through. Otherwise you know what happens—many times we want to ask those questions once they are gone, and unfortunately we did not ask those difficult questions of these *Ostarbeiter*, or at least I did not, while they were alive.

Another thing that I wanted to mention is the various communities that we should be engaging with. Two of the communities that I would like to suggest are the Mennonites and the Jews. About twenty years ago, in Winnipeg, we hosted a conference of the three communities—Mennonites, Jews, and Ukrainians in Winnipeg, or in Manitoba—and we got a lot of parallel stories in all three communities. One of the interesting things was a very strong paper on Jewish theatre. So I looked at Jars and said, "This is a similar story to our Ukrainian theatre in Canada." And sure enough, it was. It is interesting that many of our communities that came from Ukraine created a kind of ethnographic territory: they settled in patterns, for example, along Winnipeg's Selkirk Avenue. You have Ukrainians and Jews living side by side in the 1910s, 1920s, and 1930s for a good chunk of the time. We now have a Mennonite University in our province [Manitoba]: the provincial government allowed one of the colleges that was Mennonite to create a university. And certainly that university is not going to come to us, but maybe we should go to them and do some collaborative projects between the Mennonites and the Ukrainians.

NATALIE KONONENKO:

One of the things that as a scholar I find fascinating, and it has come up here again and again in this discussion, is the blending of cultures and the blending of belief. And I think that the sort of work we do (again, I will repeat what I said) can inform not just the Ukrainian community, the Ukrainian-Canadian community, but Canada as a whole—precisely because Ukrainians have been leaders in multiculturalism on a political level, as I am sure Peter Savaryn will tell you. But also because (as we just heard), as a community in a special cultural—if you want, bicultural—setting, a bicultural community, it is something for us to do.

Listening to all these people reporting on all these good projects—and they did so again in this second round—I say, as I look to our dear director of CIUS and maybe other people who work for CIUS, we need better advertising. Or maybe I should address Bohdan [Klid], because Bohdan does a great job of advertising all sorts of things, as does Halyna [Klid]. We need a better job of advertising what has been done so that the community knows, and possibly also people beyond the community know, the contributions we have made both to Ukrainian studies and to Canadian studies, history, and elsewhere.

The final thing: all of us have mentioned collaboration, coordination, and I know (and you probably do, too) that there is some very interesting material in Sudbury, including documentation of sacral heritage. We are not ignoring the east; I know very well what is going on in the east. It is just that on Sanctuary there are three of us. I would love to write a grant proposal, but we really need help, especially in this heavily bureaucratic time, when I spend more time filling out documents than I do on this interesting research in blended-belief systems and blended communities. I need help arranging coordination, making phone calls, making the whatever it is to get these things going, all these neat projects that we would love to do. Yes, we should probably have a meeting to prioritize, and having had that, maybe we can get some support to organize and do a mega-project or whatever. I would love a museum, by the way, in Ottawa—a big national one.

JARS BALAN:

About advertising better: we try, of course, to advertise what we are doing, but it is a challenge because you are caught up in the day-to-day responsibilities of work. And a lot of our scholarly projects are not done in six months, and you cannot produce results so quickly, as they are done over a period of time.

One project that I can tell you about—and again, one of those game-changing projects—we have gone through the Canadian mainstream press of 1932–33, and this is all a spin-off from CIUS's Holodomor Research and Education Consortium. We have gone through the *Toronto Star*, the *Toronto Telegram*, the *Globe*, the *Winnipeg Free Press*, the *Winnipeg Tribune*, the *Saskatoon StarPhoenix*, the *Vancouver Sun*, the *Edmonton Journal*, the *Edmonton Bulletin*, day by day. We wanted to know what did Canadians know about what was going on in Stalinist Ukraine during the Famine?

It was astounding how much coverage there was. I mean, in our community the assumption was always that the Soviets just suppressed it, nobody knew about it, and it was only in 1983, when the fiftieth anniversary of the Famine was commemorated, that more people started to talk about it.

It was shocking to discover how many Canadians (not Ukrainian Canadians) were in Ukraine in 1932 and 1933, and how many of them wrote up things. There was an engineer who came back and wrote eighteen articles in the *Toronto Telegram* about what a disaster the Five-Year Plan was. There was a Toronto journalist who travelled through the Famine areas of Ukraine in the fall of 1932 and wrote detailed accounts of her experiences there. There were journalists who went and whitewashed the whole thing. But this is going to have a big impact on the discussion of the Holodomor—it is our Canadian contribution to Ukrainian studies and the discussion of the Famine. And in Canadian studies it is going to force a bit of a re-evaluation of Prime Minister R.B. Bennett. He was the Conservative prime minister at the time; he does not have a great reputation because of the Depression. I have been impressed, actually, by many qualities the man had. You should be aware that the Holodomor Research and Education Consortium came up, and it sort of pushed us, pulled us in the direction of doing some of this work—this happens all the time.

Recently our Institute has also become very much involved in the making of a documentary film by the Ukrainian Canadian Research and Documentation Centre in Toronto on Ukrainians in the Canadian Armed Forces during World War II. This was not an immediate priority of ours. We are planning to focus more attention on the Second World War and on the broader context as well—the community during the war years. The film is focused just on Ukrainian Canadians in uniform during the war. Serhii Cipko, Andrij Makuch, and I have been very active in doing research so that the product is solidly based, and that includes doing interviews, looking at the press, and other things.

Much of what we do is often unseen because we receive many private communications via the Internet in particular, and Facebook and stuff. I do not know about my colleagues here, but we get requests regularly from all over the world with questions relating to Ukrainian-Canadian studies, especially now from Ukraine, where you have diaspora studies and people doing Ukrainian-Canadian studies asking for information, asking for help. Some of them are scholars, some are students, some are filmmakers, all kinds of areas. It is important that we try to help these people, because we do have resources at our disposal, but it is of course very time-consuming. There has been much co-operation on the personal level because we know one another, we know our interests, we run into each other at conferences, and yes, maybe we could try to coordinate better what we do, but both human and financial resources are constraining factors. I am very encouraged to see some young scholars here who can join us in this work and take it over as we go on into the future, so that is a very positive development.

QUESTIONS AND ANSWERS

ASHLEY HALKO-ADDLEY:

We have heard many wonderful ideas for the future of Ukrainian-Canadian studies today, and Ukrainian studies yesterday, and I thank you for commenting on students, but I was wondering if you could comment on one more suggestion. Students are under-represented at this conference and in its discussions and panels, so I would like to suggest that more students be engaged in discussions and decisions regarding the future of Ukrainian studies, as they are the future of Ukrainian studies.

LUBOMYR LUCIUK:

I think all my colleagues on the panel agree. I think one of the few flaws in this meeting that we are having—we have these interesting posters that I referred to—but in fact, it would have been nice to have the next generation of scholars, who represent the very great and interesting, intriguing diversity of different interests, from my generation anyway, to be presenting, to be talking about what they are interested in doing. I am an external reviewer for a PhD dissertation at Simon Fraser University right now, where a very bright young woman is doing an archaeological investigation of the Morrissey Internment Camp. This is a completely different perspective from anything that Bohdan [Kordan] or I have ever looked at. She has just recently uncovered not only the escape tunnel but the digging tools and a crucifix—a crucifix made by one of the internees out of barbed wire. What a symbol, right? So this is the kind of young scholar that I would love to have had here today to share findings with you. I am delighted that we have the seven or eight we have here, with their posters, but I would gladly have sacrificed some of my time to them.

GENIA BOIVIN:

I just would like to take up what my colleague said. I understand we are seen as the future of Ukrainian studies. However, most of us are already of a certain age, so I was wondering if any of you have been to high schools to try to interest the actual young generation in Ukrainian studies and see what they would like to study. Ukrainian studies and perhaps video games, or cinema, so have any of you done this and actually studied their culture? I think it is important to have their voice here, and, of course, none of them are here because they are not at university. But they are going to be taking your classes, so I think it would be important to acknowledge what they want.

JARS BALAN:

I was happy to get out of high school—I do not want to go back, actually. [Laughter.] Indeed, these are valid points.

NATALIA KHANENKO-FRIESEN:

I think it is a very important direction in our work: publicity, promotion. I do use opportunities to go and work with youth, maybe not through schools but through summer camps. And I do put on witch hats if I work with eight-year-olds, and I do have games for them to play that I hope eventually will settle in their heads that they can have fun with professors at the university once they grow up.

KASSANDRA LUCIUK:

I do want to start by taking the opportunity to say that I think all of us appreciate the opportunity—all of us on this student travel award. But I do want to clarify that there was no call for papers. We were not asked to speak or present our research. We were asked to come here with posters, which is fantastic, although maybe a little odd in the humanities, but we were not actually given an opportunity to present.

I find it strange that—this year I am the recipient of the Darcovich Fellowship—I actually found out about the student travel award by word of mouth after the due date. Not to be overly critical, but there is a bit of a communication barrier, and I think that maybe a student panel would have been a really fantastic idea. And something that my colleague here mentioned earlier—I do not want to speak on her behalf, but she is an undergraduate student, and I think it would also be fantastic if we created funding opportunities for undergraduate students (who were not allowed to apply for the student travel award), because undergraduate students are how we get more MAs and PhDs into programs, by engaging them at the undergraduate level. That would also have been a fantastic funding opportunity.

MANOLY LUPUL:

Okay, now this is going to be positive. [Laughter.] You see before you, in the main, part-time scholars of Ukrainian Canadians. These are either geographers, or responsible for the *Encyclopedia of Ukraine*, or people interested primarily in the theological aspect. Or people like Jars [Balan], who is responsible for almost everything to do with Ukrainian Canadians at present, running around for everything, sending books to Ukraine, and picking up money from anyone he can find who has a few cents. This will always be the case. You will never have specialists in something called "Ukrainian-Canadian studies"—I found that out when I was director. It became very clear about the third or fourth year. They will come from Canadian studies, East European studies, sociology, political science, and they will give you a chapter or an article, and that is as far as it will go.

One thing I missed in the presentation is the question of money. It is nice to hear about the projects that you are either into, or you are hoping to develop, or that somebody should take up. Various things are not being done for lack of funds. It all takes money, and none of you really said very much. I think only Roman [Yereniuk] said a little bit about money. I do believe that CIUS has a role. I do not mean that CIUS should make money available—goodness, no one knows better than I how strapped they really are. I would point out to you that the endowments that have come forward so far for Ukrainian studies have primarily come forward voluntarily. I know that there is a newsletter once a year; I know that there are reports in *Ukrainian News* and, for all I know, they may go into other newspapers. But it is not as if CIUS ever made a special effort in any way to reach out to the public for funding. We might call it massive funding, call it whatever you want. These have been largely from émigrés also, I think it is fair to say, who happen to have done fairly well and are very sensitive about helping to do something about the situation in Ukraine. There have been very few endowments for Ukrainian-Canadian studies. What I want to suggest is the following: the public, in my opinion, has to be sensitized. It has to become conscious that there is something called Ukrainian-Canadian studies, and that there are people across the land trying their best to do what they can with very limited funds.

I have a suggestion. It has been mentioned here that coordination is needed, that maybe people like you should get together. I agree. But where would you be going? What would be the point of it? You would be talking to one another, but you are talking now, and to a whole bunch of other people here who are in fact interested primarily in Ukrainian studies per se. From their good hearts, one day, they might even produce an article or two dealing with Ukrainians in Canada. Why not have the Ukrainian Canadian Congress spend a whole day on the situation in Ukrainian-Canadian studies to sensitize the UCC[5] to the fact that endowments would be appreciated for Ukrainian-Canadian studies? Instead of simply placing it before them in Winnipeg, or wherever it would be held, people who are the leaders, the heads of these various institutions, or the best spokespeople from these various institutions would meet and draw up an agenda for such a one-day session—not a session but a one-day immersion into the question of funding for Ukrainian-Canadian studies. In my opinion, this has never been done, and CIUS should bring together the heads first to draw up an agenda where they can say "these are the kinds of things"—including the young, by the way. That would be a very important function for the Institute—not to provide the money, though. They may have to fund your meeting, or a meeting of people like you. But in my opinion that is the least they can do, and that is what we should try to do if we want to get something done with Ukrainian-Canadian studies that is more than simply limping. Jars [Balan], you would have a big role in this, certainly, but it would lead to something that should make your job easier in the long run. Andrij [Makuch], you too would have a role in this, because you have been closely involved in it, and Natalie too. Anyway, that is what I propose.

NATALIE KONONENKO:

You are very much on point, and I myself was thinking about funding as we were all talking. The first thing I would like to do is thank Peter and Doris Kule, who funded my Chair and gave me the opportunity.[23] Actually, I pay for the Sanctuary Project out of my Chair endowment, so I very much thank them for that. I also thank KIAS, the Kule Institute for Advanced Study, which has funded our work, and it has been generous. Obviously we could use more, but what I would like to add to this is that I am incredibly appreciative of the donors. I am especially appreciative of Peter and Doris Kule and what they have done for me. But I think the next step we should take, especially in terms of Ukrainian-Canadian studies, is getting federal funding. Certainly our team has done it—we are applying for federal funding—and I think maybe we should have whomever coordinates this at CIUS coordinate the applications for SSHRC[78] funding.

LUBOMYR LUCIUK:

Dr. Lupul's suggestion is an excellent one, and I would like to see something like that happen at the next triennial UCC congress. I think the proposal being made now, just after the one that was held in Regina a few weeks ago, is good in the sense that it gives Jars or whomever several years to prepare for the congress, wherever it may be held in Canada. Certainly there is enough lead time to be able to coordinate the heads and representatives of the various institutes—which can be done by Skype or FaceTime, by the way. There is no need necessarily to get together physically. But I think that is a wonderful proposal, and it bears following up on.

I would like to point out, though, that in terms of funding, and this group of old people should be made aware of this, there is a $10 million fund that is now in about year eight—the Canadian World War I Internment Recognition Fund—that was a symbolic redress we secured from the government of Canada in 2008. It has already funded some very good projects. Frankly, it has also funded a few that I do not think are very good, but it has funded some excellent projects. It has another seven to eight years to run. It works off the interest, and right now we are in a positive situa-

78 A Canadian federal government granting agency, the Social Sciences and Humanities Research Council (www.sshrc.gc.ca).

tion. I am on the endowment council. So those interested in the First World War period, including the internment operations, but not exclusively, have a much easier route for securing funding than, for example, going to SSHRC, which can be quite difficult and ponderous and frustrating.

There is also a secondary fund that you should be aware of—the Ukrainian Canadian Veterans Fund (UCVF), which was based on the sale of Branch 360 of the Royal Canadian Legion in Toronto. Until recently I was a member of that committee. The sale of that property rendered about $4.5 million. It was then taken by the dominion command of the Royal Canadian Legion, resulting in a legal action; 2.4 million dollars were returned to the Shevchenko Foundation[71] for the UCVF. So, whether you are studying World War I or World War II, or indeed any aspect of Ukrainian-Canadian military history, or even Ukrainian military history, there is a fund available to you. These are two resources that, frankly, are not being used as efficiently as they could be. I am sitting on a council where we often say, "Why is no one applying? Why is no one coming to us for money?"

MANOLY LUPUL:

Because no one knows about that.

LUBOMYR LUCIUK:

There is an annual report; it has been sent to libraries. I do not think it is intentional; this is the way it is, people do not know about it in a way. And yet, as was mentioned by one of the speakers, the internment story, in broad brush, has already penetrated national consciousness.

There was an article in the *Globe and Mail* that had nothing to do with Ukrainians; it was about "whiteness" as a construct. It was very controversial, just a week ago or so, and the author of that piece (Denise, the name escapes me) mentioned the internment of Italians and Ukrainians as "whites" in the world wars in Canada.[79] So here is—I believe—a Trinidadian lady of Indian descent who is writing in the national newspaper about Italians and Ukrainians being interned in Canada. So we are out there. The endowment council maybe has not made as good an effort as it should, I do not know, but surely, having said it, now you all know about it. They have a website; look it up and apply, because the money is there.[66]

JARS BALAN:

For the record, CIUS has taken advantage of both, with our conference two years ago on internment and also now, working on this documentary film, which is funded from the UCVF. We are helping them spend their money, just as we help other people spend their money on projects that we think are important. So we are aware of these things. And Dr. Lupul, you should know that I have been talking with Paul Grod, the UCC president. He said, "We should get all our institutes, all our academic bodies, as members of the UCC," and I said, "Well, I am not sure how that would fly." He said basically to bring the academics under the UCC umbrella—to use the UCC as a venue for bringing them together to work on these common projects—and I think that is one of the issues he is going to be raising today. So it will be interesting to hear the reaction to it.

NATALIA KHANENKO-FRIESEN:

I would like to chip in, representing an institution that is by default dealing with the financial question in quite serious terms, because we are smaller. I am representing the University of Saskatchewan, the Prairie Centre for Ukrainian Heritage, which operates with a smaller budget altogether, and I did refer to finances as being a limitation and constraint in our work. Coming back to your comment on finding opportunities and reaching out for them—first, my colleague Bohdan Kordan is very effective in doing that, having set up the centre in the first place, and second, a dimension of this work is geographic distribution of funds and their availability to us if we are locally located.

But historically, we see funding gravitating toward the more established centres, which surround us on both sides. I am not suggesting we need to compete and ask for funds to support what we do in Saskatchewan. What I would like to suggest is to look back at student needs. Over the last 5–7 years, we have been graduating students with theses in Ukrainian-Canadian studies quite systematically and regularly, one year at a time. Our student work is published; it is even included in the lovely bibliography compiled recently by Orest Martynowych on Ukrainian-Canadian scholarship. Two of my students are here in the room, attending the conference on their own without being invited here. We need funding to support student work, because what we do is based on student research. The students accomplish all

79 Balkissoon, D. "Whiteness is a racial construct: It's time to take it apart," *Globe and Mail*, 10 October 2016.

the work I was referring to. We do not have enough funding to support it. Perhaps CIUS can set up a student fellowship to support Ukrainian-Canadian studies, and in small institutions like ours we will have better access to those funds to bring students on board. Otherwise I am scrambling for funding to support my incoming graduate students because they are just constrained in the wrong ways.

PAUL ROBERT MAGOCSI:

First, I would like very much to thank the panel, in particular the first two speakers, Natalia Khanenko-Friesen and Lubomyr Luciuk, the first of whom was more theoretical, the second very practical—not practical, experiential, if you will. But really what I want to do is put something on the table that was already alluded to. It reminded me of the time when I published this large history of Ukraine, which was about Ukraine and not about Ukrainians abroad. But I had a very long text insert called "the Ukrainian diaspora." After I wrote that, I felt that there was something missing, considering that my book was about all the peoples of Ukraine. So I added a second text insert called "Ukraine's other diasporas." And here—when much of the discussion has been about the desirability of co-operating, interacting with other groups, and there was reference, briefly, to Mennonites and Jews—the real question is (not only a theoretical and conceptual one but one related to your own pedagogical activity): what is the Ukrainian diaspora? Is it ethnic Ukrainians from Ukraine? Or is it diasporas from the present-day territory of Ukraine?

If you take—and this is a suggestion—if you take the second option, this opens up a wide range of possibilities of drawing into your field a whole host of other interests, which come with funding possibilities. We know that the Mennonites have chairs, and most of those Mennonite chairs come from Ukraine, and their experience in the homeland is Ukrainian. There is the question of Jews, who come from Galicia, the Right Bank, or their parents and their grandparents. I can imagine the endless opportunities. Should you be teaching not only about ethnic Ukrainian activity but also about Mennonites? There is a possibility of cross-influences and bringing a wide range of students, scholars, and others into the fold. We already have a Crimean Tatar community now, certainly in Toronto, who are part of Ukraine, and we should never forget that. So I just put this on the table for those of you who are continuing to work in this field—that your field is probably much larger than you think, and much more relevant than you think.

FRANK SYSYN:

Just two suggestions on undertaking research topics. One is that we finally realize the need to emphasize contacts with Ukraine, but what we have to admit is that for a large part of the experience of the Ukrainian-Canadian community, contacts with Ukraine were rather limited. That is a very interesting part of our development, similar to the Baltic groups, to the Lithuanians in the United States, or the Cubans, so close in Miami, right? That is a problem we should also discuss, because it explains so much, I think, about the Ukrainian communities abroad, why they developed.

I am always asked by Polish friends who complain that the Polish communities did not establish academic institutions. My answer always is, "You had Poland." We did not have Ukraine in a certain sense, so we had to do this.

The second point is whether one can really study the post–World War II immigration solely in a Canadian context. Here I would say that without development of the study of whole DP communities—not only when they were in Germany but also when they arrived in the United States—I fear that what we would do is write them into Canada in a different way than the reality of what their life was. While their children may have gone through a different experience into the 1960s and 1970s, the Toronto I knew and that generation were much more closely connected with New York, in certain ways even with Australia, etcetera. I do not want geography and national categories to take over our study, but it is another way of opening up the subject. Regrettably, because of the poor state of the study of the Ukrainian community in the United States, we may be missing a large part of the experience. I mean, it was *Suchasnist'*,[80] after all, that was getting read in Toronto and Montreal, and to a degree in Edmonton as well, and yet we are going to have no studies of what was going on south of the border.

80 A monthly journal of literature, history, and current affairs, reflecting a wide spectrum of émigré and Western opinion; published in Munich (1961–90), Newark, NJ (1990–1), and Kyiv (1992–2010, 2012–13).

PETER MELNYCKY:

I think something that is missing is any discussion of the public history that is going on in Ukrainian-Canadian studies, whether it be in Manitoba with the Historic Resources Branch, which has done very important work in recording architectural history, or here in Alberta, where we have an entire research and publications program related to the Ukrainian Cultural Heritage Village. All this is mainstream government funding, and the work being done there is very important. Somehow I think it is missing from this discussion, that indeed there are other areas where Ukrainian-Canadian studies are taking place that are directly funded by government.

JARS BALAN:

We did not address it, and thank you for bringing it up, because it is another area that needs to be understood in the context of Ukrainian-Canadian studies. I would just say to Professor Magocsi that in 1991, when we were celebrating the 100th anniversary of Ukrainians in Canada, I edited a special issue of the literary journal *Prairie Fire*. We issued a call for papers from anybody with roots in Ukraine—Mennonites, Jews, Poles, and we had all three and more—not just Ukrainians. I think that we have done things—I know of interactions with the Jewish community and the Mennonites as well. There was a conference with Mennonites, Ukrainians, and Jews in Winnipeg years ago. So we are reaching out beyond the narrow ethnic definition of Ukrainians in Canada. I have spoken to a Swedish community, the Swedes in Wetaskiwin: they are part of Ukrainian history and Ukrainian-Canadian history.

ANDRIJ MAKUCH:

I would like to add that since Ukrainian independence in 1991, it is probably more possible to address what Professor Magocsi said in terms of thinking of Ukraine in geographic terms, not just in terms of Ukrainian ethnicity. So I certainly think that Ukrainian Canadians are perhaps more receptive now to the idea that we should include other groups from Ukraine within the fold.

LUBOMYR LUCIUK:

A topic that I would like to see the new generation consider is Soviet disinformation about the Ukrainian immigration and diaspora in general. For decades, very stereotypical, inaccurate, provocative descriptions of the post–World War II immigration were provided to journalists and the media and academics around the world, and it still continues to some degree. You see it in the current conflict in Ukraine, the stereotypes about Bandera and UPA and OUN, and so on. I do not think anyone has systematically looked at that, and yet it has created a certain perception of Ukrainians in the West in the public domain, and I think it is a critical problem for our community. Every one of us, I am sure, has come up against it at one point or another. Secondly, I would like to see us consider writing about the redress campaign. It took two and a half decades to reach fruition. The only scholar I am aware of who has written about it in a sort of conceptual way is Ian Radford from the Department of History at the University of Toronto, in a paper in a book published by the U of T Press. That campaign set a standard for addressing historical injustices, and it was in fact largely set by one survivor, Mary Manko Haskett, but also Bohdan Kordan and myself: the notion that one does not ask for an apology, one asks for recognition; and one does not ask for compensation, one asks for symbolic restitution. You make the case about what happened, but you do not necessarily say, "Now pay us for it." Other communities have taken a different position, and I think comparing the approaches to redressing historical injustice is a very valid and interesting exercise that would echo throughout the First Nations community and other communities who have experienced times of difficulty in the past. Going forward, I think this would be an interesting intellectual exercise.

NATALIA KHANENKO-FRIESEN:

Coming back to Professor Magocsi's commentary on opening up the idea of identity for the Ukrainian-Canadian constituency: in Saskatchewan, in Saskatoon, we have seen the community working very hard with the new arrivals from Ukraine, and one of the fascinating observations I have made is the community's gradual acceptance of the plural makeup of the newcomers. Mostly I refer to the fact that in the provinces we have a special immigration policy separate from the federal, so we have a very steady stream of newcomers. Many have come with Russian as their lingua franca, and it is quite interesting to observe the established Ukrainian-Canadian community in interactions with this newcomer group and see gradual recognition of the complexity of Ukrainian identity. So I am all for inclusiveness and opening up the notion of what Ukrainianness is all about and where Ukrainianness is generated, be it Yugoslavia, Poland, Russia, and so on and so forth.

JARS BALAN:

We have been talking about using the latest technology, digitizing things, being cutting-edge about it. One new development, a relatively new one at CIUS, is the archiving of a lot of its publications and materials on our website. So Oleksandr [Pankieiev], if you could just bring up our website? The research reports, the issues of the journals, all of this is becoming digitally accessible to people, so scholars and students from around the world no longer have to try to track down copies or order special things in, or go to special collections to find these publications. I think this is a very exciting development, and we are well aware that this is the way scholarship is evolving in the use of high technology to make it more accessible to people.

Round Table III: Ukrainian-Canadian Studies.
L–r: Natalie Kononenko (discussant), Roman Yereniuk, Lubomyr Luciuk, Andrij Makuch, Jars Balan (moderator), Natalia Khanenko-Friesen (at the podium).

MYROSLAV SHKANDRIJ
Moderator, University of Manitoba

MYROSLAV SHKANDRIJ graduated from the Universities of Cambridge (BA) and Toronto (PhD). He is a professor of Slavic studies at the University of Manitoba. His most recent books are *Ukrainian Nationalism: Politics, Myth, Ideology, and Literature, 1929–1956* (2015) and *Jews in Literature: Representation and Identity* (2009). He has also written on the avant-garde and curated art exhibitions, the latest being "Propaganda and Slogans: The Political Poster in Soviet Ukraine, 1919–1921" at the Ukrainian Museum, New York (2013–14). His translations into English include Mykola Khvylovy's *The Cultural Renaissance in Ukraine: Polemical Pamphlets* (1986) and Serhiy Zhadan's *Depeche Mode* (2013).

This is really a continuation of the previous session, and some of the previous discussions will be continued here.

As you have heard, Ukrainian studies in Canada began around 1949. The postwar immigration started them, and many of the core programs in Ukrainian studies were housed in Slavic studies at that time. Many of these programs and courses are now shutting down. Others have survived, have morphed, have been restructured in different ways. This panel is a good opportunity for us to review some of these developments in order to see how some of the restructuring has taken place and learn about some of the new courses and programs that have been created.

Ukrainian studies within departments of Slavic studies have always been small, often just one or two people. They have always had limited possibilities. Nothing has changed within those structures. What has changed, however, is the tolerance of university administrations for small programs with limited enrolments, and there is a very great danger of their disappearing. Several have already disappeared, and many are under great pressure. Even at the University of Alberta, if you have read the recent letter circulated by Natalia Pylypiuk, you will see that this is a strong possibility. These programs have been the traditional ones. They have often fed students into graduate studies. The professors in these programs have often been the Ukrainianists on campus, the ones who lobbied for Ukrainian studies in other departments, areas, and programs. They have often been the chief spokespersons for Ukrainian issues locally—the community organizer and resource person in general. But this traditional model of Ukrainian studies within Slavic studies departments or programs is not the only one, as we have already heard in previous sessions. There are different ways of structuring these programs, ways that have now become more available. Slavic studies have always been allied to other disciplines, as they have to be, particularly in those universities that do not have chairs.

We need to become more mainstream, to be able to attract students and create programs that are interdisciplinary. This is very clear from the discussions in the previous session. Another thing that is happening is that after the Second World War there were many people in different programs, disciplines, and departments who happened to be of Ukrainian origin. They could be drawn on for various programs, but these people are now disappearing. I know that at my university, the University of Manitoba, several people have retired recently from economics, from political studies, from history. They happened to be of Ukrainian origin or Ukrainian background, and they were capable of, and interested in, teaching courses in those departments. They have now gone. This indicates that we need to look at other models, other ways of structuring the teaching and delivery of courses. Often this needs to be done, I think—as we will shortly hear from our panellists—through an interdisciplinary approach. And the key, as always in developing interesting courses, is to make them relevant, to make them in tune with contemporary developments, to

> *"Ukrainian studies within departments of Slavic studies have always been small, often just one or two people ... Nothing has changed within those structures. What has changed, however, is the tolerance of university administrations for small programs with limited enrolments, and there is a very great danger of their disappearing."*

respond to the exhortations of university administrations, and to find funding.

Each participant in our panel today can help us understand the successes and drawbacks of particular approaches and can explain the model for delivery of courses that their university has developed. Student numbers are always a great challenge, so these courses have to be attractive. But we have a wealth of experience to draw upon in Slavic studies, in fact, many years of innovative programming. We heard at the last panel, for example, of the successes of summer courses abroad, which are a big draw now and which really transform students when they visit Ukraine. We have heard about delivery of courses through distance education, through computer programming, through blended learning—that is, learning through which the community is engaged. All these are really useful, and I am sure that we are going to hear a lot more about them here.

Another theme that has come up is how to understand student interest. How do we analyze student interest, even at the high school level? We need to find out where the students are, what they want, what they expect. Lastly, it should be realized that universities will not hire instructors, scholars, or professors if the numbers are not there, so we need to think really hard about this. And these positions are required because before we can network, before we can have megaprojects, we have to have individuals who are actually teaching at the universities. Since we do not have chairs at most universities, we need mainstream positions at those institutions. ■

DOMINIQUE AREL
University of Ottawa

DOMINIQUE AREL is an associate professor of political science and holder of the Chair of Ukrainian Studies at the University of Ottawa. He received his BA from the University of Montreal, MA from McGill University, and PhD from the University of Illinois at Urbana-Champaign. Dr. Arel co-edited *Rebounding Identities: The Politics of Identity in Russia and Ukraine* (2006). He has organized the Annual Danyliw Research Seminar on Contemporary Ukraine since 2005. Professor Arel manages the *Ukraine List* (UKL), an internet academic/current events newsletter that reaches over 1,500 subscribers in thirty-five countries.

The new face of Ukrainian studies

[SUBMITTED TEXT]

As Chair of Ukrainian Studies at the University of Ottawa, I am partaking this weekend almost with a sense of filial duty in the celebrations of the CIUS fortieth anniversary. In my younger years, I had a saintly great-uncle who was a Trappist monk, and I even got to spend a summer working in the archives of their monastery on the hundredth anniversary of their foundation. I learned that the monks referred to an older monastery in France as the "Mother House," where the original monks came from. My chair may be far away from theology—our friends from the Sheptytsky Institute,[24] who alas have just left Ottawa, are covering that very well—yet I cannot but think of CIUS as our Mother House. Over the years, besides respect and co-operation, CIUS has quietly taken very concrete steps to help ensure the durability of the chair.

In my presentation on teaching Ukrainian studies, I will be making three points. The first is about approaching Ukraine through the study of problems. The second is on graduate training. The third is on providing doctoral, post-doctoral, and young scholars with a research forum. Unlike other Ukrainian studies chairs and institutes in Canada, the chair at the University of Ottawa focuses on social science. I belong to a subfield of political science called *comparative politics*, which could be defined as the study of domestic politics understood in a comparative context. What this means, in a nutshell, is that if, for example, I want to study language politics in Ukraine, I have to find out how the case of Ukraine contributes to the study of language politics more generally. And how the insights of the larger literature on language and politics help us understand the case of Ukraine. This is literally how I entered the field. My interest in language politics during perestroika almost instinctively led me to Ukraine and, with the help of the late Bohdan Bociurkiw and of Alex Motyl at Columbia, I ended up in a summer school run by a young man who would, much later, become ambassador to Canada—Ihor Ostash.

This is how Ukraine is incorporated in my teaching, as students are attracted to Ukraine through their keen interest in contemporary issues. When I teach on political systems, the model of competitive authoritarianism developed by Lucan Way is on the syllabus, with Ukraine being one of the "swing cases" (to use an American electoral analogy). When I teach on political violence, the Holodomor is the crucial case of a modern famine used as a means of mass killing. And the war in the Donbas has now made Ukraine a critical case in a very different type of political violence. When I teach on political memory in a larger course on identity politics, then the Holodomor, World War II, and now decommunization bring forward a literature very interesting to a comparative audience. When we explore social mobilization, the Joshua Tucker article of 2004 is a classic, raising students' interest in the colour revolutions, the so-called "springs," and now the *Maidan*. My students know that I am passionate about Ukraine, and they come to understand why Ukraine matters academically, not necessarily because of its sudden geopolitical importance.

My second point is on graduate training. I have five graduate students working on Ukraine, four of them at the doctoral level, and with a new round of applications for the Kule Doctoral Scholarship, perhaps one or two more in the pipeline. With a half-dozen more students or young faculty members working on post-Soviet or Eastern European topics, we periodically hold informal seminars to let them present their work. This is the upside of having a critical mass of students firmly or loosely affiliated with the chair, allowing us to build an actual community. Years ago, moreover, I decided to extend the model and make the chair part of a broader community. At the initiative of French colleagues, the chair became involved in the organization of an annual Social Science Summer School in Ukraine for doctoral students.

An intensive one-week event, the school is structured not around lectures but around the presentation of doctoral projects at various stages of completion, from preliminary to advanced field or archival work. We have a dozen faculty members and twenty students sitting around a large table, and students get to have their project discussed for a full hour, plus all kinds of informal feedback throughout the week. Significantly, the school is not *on* Ukraine but *in* Ukraine. The common geographical area of cases is East Central Europe, broadly defined, with 35–40 percent of students working on a Ukraine topic. And each day features an element of what we call "academic tourism," when we discover aspects of the surroundings that could be meaningful to our broad interests. In Kharkiv last summer, this meant visiting the OSCE monitoring mission office, the "Stantsiia Kharkiv" NGO, which cares for internal refugees, and a Holocaust site (Drobitskyi Yar) and museum, and holding a round table with local and foreign correspondents (brought in from Kyiv) who have covered the *Maidan* and the war in the Donbas. The school is held in a different city every year, namely (in inverse chronological order): Chernivtsi, Lviv, Mykolaiv, Zhytomyr, Ostroh, Dnipropetrovsk, and Uman. Strong bonds are created, and in the last five years I have ended up on the doctoral defence committees of five students whom I had met at one of these schools.

> *"The field has been revitalized from two ends: non-Ukrainians choosing Ukraine as a great field to study problems of global relevance, and Ukrainians (in a territorial, not necessarily ethnic sense here) who are increasingly part of a transatlantic community of scholars.... This shows how vibrant the field has become."*

My third and final point is on a research forum. Since 2005 the chair has been holding an annual research forum on Ukraine funded by the Danyliw Foundation in Toronto—the Danyliw Seminar. The idea was to provide scholars in the field, and particularly the rising generation, with a platform to present their research—not in a panel format like this one here, but in a seminar format where they present separately and get the full attention of their peers and older colleagues in an intense discussion. (Because of the extraordinary events in Ukraine, we had to alter the format in the past two years, but we are getting back to it this year, while keeping a large section on special events.) Essentially, the summer school adopted the Danyliw format and brought it to Ukraine, with the difference that Danyliw is about presenting research findings, not early doctoral projects.

Counting the next one on 10–12 November [2016], the twelve years of the Danyliw Seminar provide us with a fairly representative sample of the changing field of Ukrainian studies—excluding language and literature, since we are a social science chair. Our sample is 148 presentations by different academics (several have made repeat visits, but they are counted only once, and discussants are not included). Thirty-three non-academics, such as the two filmmakers who will present their film next month, are also excluded from the exercise. Of all 148 presenters, 40 percent were doctoral students at the time of their presentation. This unique database allows me to make four points.

First, in reference to Mark Von Hagen's comment yesterday about how political scientists have "abandoned us," fifty of the Danyliw presenters are political scientists, or one-third of the total. Three of them engage in the kind of modeling or advanced statistical techniques that Mark alluded to, and they all know Ukraine very well. Political scientists are in fact a very important component of the area studies discipline that we call Ukrainian studies.

The second point, however, is that political scientists comprise only one-third of presenters in an annual event whose chair is a political scientist and whose selection committee has been mostly comprised of political scientists over the years (currently three out of four). The revelation is the rise of other disciplines of social science, particularly sociology and anthropology. We have had 24 sociologists and 15 anthropologists, a little less than 30 percent combined. Even more strikingly, among doctoral students we have had many more sociologists and anthropologists (22) than political scientists (13). I dare say Professor Wsevolod Isajiw would be very proud of this development.

The third point is that from our vantage point as social scientists, the boundary between social science and history is becoming very porous. When I began the seminar in 2005, my general take was that we would leave history to our esteemed colleagues in Edmonton and Toronto, and focus solely on social science. This did not last long. Forty of our presenters have been historians, and just this year we are doing three panels on new books: by Serhii Plokhii (*The Gates of Europe*); by a French historian, Catherine Gousseff, on the Ukrainian-Polish deportations after the war; and by a historian of law, Lawrence Douglas, on the Demjanjuk trials. Our starting point is the relevance of research topics for an understanding of contemporary Ukraine, and we are inexorably and increasingly drawn to historical research. This may be self-evident to historians, but it is real and the upshot is that young social science and history scholars are engaging each other.

The fourth and final point is the Ukrainian makeup in the field. Of our sample of presenters, 53 percent are non-Ukrainian, a slight majority. Of the 69 presenters *with* Ukrainian background, 17 are from the diaspora (born or raised abroad), 25 are from Ukraine, and 27 are Ukraine-born but studying or teaching abroad. In other words, three-quarters of the nearly 50 percent of young scholars in the field are from Ukraine, revealing that the field has been revitalized from two ends: non-Ukrainians choosing Ukraine as a great field to study problems of global relevance, and Ukrainians (in a territorial, not necessarily ethnic sense here) who are increasingly part of a transatlantic community of scholars. A near 50-50 breakdown is a natural equilibrium for an area study when the political regime in the homeland allows for an open academic exchange. This shows how vibrant the field has become. ■

BOHDAN KORDAN
St. Thomas More College, University of Saskatchewan

BOHDAN KORDAN is a professor of international relations in the Department of Political Studies at St. Thomas More College, University of Saskatchewan. He also serves as director of the Prairie Centre for the Study of Ukrainian Heritage. His current research focuses on the politics of state/minority relations in Canada, ethnic conflict, and identity and minority rights issues. His publications in this field include *Canada and the Ukrainian Question, 1939–1945: A Study in Statecraft* (2001); *Enemy Aliens, Prisoners of War: Internment in Canada during the Great War* (2002); *A Bare and Impolitic Right: Internment and Ukrainian-Canadian Redress* (2004), and *No Free Man: Canada, the Great War, and the Enemy Alien Experience* (2016).

Change, challenge, and purpose: The future of Ukrainian studies in Canada

[SUBMITTED TEXT]

I. The state of Ukrainian studies: A context

In 1983, while working at CIUS as a research associate, I was tasked with writing a report on the state of Ukrainian studies in Canada. The report, "Ukrainian Studies Courses at

Canadian Universities: Trends, Prospects and Implications," conveyed a depressing picture. Academic programs were scarce, course offerings were inadequate, and enrolments vacillated wildly—but not unexpectedly, given the small numbers. I was hopeful that Ukrainian studies could and would survive despite the challenges, if only because there was a healthy crop of academics committed to instruction in this area of research and teaching. As long as there was a dedicated group of scholars and instructors, there was a future for Ukrainian studies, I thought—not a thriving future, but a future nonetheless.

I could not have predicted, however, the public policy shift in advanced education that would take place in the next two decades and its effect on post-secondary education. It was a policy shift that had as its goal increased institutional accountability in an age of public austerity, the consequence of which was the corporatization of universities and all that this entails. We have seen, as a result, the introduction of enrolment quotas, performance reviews, mission/vision statements, strategic and integrated plans, program evaluations, downsizing of faculty, tuition hikes, and the ballooning of administration, ostensibly to help streamline the delivery and effectiveness of teaching programs.

This new direction has had a profound effect on advanced education in general and Ukrainian studies in particular. We all know the story as it relates to Ukrainian studies. It is one that Professor Natalia Pylypiuk has eloquently described in her recent CAS/Facebook post regarding developments at the University of Alberta. At first blush, it seems unimaginable that this could occur at a place where, historically, Ukrainian studies excelled. But, quite frankly, it is to be expected, given the dynamics at work.

It is not just the field of Ukrainian studies that has suffered but, with few exceptions, the entire humanities and social sciences as well. Tenured faculty are being replaced with part-time sessional instructors. Courses are evaluated not on the basis of program needs but on their capacity to attract large enrolments that generate revenue. Programs and even entire departments are being eliminated. At the University of Saskatchewan, which I know best, the prospect of consigning modern-language instruction to the Division of Continuing Education as a community outreach activity was seriously discussed. Political theory in the Department of Political Studies is near elimination as one of four core competencies in the discipline—the result of a reduction in the faculty complement. What was once a proud department of fourteen is now a diminished department of nine, with its graduate program in jeopardy, given the reduction of resources.

These are distressing developments, sadly pointing to the corrosive effect of current conditions on academic programming. Sharing this predicament, the field of Ukrainian studies is now faced with competing for scarce faculty positions that are increasingly defined in terms of program relevance and needs. Instructors are hired according to university and departmental priorities, which necessarily precludes the possibility of a faculty appointment with a Ukrainian specialization. Such hires are seen as exotic and superfluous to programs that are looking to meet the core requirements of a discipline or simply struggling to survive. In a competitive environment, academics with a Ukrainian scholarly focus are neither a likely nor a desirable choice.

> *"The evidence is clear that centres matter. Who would dispute this, noting the importance of CIUS at the University of Alberta? Would Ukrainian studies be what they are in Edmonton without CIUS? It has served as the catalyst for the growth and development of Ukrainian studies at this fine university."*

The teaching situation at the University of Saskatchewan is especially disappointing because local demographics suggest that, if anywhere, Ukrainian studies should survive and thrive in Saskatoon, where census figures indicate that one in ten individuals self-identifies as Ukrainian (single and multiple origin). The phrase that applies to New York, "If I can make it here, I can make it anywhere," has equal but negative billing when speaking of Ukrainian studies in Saskatoon: "If it can't work here, it's likely impossible that it would work anywhere else." At least that is what we are inclined to believe.

And yet it is not an all-bad-news story. If it were, I would simply declare that we should all "get up and go home." I do believe, in fact, that there are measures to help address the challenges. The experience at the University of Saskatchewan helps to illustrate what might be done.

II. Ukrainian studies at the University of Saskatchewan: Coping with change

When I first arrived at the University of Saskatchewan in 1993, austerity cuts were well underway. Departments were undergoing a 10-percent reduction in their budgets, and in 1995 departments were instructed to set aside an additional 10 percent for college-wide special appointments to be allocated in areas of designated excellence. This was followed by an additional "tax" in 1997 and 1998. It was clear that traditional programs would not survive this assault, including the existing Ukrainian language and literature program. It was also apparent that if a Ukrainian program were to continue at the U of S, it had to be reimagined on at least two fronts.

First, the circumstances highlighted the importance of creating a Ukrainian studies centre that would serve as a platform for Ukrainian scholarly activity on the University of Saskatchewan campus. Such a centre would guarantee that Ukrainian studies would survive in some form, serving as a backstop in preparation for the inevitable demise and loss of the traditional Ukrainian language and literature program on campus. Financially supported by the community, such a centre also would not be hostage—at least, not at the programming level—to the vagaries of administrative fiat, ensuring some control over the fate of Ukrainian studies on campus. The proposal would be realized in 1998 with the creation of the Prairie Centre for the Study of Ukrainian Heritage (PCUH) at St. Thomas More College (a federated college of the U of S).

> *"The role and importance of centres, institutes, and chairs cannot be overestimated. The issue, however, is to use these as platforms to reimagine and rethink how Ukrainian studies as a learning experience might be delivered under challenging and demanding circumstances."*

Second, it was necessary to advocate for a reworking of the existing Ukrainian language and literature degree program on the U of S campus according to criteria that would recommend it: a program that would be innovative, effective, and sustainable. The PCUH made the case early on for a multidisciplinary and interdisciplinary program that would draw on existing resources, be attractive to students, and remain flexible so that it could adapt to changing circumstances. The proposal met with resistance from those who were still committed to a traditional language and literature model and were prepared to fight a losing battle against senior administration in its defence. Without going into the particulars, the existing degree program was discontinued, instructors reassigned, and authority subsequently granted to St. Thomas More College (STM) to create and offer an interdisciplinary minor degree in Ukrainian studies—based on the original proposal. Supported by three faculty members who work under the umbrella of the PCUH, the Ukrainian studies minor follows in the great tradition of Ukrainian studies at the University of Saskatchewan, which in 1944 offered the first university-level Ukrainian language course in North America.

I will be the first to admit that the present situation is not an optimal arrangement. The Ukrainian studies degree, after all, is a minor. But this undertaking, even in its limited form, has prevented Ukrainian studies from completely disappearing at the U of S, as has happened elsewhere in Canada. It has also satisfied the objective of providing undergraduates with an opportunity to learn and study about Ukraine (and the Ukrainian experience generally), albeit in a different format. Consequently, enrolments are healthy and the immediate future is at least stable.

Circumstances, of course, may change, which invariably raises the question of uncertainty. Retirements occur, for instance. But it is precisely the existence of a Ukrainian studies centre that guarantees there will be replacements and potential jobs for future academics. As a functioning, self-sustaining unit that contributes to the scholarly and academic identity of the university, there are compelling reasons for the centre and the minor degree program to be populated with Ukrainian studies instructors/specialists.

This points to the strategic importance of creating centres, institutes, and chairs (broadly defined) across the country. These entities serve as support mechanisms for teaching programs, without which they could easily disappear. I would argue that the announced departure of the Sheptytsky Institute in Ottawa for St. Michael's College at the University of Toronto is St. Paul University's loss. But it is also St. Michael's gain. Ukrainian studies will disappear from the curriculum at St. Paul's (despite recent claims to the contrary by the resident dean), while the curriculum at the University of Toronto will, conversely, be strengthened. The evidence is clear that centres matter. Who would dispute this, noting the importance of CIUS at the University of Alberta? Would Ukrainian studies be what they are in Edmonton without CIUS? It has served as the catalyst for the growth and development of Ukrainian studies at this fine university. Although today there are challenges at the U of A, the very presence of CIUS gives some assurance that they can be met with proper leadership and support.

III. Rethinking the teaching of Ukrainian studies

The PCUH has helped stabilize the teaching of Ukrainian studies at the University of Saskatchewan. It is considerably less than one would have hoped for, but even so there is potential for more. In this regard, I believe that it is necessary to think of alternatives and different possibilities as ways to provide a rich undergraduate experience that allows students to gain a better appreciation of Ukrainian culture and history while cultivating the next generation of graduate students and scholars. Specifically, what if the emphasis is not on teaching but on learning? Might not the same objectives be achieved? If so, then what needs to be done?

The PCUH is heavily invested in facilitating a variety of learning experiences that have aroused energy and enthusiasm among undergraduate and graduate students. The PCUH, for instance, provides partial financial support for a study-abroad program, "Spring Session in Ukraine," organized by STM with its partner, the Ternopil National Pedagogical University. The centre also awards stipends for students to participate in this overseas experience. Meanwhile, the PCUH allots an annual operating grant to the Ukrainian Students' Association to conduct activities on campus that reinforce their understanding and appreciation of Ukrainian culture, history, and identity. In addition, the centre supports and co-sponsors their events, which helps to validate the organization and strengthens the students' collective sense of identity and purpose. The association currently has 58 members, one of the largest Ukrainian university student groups in the country. Recently, several of them have gone on to serve the community both locally and at the national level.

Learning comes in different formats. It is incumbent on us to recognize the potential of each and assist where we can. This is especially important at the graduate level. The PCUH supports and offers opportunities on a case-by-case basis. Aside from traditional faculty supervision, the PCUH provides funding for Ukrainian thesis topics—work that will define the future research and scholarly orientation of these students. The centre organizes graduate seminars and round tables and facilitates and supports a teaching internship program that sees the placement of a U of S graduate student at Chernivtsi National University in Ukraine. Graduate students are also involved in the centre's various research projects, programs, and initiatives. These are opportunities that will define and potentially shape the next generation of scholars, without which their exposure to Ukrainian studies as a scholarly enterprise is greatly limited. But again, the emphasis at the PCUH is on learning and not exclusively on teaching, allowing Ukrainian studies to be relevant in the lives of our students in other but no less meaningful ways.

Our task is not simply to train the next crop of scholars but to create, with the resources at hand, a milieu and an experience that will help shape their consciousness and cultivate an awareness that will accompany them throughout their lives. This is possible only because of the creative, innovative, and supportive role that the PCUH has assumed. The PCUH does not describe itself as a "research centre"; neither is it a department or a teaching program. Rather, the PCUH is characterized as an "academic unit" at STM. This ambiguous designation was selected precisely because it allows the centre to do all of the above and more. It is an academic entity committed to research and the dissemination of findings conducted under its auspices. It supports teaching in the field, provides institutional and financial backing for student activities, facilitates and assists graduate work, and engages in outreach to help validate the community by connecting it to the university. This, I believe, is the practical face of Ukrainian studies in the university today, as well as in the future.

IV. Conclusion

Change is afoot. The need to adapt and innovate has now become imperative. The role and importance of centres, institutes, and chairs cannot be overestimated. The issue, however, is to use these as platforms to reimagine and rethink how Ukrainian studies as a learning experience might be delivered under challenging and demanding circumstances. ■

TARAS KOZNARSKY
University of Toronto

TARAS KOZNARSKY is an associate professor in the Department of Slavic Languages and Literatures at the University of Toronto. He holds a PhD from Harvard University (2001) and an MA from the University of Alberta (1994). His most recent work includes the articles "Heroes and villains in the historical imagination: The elusive Khmelnytsky," "Jews in Russian travel narratives of the early nineteenth century," and "The case of Beilis and novelistic imaginations."

Course design and promotion between and outside the lines of disciplines and cultures

My perspective here will be a little bit ambivalent. First of all, I am speaking on behalf of a Slavic department, the only one left in Canada that is kind of mainstream, normal, and therefore anomalous. Second, my position is doubly anomalous in that not only is this the only Slavic department left in Canada, it is also the only Slavic department, I think, that has *two* Ukrainianists, my colleague Maxim Tarnawsky and I. It is nice, of course, to have two Ukrainianists in one Slavic department, but again, that is a result of bureaucratic rules and circumstances. It is neither my fault nor my particular accomplishment that it happened that way.

Initially, as a second Ukrainianist in a small Slavic department, you have to do what you have to do. Teaching a number of "straight" Ukrainian courses, you have to develop second- and third-year Ukrainian language survey courses, and so on. But the problem of two Ukrainianists is that it is a small field, and having two people competing for the same pool of students is obviously not very healthy or helpful. This has led me to carve out a field for myself, and in this case my perspective will be personal. I had to design courses between and outside the lines of disciplines and various Slavic and other cultures. This task was somewhat easier for me because I studied Czech, Russian, and Ukrainian in my undergraduate years at Lviv University, and then in my graduate years at Harvard I could read Polish, which was helpful as well. But the main challenge was, and remains, to design a package and contextualize interdisciplinary courses around a certain compelling or inevitable idea, theme, or place, with the hope that they would be attractive to students. Since all the courses are taught and read in English, they are very much dependent on the availability of good texts in (preferably) good translations.

Even course titles affect their attractiveness. For example, the cultural history of Kyiv is certainly deserving of a place in any cultural curriculum, but a course title such as "After Kyiv" appears to imply ethnic limitations. As a packaging device, the title has been changed to "City of Saints and Sinners"—actually, it fits Kyiv quite well. A survey of the chief modernist and avant-garde movements in the late Russian Empire and early Soviet years was originally titled "After Filonov's *Universal Flowering*" (the "Faking It" course). At the insistence of the Faculty of Arts and Sciences, it now appears on student transcripts as "Forgery and Culture."

Other courses I have developed and taught include an overview of Slavic book culture, "Saints Cyril and Methodius to Hrabal"; an overview of Gogol, "The Ukrainian Father of Russian Prose" (of sorts); and an introductory survey of Ukrainian and Russian civilization, roughly from Herodotus to Mazepa and Peter I. Fortunately these courses qualify for several programs—for most minors and majors in our department—making them meaningful and useful to my department. In addition to creating this niche, all of them allowed—indeed, forced—me to resituate Ukrainian content within broader cultural and disciplinary frameworks.

It is certainly easier to teach a survey of Russian literature or the Russian novel or Russian short story, with textbooks, anthologies, and all kinds of resources at your disposal. It would perhaps be easier to teach a survey of the Ukrainian novel or Ukrainian short story, but times have changed. It is a matter of administrative pressure and educational marketing, cultural branding, and recognition of such brands. The Russian novel and Russian short story, literature of the Russian golden age, Dostoevsky, Tolstoy, and so on, are brands that attract students and guarantee enrolment. For example, we are likely to find Ukrainian students and Canadian students of Ukrainian descent in a survey of the Russian rather than the Ukrainian novel. The same is true for other national cultures as well: Polish drama, Czech short story, and so on. So the traditional national adjective is not sufficient to attract an audience. Are there Ukrainian novels on a par with Tolstoy and Dostoevsky? Ukrainian stories to die for? Ukrainian drama to salivate about? Well, Ukrainian literature has marvellous texts, for sure. We all can point to such examples as Krymsky, Pidmohylny, and Domontovych for novels, Stefanyk and Kotsiubynsky for stories, and Ukrainka and Kulish for drama. Certainly contemporary Ukrainian literature is on a par with anything good in any literature. But again, the only recognizable brand remains Russian. For good or bad reasons, one can imagine students reading hundreds of pages of *War and Peace* or *Anna Karenina*—they do it. By virtue of the share of the cultural market that the Russian cultural legacy occupies in the West, accumulated over the past 150 years, it is what it is. The second problem is that of translations.

> *In today's environment, which gravitates toward the relentless corporatization of learning, we still have to emphasize that culture and literature should remain and be expanded as venues for discussions on society and the human condition in general.*

The third problem is text selection and texts and reading. What was said yesterday about present-day reading habits is true. Today's students, on average, have a two-page attention span, unless there is some magic. Reading and literacy in the post-Gutenberg world—that is, Bill Gates and Steve Jobs's "Revolution Age"—are neither intensive nor extensive. They amount to the reading of captions. It is pixelated and pulverized reading: we have to deal with that and overcome it somehow. How to sustain reading and teaching—reading practices in this environment—is a major task all teachers of literature face.

Let us return to our Ukrainian packages, our material. In all the courses that I teach it is, after all, my vocation to feature Ukrainian content and frame it in a way that makes it both distinctive and attractive. A student taking the Gogol course, with five out of twelve weeks focusing on Ukrainian themes, will see the writer as an example of cultural hybridity, blackface performance, as well as a product and victim of his forked tongue. It is a little revenge, perhaps, for decades of scholarship that was ignorant or neglectful of the Ukrainian Gogol. In packaging and framing the Ukrainian content, it is usually best to zoom in on this content or open it up. That is not always easy. Building thematic courses from scratch is like doing bathroom renovation on your own. You have no idea until the end is in sight whether the framing works and the lighting and accents of your choice match your vanity. [Laughter.]

Opening up Ukrainian material, using the example of Kyiv, it is most productive to emphasize the dynamics of change, interaction, and competition in the formation of the real and virtual imagined city: grand, devastated, peripheral, metropolitan, revolutionary. "The capital of contemporary Ukraine emerges through the competition of narratives, legacies, and voices." In this context, it is possible and actually effective to teach Bulgakov's *White Guard*, framed with Kuprin's *Yama* (The Pit), Sholem Aleichem's *Adventures of Menachem-Mendl*, and Pidmohylny's *Misto* (The City). The latter two works do not suffer in comparison, and neither does Kyiv as the capital of Ukraine. By the way, Pidmohylny is available in enough English excerpts to be taught. Future possibilities might include urban experiences, literary colonizations of city-spaces in Ukraine. Bruno Schults, Bohumil Hrabal, and Yuri Vynnychuk can be put together.

Now, zooming outward into more generic thematic courses, sometimes they are most satisfactory when a Ukrainian piece provides the dessert, a concluding touch to the whole enterprise of a course. Everything suddenly comes into focus, Technicolor™ and all. These are my personal favourites. When one takes Domontovych's *Bez gruntu*[81] at the conclusion of a survey of modernism and the avant-garde, it is amazingly effective. And, of course, I provide a commentary on traditional modernist and avant-garde aesthetics, and much more—the Ukrainianness of this text has a most brilliant and poignant universality. Or, taking Valerii Shevchuk's *Eye of the Abyss* at the end of a course on forgery—when the nature of miracles manufacturing the faith and infinite recycling of stories as they bleed into life, and vice versa, are revealed in the midst of sixteenth-century Ukraine (Ruthenia), town by town, by social duress, moral depravity, and outside forces—the topic becomes historical and yet atemporal, universal.

Then, of course, packaging. Maybe the time will come for a mega-course, "The Ukrainian Novel." Who knows who will follow Yuri Andrukhovych and Serhiy Zhadan? In any case, contemporary Ukrainian literature can be successfully thematized and taught with what is available today, and I do hope to build a course on a single Ukrainian novel opened up to a broad intercultural, interdisciplinary context, namely, *Bez gruntu* by Domontovych, with the overarching thematic title of "Roots and Rootlessness." This is no *War and Peace*, but of course in some ways it is more than *War and Peace* and Anna Karenina put together, and *Natasha's Dance*,[82] and so on. The richness of this unique novel allows one to engage in a tremendous range of texts, legacies, and ideas. It has it all: commentary on a range of artistic movements, historiosophical meditation, sexual drive and indeterminacy, music, politics, infinite depths of history, infinite draws and fragmentation of culture. The main problem is the inadequacy of the translation. It exists but must be redone. Even this inadequate translation does the trick, though.

So perhaps it would be useful for the small pool of us teachers of Ukrainian literature to create a forum—I would certainly be happy to have some virtual space for sharing educational ideas, tricks, texts, experiences, trying to inspire one another. We have some venues already, and I especially want to point to my colleague Maxim Tarnawsky's page, "Ukrainian Literature," on the U of T Slavic Department's website, which has a remarkable number of sources in both Ukrainian and English. We probably need more.

The future of the Ukrainian curriculum in traditional departments will certainly be a combination of something more familiar—courses, surveys in restructured and repackaged formats, and thematic courses in which Ukraine is a main dish or a dessert. In today's environment, which gravitates toward the relentless corporatization of learning, we still have to emphasize that culture and literature should remain and be expanded as venues for discussions on society and the human condition in general. And the field is certainly worthy of life's efforts. Here I would second our presenters Mark Von Hagen, Yaroslav Hrytsak, and Rory Finnin: Ukrainian culture and literature are capable of providing access and insight into the most relevant, complex, and powerful human experiences, and we should display them with the best, without apologies or reservations. ■

ALLA NEDASHKIVSKA
CIUS

ALLA NEDASHKIVSKA is a professor of Slavic applied linguistics in the Department of Modern Languages and Cultural Studies and director of the Ukrainian Language Education Centre at CIUS, University of Alberta. Currently she is also the team lead on the Nationalities, Culture, and Language Policies cluster of the Research Initiative on Democratic Reforms in Ukraine international research project. Dr. Nedashkivska has published on Slavic linguistics, discourse analysis, gender linguistics, and political and media language, as well as on language pedagogy and second-language acquisition in Ukrainian. She is the author of Ukrainian language textbooks—one of which, *Ukrainian Through Its Living Culture* (2010) won the 2012 AATSEEL Book Prize for best contribution to language pedagogy.

Teaching Ukrainian studies in Canada: Contemporary post-secondary learners

[SUBMITTED TEXT]

Introduction and Objectives

This paper is an attempt and opportunity to engage in a discussion with those of us interested in teaching Ukrainian studies at post-secondary institutions in

81 *Bez gruntu* (Without Foundation, 1948) by V. Domontovych (pseud. of Viktor Petrov).

82 *Natasha's Dance: A Cultural History of Russia* by Orlando Figes (2002).

Canada about the challenges we face today.

Over the past few decades we have seen a steady decline in the number of Ukrainian studies courses—specifically, language, literature, and/or cultural studies—taught at the six universities in Canada that offer such programs. These institutions are: the University of Toronto, York University, University of Saskatchewan, University of Manitoba, University of Alberta, and University of Victoria. The marked decline is disheartening, with programs that were built over long periods of time and with great effort by the Ukrainian community and academics gradually unravelling. The most telling signs of these declines have been:

> Reduction in the number of faculty members teaching in the programs (retirements and non-hiring of replacements);
> Decrease in the number and variety of courses offered (owing to enrolment minimums in some institutions, such as the University of Alberta);
> Decrease in the number of courses taught in the target language;
> Lowering of levels taught (i.e., reduction of advanced-level courses);
> Curtailment of majors in Ukrainian; and
> Loss of graduate-student support, leading to a lack of teaching assistants able to train as future academics in teaching and pedagogy at post-secondary levels in this field.

Recent discussions about mitigating these declines have usually focused on returning the programs to their previous forms, reinstituting the same variety and levels of courses that existed in the past and increasing the number of students who focus their degrees on Ukrainian studies.

Such a focus, albeit laudable, may actually be faulty, dated, and limiting. Orientation toward past practices, structures, and successes does not address the needs of today's learners. Our approaches to assessing the practices of teaching and learning today must stem first of all from our understanding of the current situation of our contemporary learners. In striving to secure and grow our offerings and/or programs, we have to consider that the motivations of today's learners have shifted and continue to shift in our rapidly changing world and economy. Responses to the challenges we all face in our respective institutions must be grounded in familiarity with our students, keeping in mind that the educational and professional focus of students today is vastly different from those of learners of forty-some years ago, when most of our programs were established.

Therefore, as a professional response to the challenges we face in Ukrainian studies, including the dearth of scholarly attention to the issues of learners in Ukrainian or the above considerations, Nedashkivska and Sivachenko recently conducted a research study on what motivates and what demotivates today's students to enrol in Ukrainian studies courses. In the present paper I share selected results that are most likely to be of interest to this [audience] (for full details of the study, see Nedashkivska and Sivachenko). Primarily I offer a discussion of the main findings, concluding with some recommendations based on our empirical research work.

The main questions we pose in the study, as reported here, are the following: "Who is our contemporary student in Ukrainian studies at the post-secondary level?" and "What motivates and what demotivates students in studying Ukrainian: language, culture, folklore, literature, linguistics, and history?" In the original study, we identify and focus on four groups of students, specifically:

> Students taking Ukrainian language courses (Group 1: language enrolled);
> Those in Ukrainian content courses (Group 2: content enrolled);
> Students who took a language course at the post-secondary level in the past but did not continue (Group 3: previously language enrolled); and
> Students active in the Ukrainian community who have never taken any Ukrainian studies courses but are potentially interested in Ukrainian studies (Group 4: never enrolled).

Our objectives are to study our learners both quantitatively and qualitatively, first measuring the motivational factors for the four groups of students and then proceeding to establish motivational factors based on the actual data. Our goal is to present motivational profiles of our current, past, and potential students.

Methodology

Sixty participants were solicited for this study, 42 female and 18 male. All are from one Canadian post-secondary institution that offers courses in Ukrainian studies. "Group 1: language enrolled" was comprised of 38 participants, "Group 2: content enrolled" had 12 participants, "Group

3: previously language enrolled" was represented by 5 participants, and "Group 4: never enrolled" involved 5 participants.

Out of all the participants, 93 percent were students of Ukrainian descent. Many (33 percent) were in various humanities programs, 23 percent were in sciences, and 20 percent had not yet defined their major. The remaining respondents were enrolled in studies at the Faculty of Education (13 percent), Faculty of Medicine & Dentistry (7 percent), and the School of Business (3 percent).

In order to investigate the research objectives initially posed and establish an instrument for data collection and analysis, Dörnyei's second-language (L2) motivational framework was utilized as the main theoretical foundation of the study ("Motivation," "Attitudes"). Dörnyei conceptualizes motivation at three levels: (a) the language level (which we replace with "subject area level"); (b) the learner level; and (c) the learning situation level.

The *subject area* level is concerned with reasons to learn certain subjects and consists of two motivational orientations: instrumental and integrative (concepts originally proposed by Gardner and Lambert ("Motivation Variables," *Attitudes*). Instrumental motivation emphasizes pragmatic gains for learners, such as earning good grades, getting a better job, higher salary, and acceleration on the socio-economic ladder. Integrative motivation relates to learners' positive attitudes toward the target language community and their desire to interact with members of that community (Dörnyei, "Motivation," 274).

This integrative motivational system "is centered around the individual's L2-related affective predispositions, including social, cultural, and ethnolinguistic components, as well as a general interest in foreignness and foreign languages" (Dörnyei, "Motivation," 279). The *learner* level focuses on learners' personality traits and cognition. At this level, the motivational components focus on a learner's need for achievement as well as their self-confidence, including "various aspects of language anxiety, perceived L2 competence, attributions about past experiences, and self-efficacy" (Dörnyei, "Motivation," 279). The *learning situation* level deals with the learning environment, which includes (1) course-specific elements, that is, organizational tools such as the syllabus, teaching resources and textbooks, and the teaching and learning methodology; (2) instructor-specific factors such as instructor personality, teaching style, feedback and grading, and relationship with the students; and (3) group-specific factors that relate to the learning group's structure, its cohesion and atmosphere, as well as the relationship among peers, that is, the overall dynamic among learners (Dörnyei, "Motivation," 277–80).

This theoretical framework was used to design a motivational questionnaire for the original study. The questions aimed at gathering information about student demographics, including their past, present, and prospective educational experiences, as well as questions that focused on eliciting data about students' motivational factors for enrolling, continuing in, or not taking Ukrainian studies courses. The questions were organized according to the three levels of motivational framework mentioned above (Dörnyei, "Motivation," "Attitudes"). The questionnaires were administered during the 2014–15 academic year.

The data obtained were analyzed both quantitatively and qualitatively in order to investigate motivational and demotivational factors of students, or potential students, of Ukrainian studies, allowing for the study of data from two different perspectives. The quantitative results allowed us to measure the motivational profiles of participants, while the qualitative angle enabled us to understand the students' perspectives on how their motivation relates to their learning experiences, present or potential. In this paper, owing to space limitations, only a summary of both analyses is presented (please consult Nedashkivska and Sivachenko for full details of the analyses).

Results overview and discussion

The results of the quantitative analysis highlight that at the *subject area* level—specifically, with respect to both integrative and instrumental motivational factors—all four groups show more or less similar results. With respect to the integrative side, the crucial motivating factors were established as follows: participant's desire to integrate into the community; better understanding of culture, history, literature, music, and the like; being successful in communication with native speakers; and learning about one's heritage. With respect to the instrumental orientations, considerations of good grades, future career gains, and degree requirements were the most noticeable. Remarkably, Group 3 students, who were enrolled in language classes but did not continue, showed the highest results with respect to both integrative and instrumental factors compared to other groups. This suggests that students with the highest motivational scores could choose nevertheless not to continue with Ukrainian studies. Such results are in need of further examination, as it would be important to qualify and quantify the factors that influence students' educational choice to opt out of Ukrainian studies.

In addition, our quantitative study showed that at the *learner-specific* level, current language learners representing Group 1 showed the lowest self-confidence and the highest levels of anxiety. These results also deserve more detailed examination. In particular, do they indicate highest levels of anxiety in lower-level language classes or in lower-level (area study) classes in general? Which specific factors contribute to such low levels of self-confidence and commitment/motivation, and do these relate to the students' early term of exposure to post-secondary studies? Currently we do not have clear answers to these questions.

At the *learning situation* level, participants from all four groups reported mostly positively on the atmosphere, course load, teaching materials, and instructor's teaching approach and personality. At this level, the statistically most visible group is (again) "Group 1: language enrolled." Participants from this group voiced more concerns and demotivators when compared to other groups with respect to atmosphere, course load, teaching materials, and instructor's teaching methods.

Because the quantitative analysis in our study raised more questions than it answered, we turned to the qualitative angle of the analysis, from which the following results emerged.

At the *subject-area level*, ten main motivators and demotivators across the four groups of participants were established. The motivators were:

1. importance of preserving one's heritage, being part of the Ukrainian community, and supporting Ukrainian studies;
2. importance of language and culture for communication purposes;
3. travel;
4. further education and career;
5. enjoyment; and
6. academic gains and rewards.

The demotivators were noted as:

7. a (mis)perception of level of academic accomplishment;
8. misconceptions and lack of knowledge about course offerings, opportunities, and requirements.

The following were classified as either motivators or demotivators:

9. interest in the humanities (including Ukrainian);
10. degree requirements, scheduling, and course offerings.

What needs to be stressed here is that among the demotivators, students reported lack of knowledge about course offerings and course relevance to their degrees, which prevented or discouraged them from enrolling in Ukrainian studies courses.

At the *learner* level, students' comments reinforced their answers in the quantitative study and demonstrated that "Group 1: language enrolled" respondents, despite being mostly positively oriented, are the least confident in their learning process. These respondents often viewed their progress as unsatisfactory and inadequate. The responses also suggested that the learning expectations of respondents in Group 1 were not fully met. Such results signal that in the future, Group 1 current language learners will most likely drop out of courses and/or the program. In "Group 4: never enrolled," the comments about their perception of level of academic accomplishment were somewhat alarming. In this group, some students did not see any need to enrol in Ukrainian studies courses at the post-secondary level, as they viewed them as neither new nor challenging. In the students' view, the Ukrainian classes at the post-secondary level would only duplicate what they already knew from home, community, or secondary school experiences.

Analysis at the *learning situation* level allowed us to determine that although students were content with the group atmosphere overall, differences in proficiency levels within the group figured as noticeable demotivators. Moreover, regarding course-load and teaching resources, some participants commented strongly on the relevance and quality of the teaching materials. Particularly, in "Group 1: language enrolled," several participants expressed their desire and general need for resources that are communicatively oriented (i.e., not grammar-based) and applicable to real-life situations. Many comments related to the students' wishes for more technologically enhanced resources to be incorporated into the curriculum. For language learners, an additional demotivator was the variant of language taught—specifically, a lack of acknowledgment of existing variants of the language (in this case, the variant or language level the student uses at home).

> *It is also important to go beyond Ukrainian studies and compare the motivations of learners in other Slavic contexts, as well as more commonly taught languages, literatures, and cultures, and how they may enhance our understanding of the broader picture.*

The study summarized in the foregoing raises several important questions for us to consider in teaching Ukrainian studies. Please also note that in our original study we do not claim to provide answers to all the questions that we may have about the students and their learning experiences in Ukrainian studies at the post-secondary level with respect to motivational considerations. The next steps would be to include a larger data sample from other post-secondary programs in Ukrainian studies, thus increasing the generalizability of the results to larger populations.

It is also important to go beyond Ukrainian studies and compare the motivations of learners in other Slavic contexts, as well as more commonly taught languages, literatures, and cultures, and how they may enhance our understanding of the broader picture. The study of instructors' perspectives is yet to be carried out and will most likely yield interesting results. Do we as instructors shift and/or continue to shift, as our students do? How are our perspectives similar to or different from those of our students? In which aspects do we merge with or diverge from our students? Do we understand our students and their learning experiences? Do we understand what students are looking for in language, literature, culture, folklore, history, and other courses?

In the language classroom in particular, based on issues flagged by "Group 1: language enrolled" participants, we need to address the correlation between motivational levels of learners and their language proficiency levels: How do motivational profiles shift and change as students gain more experience in language learning? The research questions about our contemporary learners are endless but crucial to our own academic existence. So why do such studies and their findings remain on the periphery of our academic inquiries, be they individual or collective?

Recommendations and conclusions

Our original study was an initial step toward formally assessing our current situation and comprehending contemporary learners. As noted above, our results propose some practical values and applications. Therefore, allow me to conclude with some recommendations that stem directly from our empirical data and analysis. My specific recommendations, in no particular order, are as follows:

1. With respect to teaching materials:
   > The desire and need are for new, contemporary, technologically enhanced materials that are relevant to modern students, allowing them to apply the gained knowledge in real-life situations.
   > For language-specific classrooms, students' clear wishes are for outcomes that promote the ability to function and communicate in the language. Thus, learning and teaching materials need to reflect such desires and needs.
2. With respect to language teaching, and the variant(s) of the language taught in particular:
   > In our view, at the post-secondary level the language to be taught is contemporary Ukrainian as spoken in Ukraine today.
   > Importantly, teaching awareness about language variants, fostering tolerance toward different language varieties (to which some students are very sensitive), and promoting inclusivity are to be considered seriously and implemented in the learning process. Additionally, it must be underlined that language variant issues are more often related to the higher level being taught at university rather than to actual concerns over dialect.
3. With respect to instructors:
   > Students desire clear communication and transparency with respect to course objectives and expectations, as well as the establishment of a fair grading system. This recommendation may seem obvious, but it was voiced by our respondents, suggesting the need for more careful attention to these points.

4. In language teaching:
   > The factor of different levels of student proficiency in a single classroom proved to be one of the highest demotivators, which influenced the perception of group atmosphere, grading, self-efficacy, and perception of students' progress. This factor requires thoughtful consideration. Assessment techniques need to be developed accordingly, and appropriate placement tests are strongly advised.
   > In this respect, we need to communicate across campuses, across various institutions and programs, and learn from one another about possible placement and assessment practices in a differentiated classroom.

My more general recommendations are as follows:

5. Information about programs:
   > Informing students about course offerings and how these courses are relevant and applicable to their degrees and possible careers must be made more explicit and take on the form of marketing campaigns and student outreach activities. Here we must continually delve into the information-seeking methods of our students. Specifically, do our students even use the traditional information venues, and which information-sharing devices, networks, and platforms are most effective today?
6. Information about content:
   > Students need to be better educated about course content in order to be better judges of what they have already accomplished, as well as what new knowledge a particular course could contribute to their overall educational goals and professional experiences. In this respect, we must note the inadequacy of our programs in promoting the value of studying Ukrainian subjects at the university level. If completion of a given specialty—be it history, foreign language, mathematics, and the like—is sufficient at the high-school graduate level, then there really is no need to study *anything* at the university level. Yet some students consider it natural to continue their other studies at the university level but regard their Ukrainian language level, or knowledge of Ukrainian subjects, as sufficient if they have completed a high-school curriculum or have been exposed to some Ukrainian content and activities in the family or the community. We are failing to convince students that learning at the university level will lead to a higher degree of knowledge and functionality, as with their other studies or even beyond. Visiting potential students at schools and community events to inform them about available options, courses, and programs is one step toward reaching out to our potential audience and building their engagement.
7. New focus of offerings:
   > Regarding specific courses, we need to refocus the content of courses that we offer. Students are no longer interested in narrowly defined courses. We noted that the interest of today's students is in the functional use of language and knowledge. Courses of interest relate to today's Ukraine (such as "Euromaidan" at the University of Alberta and the University of Manitoba, or "Modern Ukraine and Russian-Ukrainian Conflict" at the University of Victoria), and certainly not to a philological perspective in the classical sense. Our courses must adapt to the new realities of today's world and today's learners.
8. Majors and minors:
   > The question of Ukrainian majors or minors is influenced by these new realities and shifts in students' perceptions and needs. And although the question of majors and minors was not studied or discussed above, I would like to add a recommendation, as suggested by Benjamin Rifkin, who notes on the basis of his research of foreign language departments in the United States:

> The definition of the language major should be reconceptualized to include not only literature but also history, society and social practices, politics, arts, and economics, by including readings from these disciplines in advanced-language courses....Including area studies courses would enhance language major programs and promote collaboration with colleagues in other fields....The major could also be expanded to include opportunities in collaboration with off-campus partners to facilitate experiential learning....Faculty members might consider establishing a major "track," one for language and literature and another for language and civilization (Rifkin 73).

These recommendations are relevant in light of the discussion above with respect to what students really want and need in their academic experience, and what type of knowledge they strive for. The question of majors and minors, as well as various certificates in which Ukrainian studies may play a role, deserves further study, particularly as regards testing and sharing of successful practices.

9. New direction:
   > *Adapt and remodel* is my next recommendation: *adapt* to the new realities of universities, societies, and communities, and *remodel* based on our knowledge of today's learners and their current needs. Our research, and the application of this research in our teaching and delivery of knowledge to audiences that we study and know, and to which we tailor our delivery, will most likely yield a solid basis for change or complete remodelling.
10. Audience:
   > And my final recommendation is to cultivate our audience by means of carefully planned and engaging, modern, innovative, and relevant courses and programs that are empirically informed and reflect our knowledge of today's reality, society, community, and, most critically, our contemporary learners. ■

References

Brecht, R.D., J. Caemmerer, and R.A. Walton. *Russian in the United States: A Case Study of America's Language Needs and Capacities*. The National Foreign Language Center (Washington, DC, 1995).

Dörnyei, Z. "Motivation and motivating in the foreign language classroom," *Modern Language Journal* 78, no. 3 (1994): 273–84.

———. "Attitudes, orientations, and motivations in language learning: Advances in theory, research, and applications," in *Motivation, Language Identity and the L2 Self*, ed Z. Dörnyei and E. Ushioda. Multilingual Matters (Bristol 2003), p. 9–42.

Gardner, R.C., and W.E. Lambert. "Motivational variables in second language acquisition," *Canadian Journal of Psychology* 13, no. 4 (1959): 266–72.

———. *Attitudes and Motivation in Second Language Learning*. Newbury House (Rowley, MA, 1972).

Geisherik, A. "The role of motivation among heritage and non-heritage learners of Russian," *Canadian Slavonic Papers/Revue Canadiennes des Slavistes* 46, no. 1/2 (2004): 9–22.

Kagan, O., and K. Dillon. "A new perspective on teaching Russian: Focus on the heritage learner," *Slavic and East European Journal* 45, no. 3 (2001): 507–18.

Nedashkivska, A., and O. Sivachenko. "Student motivation profiles: Ukrainian studies at the postsecondary level," in "Less Commonly Taught Slavic Languages: The Learner, the Instructor and the Learning Experience in the Second Language Classroom (The North American Context)," special thematic section, ed A. Nedashkivska, *East/West: Journal of Ukrainian Studies* 4, no. 1 (2017): 63–94.

Rifkin, B. "Learners' goals and curricular design: The field's response to the 2007 MLA Report on Foreign Language Education," *ADFL Bulletin*, 42, no. 1 (2012): 68–75.

Romanov, A. "Student motivation for studying Russian: Survey and analysis," in *The Learning and Teaching of Slavic Languages and Cultures*, eds O. Kagan and B. Rifkin. Slavica Publishers (Bloomington, IN, 2000), p. 145–66.

HEATHER COLEMAN

Discussant, University of Alberta

HEATHER COLEMAN is the director of the Program on Religion and Culture at CIUS and an associate professor in the Department of History and Classics at the University of Alberta. She is currently writing a book titled *Holy Kyiv: Priests, Communities, and Nationality in Imperial Russia, 1800–1917*. She is also the author of *Russian Baptists and Spiritual Revolution, 1905–1929* (2005), co-editor (with Mark D. Steinberg) of *Sacred Stories: Religion and Spirituality in Modern Russia* (2007), and editor of *Orthodox Christianity in Imperial Russia: A Source Book on Lived Religion* (2014). She serves as editor of the *Canadian Slavonic Papers / Revue canadienne des slavistes*.

On the contributions of Ukrainian studies to global scholarship I want to thank the speakers for some inspiring ideas, for moving forward as teachers in this area. I think that there are two key issues here. There is the issue of context, and that context is a happy story and a worrying story. It is, on the one hand, a story of certain structural pressures, the way that universities are working at the moment, the challenges of broader anxieties—the decline of the humanities, questions of whether faculty members are being replaced, questions of educational marketing—all of these sorts of questions are raised here. There is also the story of a change in the perception of Ukraine, the happy story of the normalization of Ukraine, of Ukraine being introduced into a range of non-Ukrainian courses and students recognizing Ukraine because, for better or for worse, Ukraine is in the news. And so there is opportunity, I hear, in what people are saying, as well as anxiety. I think that fundamentally there are two things.

First, there is a need for alliances—we all need to work together. And second, we are really hearing the story of the challenge—whether it is Ukrainian studies that we are promoting or the study of Ukraine and Ukrainian topics. What do I mean by all this? When I talk about normalization, I mean a different attitude toward Ukraine—people know more about Ukraine, and Anglo-Celts like me are studying Ukraine and recognizing it. And we have many people who were born in Ukraine and are now working in North America, either as students or regular visitors—and we are in constant interaction—for whom Ukraine is a given and not a question. So this changes the attitude toward the field as a whole. I think that coming from my perspective as a historian, my story is much like Dominique Arel's story in political science—it is the story of the flowering of Ukrainian studies. You know, when John-Paul Himka was a student and wanted to study Ukraine, he had to go and spend nine months in Leningrad and have his one brief trip to Lviv, because you could only go to Moscow or Leningrad, whereas I fell into Ukrainian studies because they closed the archive in St. Petersburg. I had been interested in Ukrainian studies, and because the archive in Kyiv was open, off I went to work in Kyiv. And so we have this shift.

I think that in the history department here, for example, we have a very active group of graduate students working in Ukrainian history. Students are drawn to Slavic history, and my colleague David Marples and I, and our recently retired colleague John-Paul Himka and Volodymyr Kravchenko have generally worked on mainstreaming Ukraine, putting Ukraine into all our courses. For example, when I teach second-year Intro to Modern European History, oddly enough, my example for nation building is Ukraine, and then my example for the challenges at the end of the First World War is Ukraine, and then my example for displaced persons after the Second World War is Ukraine, and so on. Ukraine works throughout as a theme in a general modern European history course. Coming out of the discussion we are hearing today, I do think that it is easier for fields like political science or history or anthropology to do this kind of mainstreaming at the undergraduate level, to pull research in, because we are teaching in English and there is an expectation that the readings will be in English. I am very interested to hear of Taras Koznarsky's efforts to do similar things through literature, and so I want to recognize that point.

Just to finish on that theme, I will say that those who are teaching languages—in Alla Nedashkivska's case, for example—face a different set of issues, because it is the language itself and not Ukraine per se or Ukrainian-Canadian studies per se, but it is the actual tools that are needed to do this work in a serious way. In first year, I ask students on the first day what foreign languages they read or speak, and I then explain that I am asking because not everything important in the world is written in English. Not all historical documents are written in English, and I cannot do my work without other languages. We need to start from the ground up, signalling the importance of language learning across the disciplines of Slavic studies. Part of the problem is that students often do not come to that realization until they advance in the program in political science or anthropology or history, and we need those language courses to be there when the students finally clue in and realize that this is a whole package. I do not know what the answer is, but I want to throw out that challenge.

I have a few small questions for our speakers, and then I will leave it to the audience. I am interested in your comments about the Prairie Centre, Bohdan [Kordan], and your view of that as a way of ensuring the future. And so I am curious about the personnel issues, because for us, I think, at the U of A, part of the issue is that we have this wonderful forty-year-old institute. But CIUS does not have any control over the decisions that departments make about hiring, and so the question is how to keep the ranks filled for the future. So I am curious about how we keep those lines of communications open with departments and show the importance of preserving Slavic studies, Ukrainian studies across the disciplines, when decisions are made at faculty and departmental levels instead of through the institutes. I am also interested in thinking about what happens to language as we make the courses more available in the ways

> *“When I talk about normalization, I mean a different attitude toward Ukraine—people know more about Ukraine, Anglo-Celts like me are studying Ukraine and recognizing it. And we have many people who were born in Ukraine and are now working in North America ... for whom Ukraine is a given and not a question. So this changes the attitude toward the field as a whole.”*

that Taras is talking about. I completely agree, for example, that Russian literature is a gateway for us to draw people in, and then they find out how exciting the other Slavic languages and literatures are. How do we balance teaching in translation with teaching how to work in the Slavic languages at an advanced level? That balance applies not only to literature courses but also to history and anthropology and politics courses: to do those subjects well, you need a high and sensitive level of language skill.

Finally, I think the emphasis that people have been making on understanding and finding ways to communicate with today's learners is a very important point, and one that we need to pursue. I want to ask you, Alla: you mentioned lack of confidence, and I am curious about why you asked that—or why that was one of your criteria. And my second question is: Does that not perhaps reflect the fact that more of your students are in lower-level classes? ■

DISCUSSION

BOHDAN KORDAN:

The question ultimately was the connection between centres and teaching programs, and specifically departments, and I think that is an important issue. The history of many of these centres is that they are isolated units, but the trick really is to make that connection in such a way that those departments see the value and necessity not only of lending support but of investing in those centres.

This is both a practical and a political question. On the practical side, we at PCUH have different categories of individuals, faculty members in the college who are tenured members of the centre, but we also have affiliates drawn from various university departments. We have people in environmental sciences, a person who is working with students on, of all things, a Ukrainian community garden in order to examine the cultural practice of growing a medicinal garden on the prairies. We have a sociologist who is working with Germans and the Mennonite community and is an affiliate of the centre. So all these individuals, in many ways, have a practical need to be associated with the centre, and in so doing they bring their experience to their respective departments and underscore its value.

The other point is really a political question. We do a lot with very few resources, and it is extraordinary how much attention we get as a result. There is a compelling reason for departments to factor the centre into their decision-making process about faculty hires. That is not always the case, but we at the centre can make a compelling case for a faculty hire in a particular department when the opportunity arises. My interest in all this has a lot to do with how we innovate. We accept the fact that Ukraine has now become a normal state, a normal society, if I can say that [laughter], and, having said that, worthy of scholarship and assessment. We do these things and we hope for the best outcome, but there is a context to consider, and that context is one of austerity and the kinds of things that have been happening in the last twenty years. I was hired not as a Ukrainianist but to teach conflict, human rights, and international organizations. I have an interest in Ukrainian studies as a kind of sidebar, but the fact is, when I arrived there and saw the state of affairs, this could not last.

So we took the initiative to change the dynamic in such a way that should Ukrainian studies disappear—in fact, in its traditional setting it did disappear—we would be there to revive them. We were there to ensure that Ukrainian studies would survive. But we had to recommend something different from what was already there, and that is where the multidisciplinarity, the interdisciplinarity comes in, what everybody is talking about. And we have done that. But at the end of the day—here is the point, the essence, the nub—it is not about teaching. It is about learning, and so the emphasis is on students. I will put my money on students every day of the week because they are the future. I have had seventeen graduate students, and three have appointments at universities, in London, Regina, and Rochester. They carry with them the experience of having studied under me with a Ukrainian focus. They integrate some of that into their teaching. But our work is not for them. It is for the students who have come to the university and will dabble in Ukrainian studies, take the odd Ukrainian class—it is the experience of *being in Ukrainian life at a university* that matters most. I, for one, took the odd Ukrainian language course at university, but my training was in political studies. But the experience of working with others in the Ukrainian students' club—with Bohdan Krawchenko, Olga Kuplowska, Roman Senkus, Myroslav Shkandrij, everybody, the Chomiak sisters—*that* became formative in my life. It informed me, and that is why I do what I do. That is what I want for this generation of students and for the next. So my purpose is not about graduate students, although we need to do that. It is about giving them the experience that they take with them into their lives and know that this is important to them, and of course to the community to which they belong.

ALLA NEDASHKIVSKA:

I will respond to the question that Heather [Coleman] posed with respect to our language students' lack of confidence, and this is not a criterion but our result, which is a bit alarming. I now teach the first level, the beginners' Ukrainian course. Do I address this question enough? This is a result of the study that may require attention: lack of confidence among our language learners may be a demotivator. We note in our study that one factor is the inequality of proficiency levels and background knowledge, as well as other factors that we discussed.

I also want to stress the need to understand today's learners. We need to adapt and renovate, as Bohdan Kordan mentioned, and Taras [Koznarsky] mentioned that perhaps Ukrainian studies could be—what did you say, a main dish or a dessert? I would say that perhaps it should be an ingredient, but I would like to stress that today's reality is changing. Our students are different; we need to learn about them and adapt to their learning needs. Again, with respect to interdisciplinarity, Ukrainian language learning most likely needs to be combined with other disciplines. We offer a business Ukrainian course at the University of Alberta that attracts a good number of students, and I believe that we should introduce courses of language and history, language and political science, language and economics, and so on. We do have administrative challenges, but we need to face those challenges, and we will do so.

TARAS KOZNARSKY:

It is a pleasure to work with historians and learn from them, as we do. But usually it is in academic venues, conference venues. It is great to have a series for this platform and co-operate—it is great that the U of T, in addition to the Slavic department, has a chair of Ukrainian studies and support for publications through our chair. What I was trying to emphasize is that it is not effective—today especially, but not only today—to shame students: "You are Ukrainian: you have to do this stuff because you have to do it"; "This is your obligation, your cross to carry." I think there are ways of showing that Ukrainian material can be a source of intellectual, aesthetic, psychological, and emotional joy. There is enough there that is valuable and *just joyous in itself*, offering the best examples of thought, of inspiration, and we should be able to communicate that. That is probably the most effective way to attract students—whether they come from studying Russian and say, "Oh my gosh, this is something different." It does not matter where some students come from, sometimes I cannot pronounce their names, but I am sure they get some useful ideas out of Ukrainian texts and culture.

DOMINIQUE AREL:

On normalization, Bohdan [Kordan] said that Ukraine has become normal, and I know what he meant, but I am sure that people on the *Maidan* would not have agreed. [Laughter.] They won the *Maidan* precisely because they were tired of *not* living in a normal country. That is not what you meant, obviously, but what has happened is that Ukraine has become very interesting to study. Look at it! The Orange Revolution was wild enough, but the *Maidan* was just—well, in terms of the consequences, obviously there is nothing "exciting" about that...but how could any country in the world go through two instances of mass mobilization in ten years? It is massive, and we all know the details. It is just amazing, so it draws people in, and that is the most spectacular example.

Obviously we have a whole community of scholars who are interested in war, civil wars, and so forth, and they are looking at the Ukrainian case because it is the second-largest case in Europe since World War II (after the Balkan war), and it is happening in Europe. That is the kind of normalization we see very much in the social sciences. I tried to explain very broadly how it can be defined, and it surprises even me how broadly it can be defined.

Since we keep mingling with historians, let us address the situation with archives: no matter how problematic issues always are in Ukraine, they are infinitely better than in Russia, and I think your own personal experiences are not just anecdotes; they reflect a trend. If you want to study the Second World War or memory politics in Russia, well, good luck, everything is completely closed, and anyway you will be followed by the FSB[83] if you do that. Whereas in Ukraine, with all the controversy, there are actually a lot of archives that are open, which means that in practice the literature and research being produced are qualitatively (if not quantitatively) at a very high level for anyone interested in these broad historical matters.

From my vantage point, I see Ukrainian studies indeed experiencing a period of remarkable growth across the board. But obviously we are talking about the study of Ukraine, not the study of the diaspora in Canada; these are two different worlds that intersect at some level, but not always, as they are two different experiences. This means that students, whether of Ukrainian background or not, are being drawn into Ukraine because it is—I think Professor Kononenko said "cool" this morning. She is a "Kule" scholar herself, K-U-L-E [laughter], of cool students, in both terms, but that is just the reality.

Now my reality is that, unlike the University of Alberta or Toronto, where there are more resources despite all the constraints, and the possibility of actually having courses in the Ukrainian language, we unfortunately do not have such courses at the University of Ottawa. But there are ways to remedy that. There are all these booming summer schools in Ukraine—that is how I learned Ukrainian. I just went to Ukraine, and there you go. Ostash put me on a radio program the day I arrived in Ukraine. I had never really spoken Ukrainian in my life [laughter], but I could read it, so I had enough words to say—and I was very happy to be there.

The last point I would make, since it was raised, is indeed a serious issue, and I can see that with regard to the younger generation, people very close to me—that is jobs. It is great to have this young cohort, but will there be overproduction, as Bob Magocsi said? It is a real problem, but I looked at my little database yesterday and realized that of the 50 doctoral students we have had over the years, I could count 14 who found jobs. Now, of those 50, many are still doctoral students, and some are post-docs or are still around. I mean, who got a job immediately, first year on the market, right? And of those 14, 5 were in anthropology, so you have Ukrainian studies now growing in non-traditional fields.

HEATHER COLEMAN:

Anthropology is really big.

DOMINIQUE AREL:

Yes, it is big. There are terrific things that can be done. It is also big in Russian studies—that is the one thing that can probably still be done in Russia without the FSB running after you. We see that in Europe the job market is very difficult as well, in Western Europe in particular, but somehow there is a critical mass of young people who either get regular jobs, or in Europe, where they have a very different system, they can get permanent research positions in Germany or in France. We do not have that here, except perhaps in some institutes, and there are quite a few who manage to find themselves a niche. Enough for me to witness a quantitative growth in Ukrainian studies on the basis of my own experience.

MYROSLAV SHKANDRIJ:

I have taught languages and literatures for almost forty years, in four different universities. I have always been pretty much the only person in those programs. Sometimes I have been the only person who taught the language as well as the literature. Small programs have a special difficulty; it has always been like that, as I said in my introductory comments. But now the climate at universities has changed, and this poses a very different set of problems.

This year our university cut all languages that were not on a departmental banner. Arabic, Hebrew, Yiddish, Icelandic, anything that was not linked to a banner program disappeared. So we are in a different climate—we have to be aware of that. That said, we can learn from the Germans, from the Russians, from the Poles. I am in a department where all those languages are taught, and when I was head, they wanted to cut German; they wanted to cut Slavic. We survived, and German is now booming. But there are special things that can be done to improve language-teaching programs, the way they are delivered, taught, and conceived. And part of that has to do with high schools. German survives and is booming because they have German in high schools all the way up to university entrance, and there is a very easy move for students: you can contact them in the last year of high school, and they just go immediately into the university courses.

One of the things that repeatedly comes through, and that I agree with completely, is that you cannot just teach language alone; there has to be a reason for a student to

83 Post-KGB Russian state security service.

learn the language. Sometimes it comes from the content, the issues, sometimes the other way, but that means there has to be a link between language teaching and other instruction so that students see the need for it. On the good side of things, literature is now anything you want it to be. It can be political studies, history, cultural memory, psychology, whatever you want, and it is all over the map. We can now shape courses in interesting, exciting ways, the way Taras [Koznarsky] and other panellists have suggested. It is not all terribly dark.

QUESTIONS AND ANSWERS

GENIA BOIVIN:

I do have a question concerning the programs. As Dr. Shkandrij said, all our programs are small, and my question is that of addressing the competition between them. Right now, all of you are from different universities, so this is not really a problem. But sometimes, within the same university, you have Ukrainian studies in language, literature, and folklore, and all these programs competing with one another, and the reason I am asking this question is that one of you (I cannot remember who) said that the Ukrainian language is not Ukrainian studies per se but a tool for doing Ukrainian studies. It seems to me that this is already a bit of a problem. So how would you address these competing programs within the same university all dealing with Ukrainian studies?

BOHDAN KORDAN:

I do not remember who said it, but we do not have competing programs. They have all disappeared! [Laughter.]

HEATHER COLEMAN:

I said "tool," but I guess I actually meant that it may not be apparent to students at the beginning, but in fact language is the glue, and language is what we share in common and need in common to pursue our field in a sophisticated way, in order for our students to do advanced work in our field. I see it as the "net" in the "network," as well as being a subject of study in and of itself. One of the things that I think we can be very proud of here at the U of A is the really innovative work that our Ukrainianists have done in language study. Alla has published a textbook, and I know there has been a lot of innovative work in language teaching. And that is critical.

NATALIYA BEZBORODOVA:

I would like to address a topic that was also discussed yesterday and today, about Ukrainian studies and the students who register in the program. Three years ago I came as a Master's student and knew through private sources about this program, and when I was at the university, I had heard that there were not so many students there from Ukraine. I wondered how they managed to bring those students to Canada. In Ukraine, interest in studying abroad is increasing greatly; there are a lot of educational fairs and exhibits, but Ukrainian studies and the humanities are not represented at all at those fairs. There are MBA programs, there is IT and maybe English language for those who would like to stay in Canada or somewhere else. So I think it is probably a task of the university administration and of Ukrainian institutions and programs to advertise opportunities for study abroad more widely in Ukraine, especially if they include Ukrainian studies.

MYROSLAV SHKANDRIJ:

I think that has been addressed in part. Many students from Ukraine can get recruited and brought to Canadian universities, and we find grants for them. This is one way in which these programs have survived. The University of Manitoba cannot access some of the money that is made available through CIUS because it is earmarked in specific ways, but we find money in different ways. So we have brought students, and there is interest, of course, and it is a very good way of blending students from Ukraine with local students. It really improves the educational experience.

NATALIYA BEZBORODOVA:

I actually did not refer to money in my comment, and I know that those graduate students who are accepted and registered usually get assistantships or scholarships, really great support. But my comment was about advertising opportunities more actively in order to attract *more* students.

MYROSLAV SHKANDRIJ:

Well, that is a possibility, yes. To be honest, we are a very small program, we get more than enough applications, and even word of mouth seems to work. But you are right—we probably need to publicize it more and maybe think about funding this in a more systematic way.

PAUL ROBERT MAGOCSI:

It was very nice to hear that at the University of Toronto, where I teach, this is the last department of Slavic studies, but believe me, as I am sure Taras [Koznarsky] will say, that department also has problems in recruiting students.

Let me say one thing. You cannot be a Ukrainianist—you cannot be interested seriously in Ukrainian studies—unless you know the Ukrainian language. I very much sympathize with teachers of the Ukrainian language, who have an incredibly difficult task in preserving the pedagogy of teaching Ukrainian. But without knowledge of the Ukrainian language, forget it—you can never pursue anything in Ukrainian studies. Minimum is Ukrainian language, let us throw in some Russian perhaps, let us throw in some Polish. We have heard here, however, that we have a crisis, departments are closing, etcetera. Yesterday I said in one of our discussions that academics should be doing scholarly matters and not be concerned with political activity. Well, that was yesterday. [Laughter.] Today I am going to at least mention the imperative of being politically active—within one's institution and outside one's institution, in the larger society. Whether that political activity is carried out by any one of you sitting there, or any of us sitting here, or the leaders of the institutions with whom we are associated is a different story. But why is political activity necessary? We have already heard, *en passant*, from our instructor of the Ukrainian language that she offers a course in business Ukrainian. The real name of the game within institutions is in fact to co-operate aggressively with business schools, with all those departments that do practical things. But even that is not going to help, because the real battle was lost probably 20 or 30 years ago. I had this discussion yesterday again with former ambassador [Derek] Fraser. The real battle is that universities have *removed language requirements* across the board. Once those language requirements go away, you have lost. There is literally, I am sorry, nothing you can do to save the teaching of language unless it is required.

In order for that to happen, there has to be lobbying at the political level *outside* the university to convince the funders of universities at the provincial level that *language is an economic imperative*. Let us be very practical here. The argument that it is nice to learn about the Ukrainian language and culture, or Spanish, and so forth is not going to fly. The only argument is that future Canadian generations want to be competitive in the outside world, in a global economy. One needs to know languages—not a smattering, something that you have heard in kitchens at home, but formal knowledge. That is where the battle is. It is not even within the universities, though you can do a little bit with business schools and IT programs. It is outside the university, and who can take that initiative? You cannot take it, we cannot take it, but the directors of institutions, lobbying, and those political activists, including some of them from the past and from the present and future, who are sitting there—that is who. We have to engage these people to convince provincial governments to reinstate language instruction for every student as an economic imperative.

NATALIA KHANENKO-FRIESEN:

I regret to inform everybody that my question is again about language instruction. In our ladder of university courses, we begin with the recruitment of students into Ukrainian studies with language instruction. In fact, at our university Ukrainian studies enrolment is highest in the first-year Ukrainian language class, and I think it is probably the highest on this continent. Alla [Nedashkivska] will later correct me if I am wrong. And yet we are in a conundrum as academics motivated to advance and pursue Ukrainian studies, mostly because we are not professionally equipped to do so. Alla, I think, is the only professional at CIUS fully equipped to teach and deliberate and talk about how language needs to be taught. The rest of us are split between our main foci in literature or history, or we have no full-time faculty teaching the Ukrainian language. So I have a very practical suggestion. A year ago, the University of Victoria, I believe, organized a workshop or seminar on how to teach Russian in North America, and I have been waiting for such an opportunity for our sessional and part-time faculty who are involved with the foundational task of exposing our students to Ukrainian studies through the language itself: how to do it in a more coordinated manner.

That is where CIUS can come in, with the leadership of professionals in the field, and start a conversation about sharing resources and using the textbooks developed here. We also need to recognize that often students come into these classes to study language for its cultural or symbolic value rather than for its practical application. So there is always the challenge of teaching heritage students here and then sending them to Ukraine, where they face the very different task of acquiring the language for practical use, as a means of communication.

MYROSLAV SHKANDRIJ:

We do have a methodologist trained in language teaching in our program at the University of Manitoba. And there is plenty of experience in other languages that we draw on. We have trained methodologists in German as well, and we share. So it is not quite as bleak as that.

BOHDAN KLID:

I would like to return to the idea of contexts, and direct attention again to the question of language teaching, and of course to the situation here at the University of Alberta, where we have seen a program basically abolished. In the context of multiculturalism, of course we remember that the Institute was founded in the wake of the adoption of the multiculturalism policy, and of course the favourable political circumstances that existed at that time made it possible here at the University of Alberta. We have all these Ukrainian specialists here at the university, and yet we now have a crisis here. You have to ask yourself, how could it have happened? We have this Institute, and it seems that if we are going to save anything that has to do with language, then it should be done here, right? But it did not happen. Our administrators decided to go ahead and cut, and it happened to hit the Ukrainianists pretty hard. In the context of multiculturalism, though, it does not make sense.

I was at the Ukrainian Canadian Congress meeting about two weeks ago, and I heard a very interesting comment by Minister Dion[84] about multiculturalism in particular. What he said was striking, because he was a student when the multiculturalism policy was being adopted. His father was on the Royal Commission on Bilingualism and Biculturalism, and he stressed that Ukrainians were the key to the government's adoption of the multiculturalism policy. And he thanked the Ukrainian community. He said, "Your work helped us not just to adopt the policy, but also you have helped identify the Canadian identity, or you have made a contribution toward that."

How does that make sense? You hear the politicians say that we are stressing diversity, that Canada is a place of tolerance, of understanding—so, in this context, all these cuts just do not make sense. What I would like to state here is that the university itself should be a reflection of society: if we really are a multicultural society, then the university should reflect that, here in Edmonton in particular, where the Ukrainian factor is very important. We have to work to get language classes re-established or a program re-established because *at least the Faculty of Arts* should reflect the principle of multiculturalism.

DOMINIQUE AREL:

On the student's comment about better promoting programs in Ukraine, I think she is right. It is on my mind all the time, and I think we could do infinitely better using the new technological tools, social media, and so forth, as a community in Ukrainian studies. On Bohdan Klid's [recounting of Minister Dion's] comment, I found it very revealing that it came from a Quebecois, because multiculturalism is not very popular in Quebec. But the reality is that both the Quebecois and the Ukrainians have been extremely influential in forging the Canadian identity without really realizing it, and here I am in Ukrainian studies. On Bob Magocsi's point about the absolute necessity of learning languages, in comparative politics it *is* an absolute necessity, though also misunderstood by our own colleagues in other subfields of political science. If you want to study the Middle East, you have to know Arabic; if you want to study China, you have to know Mandarin, etcetera. If you want to study Ukraine, you have to speak Ukrainian (and Russian, not only Ukrainian). That means, in our case [at the University of Ottawa], we cannot learn Ukrainian on campus, but there are other ways—the "scenic route," and usually you just go into the field and learn it. Again, that is a constant battle, and often it is a battle even within disciplines.

84 Stéphane Dion, Minister of Foreign Affairs, Global Affairs Canada.

Round Table IV: Teaching Ukrainian Studies.
L–r: Heather Coleman (discussant), Dominique Arel, Taras Koznarsky, Alla Nedashkivska, Bohdan Kordan, Myroslav Shkandrij (moderator, at the podium).

ROMAN YERENIUK

Moderator, St. Andrew's College, University of Manitoba

ROMAN YERENIUK is an associate professor of church history at St. Andrew's College in Winnipeg and a sessional instructor in Eastern Christianity at the Centre for Ukrainian Canadian Studies and Dept. of Religion, University of Manitoba. He has also been a long-time administrator with both units of the university. Roman has written two volumes, published some 50 studies/articles, and has organized and participated in numerous conferences/symposia in Ukraine and Canada on the theme of the Ukrainian-Canadian diaspora. In addition, he has done extensive research and publishing on Ukrainian Orthodoxy, including the Ukrainian Orthodox Church in Canada, and is the editor of the journal *Faith and Culture* at St. Andrew's College.

I think it is very apropos that we left this session to the very end. At the same time, I want to tell you how proud I am: we have a very rich session with four of the finest people CIUS could have found, plus a commentator who is coming from the national convention of the Ukrainian Canadian Congress. Ladies and gentlemen, let us begin with a couple of general remarks. First of all, I want to say that I was told by the organizers of this auspicious event that community outreach can be defined very broadly, but we can also make it as narrow as we wish, and it will be up to each of our speakers on the panel to do this. We want to work with community institutions to advance higher education, to find agencies, endowments, and others that could continue the great work of CIUS to support Ukrainian studies through some of our smaller community grants and scholarships and library funds. All of this will be part and parcel of this panel on community outreach.

Everybody on this panel has received two questions: (1) How can we improve community outreach and provide new incentives for our academic life across Canada? (2) How do we provide further and new co-operation with the Ukrainian community and the community at large? We are going to give our presenters fifteen minutes each, and our discussant will also have fifteen minutes. At the end we are going to open it up to the community at large, beginning with some responses from graduate students. We have to end this session by a quarter after five to allow for the final conference conclusions and statement. I remind you that the biographies of all the presenters are at the back of our program. First of all, Andrew Hladyshevsky, an Edmonton lawyer, is going to speak to us on behalf of the Ukrainian Canadian Foundation of Taras Shevchenko. This is the paramount foundation of the Ukrainian community in Canada. ■

ANDREW HLADYSHEVSKY

Ukrainian Canadian Foundation of Taras Shevchenko

ANDREW HLADYSHEVSKY, QC, focuses on providing corporate and commercial advice to Alberta businesses, whether operating locally, nationwide, or internationally. A partner of the law firm Dentons LLP, he is experienced in a variety of corporate transactions and acts as general counsel for companies listed on the Alberta, Vancouver, Toronto, US, and NASDAQ Stock Exchanges. He was appointed queen's counsel in January 2000. He has lectured extensively, appeared on Global TV, CTV, and CBC Radio, and given interviews to print media. Andrew was a recipient of the Queen's Diamond Jubilee Medal for his extensive pro bono work (2014), and he received the International Award of Merit from Ukraine (May 2008).

Stewardship, leadership, partnership: The Shevchenko Foundation view of the Ukrainian Canadian community over the past fifty years

Nice to see everybody here, *Slava Isusu Khrystu*. Wonderful to see [Bishop] Dr. Borys Gudziak, welcome, thank you for bringing us such wonderful weather. We will talk about it over dinner. [Laughter.] We spare no expense for our guests here in Alberta. The Shevchenko Foundation—how many have heard about it? Okay, very good. How many of you received the last annual report from the Foundation? That is not bad. One of the first lessons in community outreach is to make sure that your message gets to the people that you think you are talking to. So those of you who have heard about us, that is great, because that is a lot of you. All of you can have a pen from the Foundation if you come and talk to me later.

[…] If you go to our website, www.shevchenkofoundation.com—all of you in this room have directed students there to ask us for grants—now you can actually download them, and add a bookmark: if they want to apply for a grant, they can just go there and apply for a grant in about two minutes.

Or perhaps you are interested in donating to the Foundation. You will see on the website how to do that before you die. Because we know that when you die, the Canada Revenue Agency will immediately take taxes from you, and then whatever noble thing you left the money for—for instance, "a hundred percent of my money to CIUS"—the government is already taking its share before CIUS gets there. Had you known that, you could have donated the money in your lifetime, reduced your immediate taxes, and increased your donation to CIUS and other organizations. That would have been very beneficial to the Ukrainian community and to the cause of Ukrainian education in the world. Now that you know, hopefully you will never be able to sleep peacefully again until you have done your wills and started to donate.

Community outreach is getting the message out to stakeholders. It is trying to get your message to people who may not understand who you are and what you believe in. The Shevchenko Foundation is interested in being the best foundation in the country—not Ukrainian-Canadian foundation, but the best in the country, with a vision of ensuring that Ukrainian culture in Canada is promulgated, accepted, celebrated for the benefit of all Canadians, because our culture is part of Canada. The stories we have are part of Canada, so we market the Shevchenko Foundation not only to the wonderful people in this room, who are part of the educational elite of our country, but everybody. Because everybody has an interest in the Shevchenko Foundation. How does it tie into education? That is a good question.

> *"There are others who would like to connect with their culture and heritage, some of whom will have very "un-Ukrainian" parents but will be turned on to the subject matter even though it is not necessary for them. One of my preoccupations is making that "unnecessary" element a part of their lives."*

We have four pillars of activity in the Foundation: arts, education, community development, and heritage. In the arts, you probably know what that would entail: lots of people who like to sing, lots of people who like to dance, but there are also visual artists; there are a few of them in the room here I know very well who have collaborated with the Shevchenko Foundation. That also encompasses the world of literature: some of the people in this room have applied to try to win the Kobzar Literary Award. At the time we announced that award, twelve years ago, it was equal to the highest Canadian book prize of $25,000. It is awarded to a Canadian writer who writes on a Ukrainian-Canadian theme, or in whose book that theme is important. Since then, people such as Dr. Myroslav Shkandrij have submitted some of their non-fictional works. The recent book on [Vasyl] Avramenko was actually short-listed. So the award encompasses fiction, non-fiction, poetry, and even theatre. Why is that important? Well, we want to encourage our writers. We want to encourage our academic writers to inspire other people. If nobody ever reads your book, how do they get inspired? So one of the motives behind the Foundation is: "Let us get this out." That is part of community outreach.

You have to ask yourself, in your own organization, how are you doing—to get that out there. The pillar of education seems like a no-brainer, because the Shevchenko Foundation has been around since 1963. Its first grants totalled about $500,000, and since then we have given almost $10 million back to the community, investing in the community. But education has always been a pillar. Some people in this room would have received bursaries when enrolled full-time in a Ukrainian program. But we are concerned about people who are fairly young and do not understand how to get involved with Ukrainian education in Canada, or why it would motivate them, so we have a small subsidy program for students. We have had over a hundred take advantage of this, allowing them to go to Ukraine: they get a small subsidy toward their tuition, toward courses in Lviv and Kyiv.

The theory is that young and energetic men and women aged 18 to 26 will meet other young men and women in Ukraine while they study and not only get excited about their Ukrainian heritage but perhaps also be inspired to pursue that education further. We just have to do more of that, which is why we have a $20 million capital campaign underway. In fact, I am going to ask for money now: why delay it, why spoil your supper? I will ask for it now: I am trying to get *you* involved in community outreach.

The third pillar is heritage. We have archives all across the country that are slowly decomposing into dust, and part of the Foundation's role is to assist in preserving some of them. Not only preserving those archives but potentially working with museums and creating new museums so that those things can see the light of day and go across the country. It is a remarkable achievement—Nadia [Jacyk] remembers this, and so does Olya [Kuplowska]—that one of the greatest exhibitions ever was at the Royal Ontario Museum, largely spearheaded by James Temerty. I remember the first conversations with the ROM, which said, "Why would we ever do a Ukrainian exhibit? Who would be interested?" Mr. Temerty stuck his neck out, but he also came to the Foundation and others, and said, "We need to see that there is broad-based community support." As a result, that exhibit broke all the records of the ROM—all records from its inception. The Ukrainian-Canadian initiative (it was the Scythian Gold exhibit) was so popular with non-Ukrainians in this country and in the United States that it broke all records. We have something to share in our music, in our dance, in our culinary arts. We even share how we pray to God, through our sacred music. So there is a lot to share.

> *"Of the $3 million that we have ... 60 percent of the funds come from modest donations, ranging anywhere from $50 to $1,000, that have been collected over the years. Virtually all of the donations, be they major or modest, have come from individuals of modest means."*

My son Roman Hladyshevsky is in grade twelve. He has met very few academics other than his teachers in school. The exception is Alla Nedashkivska, whom he has seen a few times, who has made a few cruises through high schools and elsewhere. Think about it: why is the course in witchcraft one of the highest-rated and desired by university students? It means nothing to an engineer to have witchcraft to build a bridge, or to a lawyer (though some may argue otherwise); modern medicine no longer requires it. It is an unnecessary course. The problem for the average young adults who come to university—in this university, there would be three or four thousand students of Ukrainian heritage—is not that they don't like Ukrainian but that it is just not necessary to what they have to do as engineers, doctors, lawyers, or dentists. But there are hundreds of people of Ukrainian heritage in education programs in Western Canada who will become teachers, and Ukrainian studies are relevant to their teaching. Somehow we need to get in their faces.

There are a few hundred students in the university students' Ukrainian club here. How are we meeting with them? How are we encouraging them to study? What are we doing? Are we actually interfacing with them, the brilliant minds in this room—with the young people who would love to talk to you if they only knew how they could approach you? Well, that is a tough thing to do as a volunteer. I do it all the time. It is very tough just to stand here nervously and talk to you. But you have to overcome that and be the driving force in that young person's life. Unless *you* do that [pointing], or *you* do that, or *you* do that, nobody else is going to do it for you. The future of all these programs will never be as bright as it really could be.

To me, somehow this issue of strict MA- and PhD-driven students will always be there. The Shevchenko Foundation will always be there to assist them by providing bursaries and scholarships. But there are others who would like to connect with their culture and heritage, some of whom will have very "un-Ukrainian" parents but will be turned on to the subject matter even though it is not necessary for them. One of my preoccupations is making that "unnecessary" element a part of their lives. It is interesting: we do not seem to have any problem with Ukrainian priests going out into the bilingual programs to talk to the kids in elementary school, in junior high, in high school. Why would they go there? Well, because they are actually talking to Christian children, and they actually have something to say to them, something that they would like to be part of their lives. Well, education never really leaves us, so we have to be part of their everyday life, and we have to meet them. That is the challenge I throw out, and we can talk about ways to get out there through multimedia and new media. I want you to spend some time, though, on that Shevchenko bookmark that you just put into your phones, and look at it seriously to see: "Where do I fit in here?" Either as a consumer or a donor, because that is part of my community outreach to you. ■

ROMAN YERENIUK:

Andriiu, I was looking at some of the faces in the audience, and an image that comes to mind is that probably in your law studies you took salesmanship…I think it comes across very well. [Laughter.]

OLGA KUPLOWSKA

Canadian Foundation for Ukrainian Studies

OLGA KUPLOWSKA is a graduate of McGill University (BA) and the University of Toronto (MA in applied psychology). Her professional career has spanned two different fields: evaluation/communications research and corporate governance. She spent 32 years at Ontario's educational media organization, TVOntario, where she was the director of research for many years, and later its corporate secretary. Since retiring from TVOntario in 2006, she has continued working part-time as a corporate secretary, first for TFO (Ontario's French-language educational media organization), and since 2011 for the OmbudService for Life & Health Insurance. She has been an active member of the Ukrainian-Canadian community all her life, including serving on several Ukrainian-Canadian community boards. She has been the president of the Canadian Foundation for Ukrainian Studies since 2001.

Canadian Foundation for Ukrainian Studies: Who we are, what we do, challenges we face

I am going to be a little bit more low-key than Andrii [Hladyshevsky]. [Laughter.] I think most people have heard about the Foundation, but I know sometimes there is a lot of confusion as to what we actually fund and how we are set up. I would like to address some of the issues and challenges before us. Many of them are actually similar to some of the issues and challenges raised in the last two days.

First of all, some background information on the Foundation itself. The Canadian Foundation for Ukrainian Studies[85] was established in 1975 by the Ukrainian Canadian Professional and Business Federation, and we are actually one year older than CIUS, so we celebrated our fortieth anniversary last year. We were incorporated under federal law as a national non-profit charitable body, and as of February 2014 we have been continued corporately under the new Canada Not-for-Profit Corporations Act, with no changes to aims and objectives. Under the new act we are required to overhaul our constitution, and this has some implications for some of our governing practices, which therefore affect our operations.

The general objectives established for the Foundation were: first, to be recognized by the community, by institutions of higher education, and by governments as a body that, through funding and other means, supports the development and enhancement of Ukrainian studies in Canada and elsewhere. Second, to build a base of endowed funding that consists of the Foundation's general endowment fund and also of individual endowments, the annual proceeds from which would be used to support Ukrainian studies in perpetuity. Priority is to be given to projects that initiate or expand Ukrainian studies at Canadian universities, all other considerations being equal. To reiterate, the Canadian Foundation for Ukrainian Studies focuses first and foremost on activities at the post-secondary level. There have been some exceptions in the past, and I guess it does not mean that there cannot be any in the future. But by and large, our focus is on Ukrainian studies at the post-secondary level.

As to the structure, the Foundation's work is guided by a national board of directors, currently comprised of ten individuals from Alberta, Manitoba, Ontario, and Quebec. We do have several vacancies to fill, and normally we would have people from some of the other provinces as well. Historically, members of the board have been drawn from the ranks of the Ukrainian Professional and Business Federation, and this began to change in the late 1990s as local chapters of the professional and business clubs either

85 www.cfus.ca.

became less active, began to redefine themselves, or moved in a different direction. Most of the current members of the board, though active and very prominent in the Ukrainian-Canadian community, are not necessarily members of the P & B associations,[27] and that is another issue that comes up when we are recruiting members for the Foundation. In addition, and this was the case until recently, we also used to have three ex officio members on our board—the director of CIUS, the president of the Ukrainian Canadian Professional and Business Federation, and the editor of the *Encyclopedia of Ukraine* while it was being published. But under the new Not-for-profit Corporations Act, ex officio positions have been disallowed, and we are now in the process of exploring different ways to incorporate academic guidance, possibly through an academic advisory committee attached to the Foundation.

At this point, I would like to thank Professor Frank Sysyn for his years of invaluable service as proxy for the CIUS director: he has served for many years, coming to all of our meetings, and his service has really been invaluable.

The executive committee is responsible for day-to-day activities. All board members serve as volunteers, and no one receives any financial compensation for their time, other than travel expenses to annual board meetings. I mention all these things because very often people want to donate money, and they like to know how the Foundation operates. We are very professionally managed: we have audited statements, comprehensive records, all meetings are "minuted"—in other words, we are very transparent. We do have a website, perhaps not yet as energetic and maybe as interactive as yours [referring to the updated website of the Shevchenko Foundation], but we will get there. It does have all the information about our various programs. The head office is currently in Toronto, where it has been since the 1990s. Previously the head office was in Edmonton, Vancouver, and in Winnipeg, depending on where the presidents were. I am happy to say that Mr. Peter Savaryn was one of the early presidents of the Foundation [acknowledging Mr. Savaryn in the audience], and he has left an impressive legacy.

In terms of our net assets, as of the end of December 2015, our assets were nearly $3 million, and this does not include the $300,000+ that we transferred over the last twenty years to Canadian universities to take advantage of matching-fund programs. I will speak about that a bit later.

Of the $3 million that we have, 40 percent are from larger or major donors, and these donations have been used to establish funds that in most cases carry the name of the donor. However, 60 percent of the funds come from modest donations, ranging anywhere from $50 to $1,000, that have been collected over the years. Virtually all of the donations, be they major or modest, have come from individuals of modest means. This echoes what Bishop Borys said earlier about our chairs and institutions being founded and built by ordinary, hard-working people in the community who believe in education, have a sense of mission, and respond with passion. That fact has never been forgotten by the successive boards of the Foundation. It has always been front and centre when key financial and other decisions have been and continue to be made.

How is this $3 million broken down? We have thirteen programs or funds, all of which, except for two, are restricted or designated for specific purposes, and the designations were made by the donors who set them up. In all cases, be they designated or not, the programs are for the most part endowed, meaning that we can only disburse the earned annual income. Both of these conditions present challenges or issues that I will be addressing shortly.

In addition to the funds that we hold and manage, there were four other funds that we used to hold but transferred to universities to take advantage of matching-fund programs. One went to the University of Toronto, two went to the University of Alberta, and one to the University of Victoria. These transfers involved substantial funds in each case. In three cases it was $100,000, and each of these situations presented us with some learning experiences, which I will also bring up shortly. While there are obvious benefits to arrangements where we transfer funds to universities in order to obtain matching funds, there have also been some challenges.

I would like to say a few words now on how much the Foundation has disbursed over the years. Since its creation in 1975, the Foundation has disbursed close to $3.5 million in grants. On average, that would be about $87,000 per year, although probably we disbursed less in the earlier years. But certainly for the last five years, since 2011, we have been disbursing over $100,000 annually, and last year, in 2015, we actually disbursed a record $125,000, the highest amount to date. What has been supported with all this money? I am happy to say that in spite of program restrictions or designations, a wide diversity of projects and activities have been supported, and they are wide-ranging: various academic press publications, academic conferences or symposia, public as well as more student-oriented lectures and seminars, academic exchanges, scholarships, fellowships, library collections, teaching of new university-level courses, research activities, and distribution of educational films. The Foundation was the primary financial supporter of the *Encyclopedia of Ukraine*, and now continues to support, in a significant way, the *Internet Encyclopedia of Ukraine*.[8] In terms of geographical or institutional diversity, over the years the Foundation has supported activities and scholars at pretty well every university in Canada where Ukrainian studies take place.

It is true that projects and scholars at the University of Alberta and the University of Toronto have been beneficiaries more frequently and have received possibly close to 60 percent or maybe more of all of the distributed funds. This is not surprising, since most of the funds that we have are targeted or tied to specific programs at these two universities. We also have two funds designated to support activities at national universities of Ukraine, the Kyiv-Mohyla Academy and the Ostroh Academy. But other than that, all our funds are directed toward activities in Canada. Looking at all of this, we can say that the Foundation has definitely been fulfilling its mandate, and at quality levels.

> *"The reason why many donors are so specific ... is that in their opinion, the particular area they would like to fund is not being ... sufficiently addressed by academics ... We are considering whether short-term specificity might be built into our terms of agreement, or allowance made for periodic reviews and updates."*

However, we are also facing issues and challenges, and, not in any order of priority, some of the things I am going to mention have actually come up on earlier panels. The first one is matching existing funds, the ones that we have, with new and emerging needs and various incoming requests. As I have mentioned, most of our program funds are designated: they support existing programs or activities at universities, or specific scholarships. This means we have next to no flexibility to address new priorities, new needs with the funds that we have. And yet, as we have heard from the other panellists, priorities are shifting. It also means that we have few discretionary funds for small, one-off projects: a seminar, a visiting lecturer, a small publication, a student scholarship, anything that does not fit into what we already have.

At the same time, we have a couple of designated programs—and both of them deal with the fields of communications and journalism—for which in recent years we have actually had difficulties attracting qualified candidates. There are different reasons for this, which I can go into later. But it means that those funds have been sitting idle when there are no qualified candidates, yet we cannot redirect the funds toward other purposes because there are signed agreements and we need to respect them. We are currently reviewing other aspects of those programs to see what can be modified or tweaked or maybe looked at in different ways. So this brings up the issue mentioned the other day by Professor Marples, and I think others as well—the need, perhaps, for less restrictive or more open terms of agreement. However, the reason why many donors are so specific, and I am talking about those who have approached us, is that in their opinion, the particular area they would like to fund is not being addressed, or sufficiently addressed, by academics, and they feel that their fund may encourage work in a certain direction. On the one hand we would like something less restrictive, and on the other hand people feel that gaps need to be filled, and that is why they are giving money. We are considering whether short-term specificity might be built into our terms of agreement, or allowance made for periodic reviews and updates.

The next question is whether or not all funds should be endowed. With endowed funds, as you know, we can spend only the earned income and cannot touch the capital. But we have asked ourselves, when there are pressing needs, whether it always makes sense to safeguard the capital. At times we have dipped into our endowment fund beyond the earned income in order to respond to a need.

Another issue is monitoring—I mentioned that we have transferred some funds to universities. One would usually think that once you have transferred, you do not have to worry about it anymore, but we have learned from experience that you need to continue monitoring the management and status of funds transferred to universities. To give two examples, there is the Clark Graduate Fellowship in Ukrainian Language and Literature at the University of Toronto. For twenty years there was no problem in the way it was disbursed—it went to the most qualified students. And then suddenly, last year, we were told that there is a residency requirement: unless you are an Ontario resident, you cannot qualify for that fellowship. Without going into all the details, this took many meetings, looking through files, pulling out old documents, discovering that certain documents were missing. In the end, after all that, the university agreed to waive all residency requirements from now on: as long as the student is qualified and is recommended by Professor Koznarsky or his colleague, he or she will get that fellowship. Had we not been monitoring it closely, such things can slip, and then, because many of the students getting that fellowship have been from Ukraine, they would not qualify for it.

The other one is the Struk Fund that we transferred to the University of Alberta, with the promise that there would be matching funds, and we are still waiting. To date we have not heard anything from the University of Alberta, and I have heard informally that the matching fund program has been closed, but that needs to be followed up.

As for redirect clauses, we have learned that you have to be very specific—in the event that a program ceases to exist, the university will not only *not* redirect the funds on its own but will consult with the original donor. If you do not put that in, they have the freedom to redirect, and even though they say that it will be in the spirit of what was intended, the spirit may be defined differently.

Raising new dollars is also a challenge for us. To tell you the truth, when we raise funds, the response is not always great. It is the same people who give, and many of these donors are passing on; they are being replaced very slowly. We hear different reasons why younger people are not prepared to donate or support, and those are topics we need to discuss with people at the universities. Very often people say: "I do not see what I believe should be happening. What are the priorities? Too much attention is being focused on Ukraine. We want Ukrainian-Canadian research, or diaspora research...or something else." Or you have the reverse. So there are all kinds of discussions taking place at the community level, and we need to find some good way of reconciling their concerns with what is needed so that people feel they are getting a good return on their investments.

The last challenge is really an internal one for us, but it is important because the Foundation has now been around for 41 years and hopefully will have a long future. We need to look at the board composition and the challenges this can present. We need to look at drawing on different skills from those we had in the past—people, perhaps, with a greater emphasis on marketing, communications, governance knowledge to help us meet new challenges and raise more funds.

In closing, I would like to reiterate what Professor Lupul alluded to in his introductory remarks the other day—that Ukrainian studies are not like other academic studies. They are not independent of the community that made them possible, that nurtured them through difficult times. This does not mean that the community does not believe in or respect academic freedom, but it does expect a return on its investment. The relationship is a delicate balancing of interests, and I am reminded of this whenever I read old Foundation minutes, the minutes of board meetings of the 1970s, 1980s, and 1990s. The debates and discussions recorded in considerable detail in those minutes all bear testimony to the passion, sense of mission, and dedication that have always driven this Foundation.

So I feel that as CIUS celebrates its fortieth, and we our forty-first, this is indeed an opportune time for us to review our successes and our disappointments, and to see how we can work together to meet the new challenges and address some of the problems identified here, so that we can continue to provide some of the financial support required to ensure that Ukrainian studies have a long and prosperous future. ■

W. ROMAN PETRYSHYN

Founding director of the Ukrainian Resource Development Centre, MacEwan University (1987–2015)

ROMAN PETRYSHYN is an adjunct assistant professor with the Department of Educational Psychology, Faculty of Education, University of Alberta, where he is researching the reform of the university system in Ukraine. From 1987 to 2015 he was the director of the Ukrainian Resource and Development Centre (URDC) at MacEwan University. He holds a PhD in the sociology of race and ethnic relations from the University of Bristol and a diploma in social sciences from the University of Birmingham, as well as master's and bachelor's degrees in clinical psychology from Lakehead University (Thunder Bay, ON). Dr. Petryshyn edited *Changing Realities: Social Trends Among Ukrainian Canadians* (1980) and has authored a number of articles on different themes in Ukrainian community and international development.

Cultivating our legacy: Both a "Consortium of Directors of Ukrainian Studies" and a "Network of Fundraising Organizations Promoting University Endowments" are needed now to help protect and expand institutional endowments for Ukrainian studies at Canadian universities

[SUBMITTED TEXT]

Introduction

The celebration of the fortieth anniversary of CIUS is an appropriate occasion to reflect on what has been achieved in Ukrainian studies. Throughout that time, Canadians of Ukrainian ethnicity remained involved in the Ukrainian community and created a variety of Ukrainian institutions, among which are ten centres of Ukrainian studies at universities across Canada.

Funding is central to every organization, as it defines the capacity and range of programs it can undertake. It is therefore vital that discussions about future planning of Ukrainian studies examine the nature and amount of funding that is available. It is useful to look at this subject historically, comparatively, and critically before planning future activities.

This paper will summarize information and draw on data recently collected in the three Prairie Provinces of Alberta, Saskatchewan, and Manitoba that can inform us about trends relating to *institutional endowments for Ukrainian studies* (IEUS). The focus is on several key questions regarding the endowments that fund the core administrative finances of Ukrainian centres, institutes, and a college (i.e., excluding the costs of courses, curricula, library, or archives), namely:

a) What is the nature of the governance system overseeing IEUS, and what degree of influence do donors and community organizations have to protect their endowments at recipient universities?

b) How many IEUS exist at the four Canadian Prairie universities in this study? How do they differ from one another, and what is their market value?

c) How much revenue do these endowments yield annually, and how many Ukrainian studies faculty and support staff positions receive guaranteed funding from IEUS?

d) Are the terms of agreement for IEUS being fully respected? How can donors be assured that their donations for Ukrainian studies will continue to be used for their stated purposes in generations to come?

e) How can a more positive climate for giving be built up within the Ukrainian-Canadian community?

f) Should a national network of individual donors and foundations be created to establish greater co-operation with Canadian universities and facilitate closer monitoring and promotion of IEUS?

g) What priorities should donors engage to help protect existing IEUS and raise funds for future endeavours?

We will look at the history and growth of the financial capacity of Ukrainian studies in the Prairie region of Canada and identify some lessons learned that can benefit future donors. Answers to these questions were collected via published annual reports and two dozen interviews with selected knowledgeable respondents over the past eight months in order to consolidate information from six centres at four Canadian Prairie universities.

Historical perspective

Over the past 125 years, Ukrainian Canadians have carried the bulk of financing the many organizational systems that have made up the "Ukrainian community"—or, more accurately, our *community of communities*. Anecdotally, we know that Ukrainians have financially sustained several major community structures that stabilize the community. These include multimillion-dollar financing for: (1) religious institutions, (2) community centres based on various ideologies, (3) credit unions, (4) dance and arts organizations, and (5) Ukrainian studies teaching, research, and publishing institutions at Canadian universities.

Of the foregoing five categories, the latter is the most recent, having sprung up in the 1960s and continued to the present. It is also the least coordinated one of the five mentioned at the national level. This is the case even though annual expenditures in Ukrainian studies are comparable with other categories that do have significant national coordination.

Since the 1950s, individual Ukrainians in Canada and the USA have donated sums of money to create endowments at universities that generate annual investment revenues used to finance projects and institutions in Ukrainian studies. To date, such institutions exist in seven cities of Canada and at least three in the United States. In Canada these endowments can be found in Edmonton, Saskatoon, Victoria, London, Winnipeg, Toronto, and Ottawa. In the United States, institutional endowments in Ukrainian studies exist in Cambridge, Mass., New York, and Chicago.

Donated endowments have financially supported centres, institutes, and a college that teach, research, and publish about the religions, history, languages, literature, folklore, social sciences, and development of Ukrainians in North America and Ukraine. Prior to the creation of these endowments, Ukrainian-content courses were not taught at universities, despite the fact that Ukrainians had settled in North America since the 1880s.

The information that follows is from a study that focuses on four universities in Western Canada, namely: the University of Alberta and MacEwan University in Edmonton, the University of Saskatchewan in Saskatoon, and the University of Manitoba in Winnipeg.

To the best of our knowledge, this is the first study of its kind. Its purpose is to begin a dialogue among Canadian professionals in Ukrainian studies that could result in coordinated action enabling Ukrainian Canadians in the twenty-first century to develop a strategic plan that will serve to protect and expand IEUS. I will make two specific and interrelated recommendations for action at the end of the paper.

The capacity for institutional endowments in Ukrainian studies on Canadian campuses emerged in the context of the generation and circumstances of the donors. This report provides empirical evidence that endowments have proven to be central to the creation and development of Ukrainian studies at Western Canadian universities. The history of six centres in Prairie Canada demonstrates that endowments for centres and institutes have been established in three periods, with three different sets of objectives. From the 1920s to the 1960s, donors focused on financing religiously based institutions. In the 1970s and 1980s, new Ukrainian institutions were endowed to enhance community participation in multiculturalism. Most recently, from the 1990s to the present, the gifting of endowments has been motivated largely by the desire to build Canada/Ukraine inter-university relations. This enables academics to study and promote the independence and sustainability of Ukraine as a democratic state and society that aspires to join the European Union.

The institutions that emerged in these three periods all continue to exist today and play their specific roles individually and simultaneously. However, each is structured differently, depending on its purpose, with different operating methods and different expected outcomes and products. Table 1 compares the governance models and community influence of the six institutions.

TABLE 1. COMPARISON OF GOVERNANCE MODELS AND COMMUNITY INFLUENCE SUPPORTING UKRAINIAN STUDIES AT SIX WESTERN CANADIAN INSTITUTIONS

Institution	Degree of community influence	Mechanism for monitoring	Investment with community foundation
St. Andrew's College in Winnipeg (SAC) at the University of Manitoba https://umanitoba.ca/colleges/st_andrews/	The College was created through provincial legislation, and since 1963 has had a signed land-lease agreement with the University of Manitoba. It has its own board of governors, drawn from the Sobor of the UOCC. +++	Annual report to College donors. The College contributes budget costs through fundraising, support of the UOCC and SUS, and its own foundation.	St. Andrew's College Foundation has $5.9 million with the Shevchenko Foundation, which invests and manages the fund to produce annual revenues.
Centre for Ukrainian Canadian Studies (CUCS) at the University of Manitoba http://umanitoba.ca/faculties/arts/departments/ukrainian_canadian_studies/index.html	A university-approved agreement with St. Andrew's College in 1981 established this jointly managed (unincorporated) centre. Of the ten members on the Policy Council, six are from the Ukrainian community. ++	Annual report submitted to Dean of Arts and to SAC. The Arts Faculty contributes to budget costs, along with CUCS endowment revenue.	CUCS has $1.8 million in endowments. These funds are managed by the University of Manitoba Foundation under the authority of a Policy Council.
Kule Folklore Centre (KuFC) at the University of Alberta ukrfolk.ualberta.ca	The university signed an agreement establishing the KuFC in the Department of Modern Languages and Cultural Studies. A board of directors draws 3 of its 8 members from the Ukrainian community. ++	An annual report is submitted to the Board of Directors and UofA Provost and Dean of Arts. Both endowment revenues and the university contribute to budget costs.	Friends of the Ukrainian Folklore Centre (a casino-funded society) are planning to set up a designated fund with the Shevchenko Foundation.
Ukrainian Resource and Development Centre (URDC) at MacEwan University http://www.macewan.ca/wcm/SchoolsFaculties/ArtsScience/CentresandInstitutes/UkrainianResourceandDevelopmentCentre	The university president signed a 5-year agreement (2015–20) with president of the Ukrainian Foundation for College Education (UFCE) regarding its role in URDC projects. ++	URDC reports to MacEwan Provost; its Kule Chair reports to the Dean of Arts. Both endowment revenues and Arts Faculty contribute to budget costs.	UFCE has $312,000 in a designated fund with the Shevchenko Foundation. Annual revenues are paid to UFCE, which directs the funds to URDC.
Canadian Institute of Ukrainian Studies (CIUS) at the University of Alberta cius.ca	With a commitment to annual funding from the Government of Alberta, the university's General Faculties Council approved the establishment of CIUS, subsequently endorsed by a Board of Governors resolution dated 18 June 1976. + CIUS's original two offices (Edmonton, Toronto) expanded after 1991 to include Ukraine (Lviv, Kharkiv, and Zaporizhia). Organization includes CIUS Press and the Internet Encyclopedia of Ukraine.	Originally under the U of A's VP for Research, since 2011 the CIUS Director has reported to the Dean of Arts. CIUS activities are facilitated by the Faculty's Arts Collaboration Enterprise (ACE).	CIUS endowments are managed by U of A Financial Services. Contributors include CFUS, the Petro Jacyk Education Foundation, and other major individual donors, as well as community organizations that receive casino funds. The Alberta Society for the Advancement of Ukrainian Studies was founded in 2008 with the objective of fundraising to support CIUS.
Prairie Centre for Ukrainian Heritage (PCUH) at St. Thomas More College (STM), federated with the University of Saskatchewan pcuh.stmcollege.ca	An academic unit of STM. +	Director is a faculty member, appointed by and reporting to the Dean of STM.	Some potential donors to PCUH are considering investing in the Shevchenko Foundation, directing revenues to benefit PCUH.

Host or partner universities have used different kinds of legal agreements to govern the Ukrainian centres associated with their organizational structures. As a result, the centres have varying degrees of autonomy, and endowments have been established for different subjects within Ukrainian studies (e.g., Ukrainian history, Ukrainian-Canadian studies, Ukrainian folklore, Ukrainian language, Ukraine, and theology) and different purposes (e.g., operating costs, student awards, publishing, etc.). Moreover, over time, the various centres/institutes in Ukrainian studies have developed different administrative models regarding (a) how much community control is written into the legal agreements (high +++ or medium ++ or low +; see Table 1); (b) what kind of mechanisms are established to monitor those agreements; and (c) whether Ukrainian studies are supported by a community foundation.

Table 1 shows that St. Andrew's College has negotiated the most comprehensive agreements of the six institutions examined in the Ukrainian studies field. The college was created by an act of the Manitoba government. It joined the University of Manitoba on terms similar to those that govern other confessional colleges (Anglican and Roman Catholic) and has a land lease as well as benefits from internal university financial and administrative structures.

Typically, other Ukrainian studies institutions were formed internally at their respective universities and have fewer written legal documents of incorporation. Their existence depends on resolutions of general faculty councils and/or decisions of university boards of governors. The remaining five institutions have been established in this way. Three of the five institutions—CUCS, KuFC, and URDC—were created as internal constituents of their universities but are also supported by community fundraising groups that have established endowments to benefit their institutions. Two of these three community organizations (KuFC and URDC) are investing their endowments externally with the Shevchenko Foundation, rather than only with the university.

These community fundraising organizations have developed a working relationship with the recipient Ukrainian studies institutions but remain independent registered societies outside the university. This enables such community groups to familiarize themselves with the internal work priorities in Ukrainian studies, as well as to continue their fundraising efforts externally.

This model is emerging as the most effective way to ensure university autonomy in internal decision-making while giving donors some involvement and influence in the evolution of Ukrainian studies, both locally and nationally. Currently fundraising occurs in a shrinking pool of donors who have traditionally supported religiously based and multicultural Ukrainian institutions.

TABLE 2. SUMMARY OF ENDOWMENTS FOR UKRAINE-ORIENTED AND UKRAINIAN-CANADIAN STUDIES AT FOUR PRAIRIE UNIVERSITIES

Institution	Total endowments for Ukraine, 2015 market value	Total endowments for Ukr-Can, 2015 market value
St. Andrew's College (Winnipeg)		$5.7 million
Centre for Ukrainian Canadian Studies (Winnipeg)		$1.8 million
Canadian Institute of Ukrainian Studies (Edmonton)	$22.5 million (estimate)	$2.5 million (estimate)
Kule Folklore Centre (Edmonton)		$12.4 million
Ukrainian Resource and Development Centre (Edmonton)	$7.5 million	
Prairie Centre for Ukrainian Heritage		$1.9 million
Total	**$30.0 million**	**$24.3 million**
Grand total	**$54.3 million**	

This report examined only six of fifteen Ukrainian centres in North America. The total values of endowments at six Ukrainian centres/institutes at four Western Canadian universities are presented below in two categories: (1) for studies on Ukraine and (2) for Ukrainian-Canadian studies.

The market value of endowments for research and other activities on Ukraine is estimated to be approximately $30 million in 2015. The market value of endowments for Ukrainian-Canadian studies is approximately $24.3 million.

The total market value in 2015 of endowments at the six centres is approximately (at least) $54.3 million. More detailed research, using annual financial reports, is necessary to establish precise figures.

TABLE 3. ESTIMATED ANNUAL EXPENDITURES OF SIX UKRAINIAN STUDIES ORGANIZATIONS IN 2015–16

Institution	Estimated budget expenditures in 2015–16
St. Andrew's College	$1,200,000
Centre for Ukrainian Canadian Studies	$200,000
Canadian Institute of Ukrainian Studies	$1,500,000 *
Kule Folklore Centre	$621,000 *
Ukrainian Resource and Development Centre	$264,000
Prairie Centre for Ukrainian Heritage	$56,000
Total	**$3,410,000**

* includes costs of salaries paid from university general funds, as per agreements in place

Summary data indicate that expenditures at the six Ukrainian studies centres/institutes in 2015 were approximately $3.8 million. The majority of these funds were spent at the University of Manitoba and the University of Alberta.

Table 4. Summary of endowment sources of funding for academic and non-academic staffing in Ukrainian studies at four western Canadian universities (FTE)

Centre/Institute	Academic faculty		Support staff	
	Endowment revenues	University funds	Endowment revenues	University funds
Canadian Institute of Ukrainian Studies, U of A	3.5	2.0	1.0	4.0
Kule Folklore Centre, U of A		2.0 (+0.5**)	2.0	
URDC, MacEwan University	1.0		1.0	
Prairie Centre for Ukrainian Heritage, U of S	0.3		0.2	
St. Andrew's College, U of M	2.0		5.5	
Centre for Ukrainian Canadian Studies, U of M	3.0	0.5	0.2	0.8
Total by column	**9.8**	**5.0**	**9.7**	**4.8**

Total Academic faculty – 14.8

Total Support staff – 14.5

* Full-time equivalency for one position equals four full courses (or eight one-semester courses)

** 0.5 position is for French Canadian studies managed by KuFC

Academic and non-academic staff in Winnipeg and Edmonton

Number of full-time equivalent (FTE*) positions funded by university (base) funds and revenues from institutional endowments at Ukrainian institutions in four Prairie universities. Contracted faculty are not included in this list of endowed positions.

The summary indicates that a total of 14.8 academic positions in Winnipeg and Edmonton are secured by endowment and negotiated agreements. There are also 14.5 ongoing support positions in Ukrainian studies.

Altogether the total is just over 29 positions in the four universities of Prairie Canada.

Table 5. Comparison of Winnipeg and Edmonton Ukrainian studies academic and support staff, 2015–16

Institution	Academic staff		Support staff		Total
	Endowment	University	Endowment	University	
Winnipeg					
St. Andrew's	2.0		5.5		7.5
CUCS	3.0*	0.5**	0.2	0.8	4.5
Total	**5.0**	**0.5****	**5.7**	**0.8**	**12.0**
Edmonton					
CIUS	3.5	2.0	1.0	4.0	10.5
KuFC		2.5	2.0		4.5
URDC	1.0		1.0		2.0
Total	**4.5**	**4.5**	**4.5**	**4.0**	**17.0**

* Approximately 3 FTEs are funded by the CUCS endowment and student tuitions for courses. The courses are taught by qualified academic sessional lecturers specializing in Ukrainian studies.

**The Faculty of Arts provides funding for a 0.5 academic director.

When we compare the two endowed centres in Winnipeg with the three endowed centres in Edmonton (taking permanent and contract staff into consideration), the distribution of academic and support staff is similar in both cities. Funds allow for 17.0 full-time equivalency (FTE) positions in Edmonton and 12.0 in Winnipeg.

As for academic staff conducting teaching, research, and publishing work in Ukrainian studies, there are similar numbers in Winnipeg (5.5) and Edmonton (8.5). However, a greater number of academic positions exist in Winnipeg on a part-time basis than in Edmonton.

In support staff, Winnipeg has 6.5 positions, while Edmonton has 8.5. The University of Alberta provides somewhat more financial support for support staff than does the University of Manitoba.

The total number of people working in Ukrainian studies in 2015–16 was 12.0 in Winnipeg and 17.0 in Edmonton. This includes faculty sessional lecturers paid by endowments and departmental budgets.

[PowerPoint texts presented at the CIUS@40 Conference Round Table]

Challenges with the "Corporate University"

Universities have become more corporatized in the last two decades. Today's corporate university structure has made administrative processes more centralized and put more control into the hands of administrators than of faculty members. One consequence is that major changes have weakened the administrative authority and structure of Ukrainian centres and institutes.

> Constant administrative restructuring
> Corporatization of university structures
> Recapitalization of endowments
> Institutional memory is inadequate
> The danger of endowed positions in Ukrainian studies being changed to other disciplines
> Little co-operation on financial matters among Ukrainian centres
> Defining whose role it is to promote and raise new endowments
> The internal organizational structure of universities is in perpetual change.

Administrative structures at universities change continually with circumstances in programs, growth in the number and types of students, and the amount of financing provided by public and private sources. With decreasing numbers of students, Ukrainian studies lose out and have less access to senior decision makers at universities.

Corporate fundraising has become the central mechanism for university fundraising. The relationship between Ukrainian studies professors and university endowments is no longer available as the principal way for universities to raise funds for Ukrainian studies. Where Ukrainian studies have not been made a priority by the corporate university, it is unlikely that the centralized fundraisers will raise money for Ukrainian studies. Instead they tend to target Ukrainian studies donors for general university needs.

Some universities have eliminated the process of recapitalization. Unless endowment agreements specifically include clauses on recapitalization from revenues, universities may refuse to carry out this function.

This experience teaches donors that they would be wise to include a written clause on recapitalization in their endowment agreement if they wish the practice of recapitalization to be applied. Practice has shown that donors might best be advised to choose 20 percent as the portion of annual revenue that should be returned to capital to continually enhance the capital fund.

The number of staff and the authority of offices for university advancement (fundraising) have been growing in administrative authority but, arguably, not in their understanding of the field of Ukrainian studies. As university staff is constantly changing, verbal or undocumented decisions can easily be forgotten when personnel change. Even documented decisions can be forgotten, misconstrued, or intentionally overwritten.

Corporate memory of endowments for Ukrainian studies is relatively poorly documented, both at the universities and in the Ukrainian centres themselves. Even signed agreements get lost, and documents from years ago have been misplaced at universities. On the other hand, donors may have signed documents while still alive, but such documents are not necessarily passed on to family members. Moreover, typically copies of such agreements have not been given to community organizations. Unsurprisingly, there is no central depository for endowment agreements (or copies) in Ukrainian studies.

Problems arise with regard to earned revenues when there is little corporate memory of the donors' wishes. Unless some agency or program is made responsible to remember the purpose of endowments, the donors' families or their proxies will become disconnected from the annual reports and unable to assess the university's use of earned revenues based on their donations.

I believe there is an urgent need to compile and maintain a central databank of agreements (signed in the past by donors with university and community foundations), as well as duplicate annual investment reports released by donors to their proxies, to ensure that their donations for Ukrainian studies will continue to be used for their stated purpose for generations to come.

University foundations vary their policies over time and do not always honour the terms of endowment agreements in the long term. Consequently, there is a danger that some endowed positions in Ukrainian studies may be diverted to other disciplines.

For example, teaching positions in Ukrainian studies depend on sufficient student enrolment in courses. The tendency to require larger and larger numbers of students for classes has negatively impacted minority interests such as classics and Ukrainian studies. If student numbers are not sufficient, the university reserves the right to reassign faculty members to courses other than those with Ukrainian content. Thus, specialists in Ukrainian studies may end up teaching general history or cultural studies in classes unrelated to the original terms of the corresponding endowment. In this way, the university retains its permanent faculty member; however, the terms of reference signed by the donor (i.e., specifically supporting Ukrainian-content courses) may be disregarded.

To make matters worse, there is little sharing of information on financial details among the universities and their Ukrainian centres.

Lack of a formal coordination agreement among directors of Ukrainian studies to meet, share, and discuss endowments has meant that there is little communication and less planning than would be possible if they co-operated. It has also meant that no formal meetings or planning between directors in Ukrainian studies and all the Ukrainian community foundations have taken place. This gap has weakened the message from the universities to community donors about the need for new endowments in Ukrainian studies.

Since ten Ukrainian centres and institutes in Canada have already set up their founding endowments, a coordinated plan could negotiate that further donations might be invested with a community foundation, where disbursed earned revenues are higher than the 3.5 percent generally offered by universities. It is also possible to imagine a negotiation whereby community foundations would provide some matching funds for new endowments in order to keep new endowment funds under the investment control of Ukrainian institutions.

Whose role is it to promote and raise new endowments?

IEUS have previously been raised by community leaders and faculty members who championed specific fields. Major donations have rarely (if ever) been sourced successfully by the staff of development or advancement offices at Canadian universities.

In the past, the driving motivation for fundraising has been the community's traditional need for affirmative action in academic work because of the destruction and oppression of Ukrainian scholars in Ukraine over several generations. Scholarly work in Ukrainian studies is central to understanding and honouring the donor's identity (i.e., Ukrainian history, language, literature, and folklore content). This model of fundraising for Ukrainian studies resonated within the ethnic community, which was devoted to protecting its Ukrainian identity.

Nowadays the recent independence of Ukraine has posed a different set of economic and scholarly needs and opportunities. Ukrainian scholarly work has been enriched with opportunities for academic exchange in all disciplines (e.g., agriculture, medicine, law, and engineering). Universities in Ukraine are seeking to adopt Western program standards, with appropriate pedagogy in a wide range of specialized fields of study.

> *"Achieving community oversight requires bringing the full diversity of Ukrainian-Canadian organizations into a common effort.... The effectiveness of the oversight program and strategizing requires drawing upon all the resources that can be gathered together in Canada, along with whatever help can be obtained from Ukraine."*

These new circumstances raise questions about the future direction of Ukrainian studies in Canada. Should fundraising for Ukrainian studies shift its current focus on the humanities to include other fields in addition to questions of identity? Whose role is it to decide on priorities and locate the financial resources for such a change?

What should be done to protect and grow IEUS?

The foregoing cases outline some of the current challenges facing fundraisers for new Ukrainian studies endowments. The original trust relations between donors from various Ukrainian communities and Ukrainian professors, which were key to fundraising for Ukrainian studies and facilitated giving, have deteriorated.

A new kind of relationship has to be created. It could become a relationship between a community of fundraisers and the corporatized university—one that would ensure corporate memory, monitor and compare the financial management of endowments, avoid administrative pitfalls, and take advantage of investment opportunities when they emerge.

Let us examine two interlocking proposals for strengthening the financial capacity of Ukrainian studies at the universities and fundraisers in the Ukrainian-Canadian community.

One proposal is to establish a "Consortium of Directors in Ukrainian Studies." The other is to strengthen the relationship between "town and gown" by linking existing fundraising organizations to create a new national network of fundraising organizations that promotes IEUS.

Two steps toward the creation of a working relationship between town and gown:

A. Establish a "Consortium of Directors of Ukrainian Studies"

B. Create a national "Network of Fundraising Organizations Promoting IEUS"

Establishing a "Consortium of Directors of Ukrainian Studies"

A formal "Consortium of Directors of Ukrainian Studies" should be established through a partnership agreement. The partnership can be signed on the basis of mutually agreed principles of co-operation and joint interests. The political objective underlying the creation of such a consortium would be to share knowledge about existing IEUS in Canada and to create new ones.

The way to build greater capacity is to look after harmony and order inside the Ukrainian donor community. No one group (Catholic, Orthodox, nationalist, newcomers, established generations, etc.) should have a monopoly over a national endowment oversight process. The same is true of the centres/institutes/colleges in Ukrainian studies. Respecting the principles of unity and diversity will strengthen the capacity of Ukrainian studies and increase donations from the national Ukrainian-Canadian community.

Annual revenues from IEUS investments, although fluctuating with market conditions, have generally provided a stable source of funding. More than sixty years have passed since the first endowments for Ukrainian studies were created. It is time that our Ukrainian studies centres coordinate their efforts to study and better understand their situation, as well as to learn how challenges have been overcome and which others still exist. Most importantly, research is needed to develop a strategy to assure donors that their endowment contributions are secure, that revenues are funding intended purposes, and that academia will continue to attract new donors and grow Ukrainian studies in the future.

Once established, the "Consortium of Directors of Ukrainian Studies" should initiate and endorse joint activities to collect and share information about available matching dollar programs and research grants available at universities, including revenues from small endowments. This information should be shared among the Ukrainian centres and provided to all Ukrainian-Canadian community foundations on a regular basis.

Creating a national "Network of Fundraising Organizations for Promoting IEUS"

Given that existing IEUS in Ukrainian studies are likely the largest investments ever made for the development of Ukrainian culture in Canada, an institutionalized national program needs to be created to oversee the well-being of these investments.

As only donors or their proxies have the right to receive financial reports on their gifted investments, individual donors and organizational fundraisers need to create a program to monitor investments on behalf of those donors no longer able to do so. The initiative for a Network of Fundraising Organizations can be led by two of our established foundations that have a national mandate and the capacity to undertake such a community-development project.

Two foundations well suited for the task are the Canadian Foundation for Ukrainian Studies (CFUS) and the Ukrainian Canadian Foundation of Taras Shevchenko (Shevchenko Foundation). The former has a mandate to foster Ukrainian studies across Canada, while the latter has the infrastructure to undertake the development of such an initiative. Together these two national foundations can also engage the co-operation of a variety of existing local and family foundations that have demonstrated their commitment to expanding IEUS at Canadian universities.

Both CFUS and the Shevchenko Foundation have a policy on Ukrainian higher education, and both have invested donor endowments in Ukrainian studies. Together, along with local community foundations, they are capable of harnessing expertise (e.g., in law, accounting, investment, and donor relations) that would allow them to create a national network and enable them to assist donors, new and old, across Canada.

In my opinion, the Canadian Foundation for Ukrainian Studies should lead the co-operative initiative because this activity corresponds to the bulk of CFUS's central mandate and purpose. Certainly the Shevchenko Foundation also has endowments in this field; unlike CFUS, however, IEUS are a minority portion of the range of activities carried out by the Shevchenko Foundation. Finally, other foundations raising funds for institutional endowments in Ukrainian studies are of a regional character and do not manage funds from across Canada.

The network could carry out a program of activities such as the following:

Proposed activities of the Network of Fundraising Organizations Promoting IEUS

> Ensure that legal proxies from donors are arranged;

> Compile and maintain a central data bank of duplicate donor-signed agreements (signed in the past by donors with university and community foundations), as well as duplicate annual university investment reports released by donors to their proxies;

> Offer advice to new donors for ideas and wording of new agreements;

> Propose to new donors that CFUS and the Shevchenko Foundation co-sign all new agreements and hold the donors' proxies in perpetuity;

> Partner with regional foundations to assist them in their work with local IEUS and ensure their participation in national projects and meetings;

> Compare investment portfolios and revenue performance of IEUS at different universities;

> Establish an inter-university network among donors in specific cities/regions (e.g., Edmonton) where Ukrainian studies are offered at more than one university;

> Offer major donors membership in the "Network of Fundraising Organizations Promoting IEUS" and the right to participate in national conferences and seminars concerning IEUS;

> Provide necessary foundation staff time and sufficient funds to carry out, on a biennial basis, summary financial reports and workshop programs;

> Ensure that endowment revenues paying for university teaching positions respect the terms of endowment with regard to teaching Ukrainian studies courses; and

> Arrange regular meetings between the Consortium of Directors and the Network of Fundraising Organizations.

As generations change in Ukrainian studies, a national Network of Fundraising Organizations can provide continuous oversight of IEUS that is rooted in Canadian law. The process of national oversight will require the capacity to use the court system, deal with university regulations, understand investment strategies, and collaborate with and respect diversity within the Ukrainian-Canadian community, as well as other professional skills.

The Network could also:

> provide greater insight into the comparative financial performance of IEUS;

> build a much-needed bridge between universities and Ukrainian-Canadian fundraising organizations;

> empower donors or their proxies to increase their influence with university offices of advancement;

> stimulate trust relationships with new donors and open a continuous dialogue between fundraising organizations and employees at Ukrainian centres; and

> facilitate greater corporate memory and exchange of information on IEUS among the Ukrainian centres themselves.

Finally, I recommend that Ukrainian-Canadian foundations themselves consider, either singly or jointly, whether they wish to establish their own matching dollar programs for Ukrainian studies at universities; for example, a program of matching endowment gifts, such as $1 for every $5 donated, would stimulate donations. It is also conceivable that a program of community foundations "co-matching with universities" could be established. All of this, of course, requires strategic planning.

Strategic planning

Achieving community oversight requires bringing the full diversity of Ukrainian-Canadian organizations into a common effort. Creating a "community of communities" would facilitate the emergence of a collective (i.e., federated consortium) perspective. The effectiveness of the oversight program and strategizing requires drawing upon all the resources that can be gathered together in Canada, along with whatever help can be obtained from Ukraine.

This new relationship can be achieved by establishing a more complete dialogue among three categories: the Consortium of Directors of Ukrainian Studies, Ukrainian community foundations, and individuals who donate to endowments in Ukrainian studies. New attention and a greater amount of time and money should be spent in bringing endowment specialists and volunteers from the Ukrainian community together. The new Kule Legacy Monitoring Program created in June 2016 by the Shevchenko Foundation is a good first-step example of this approach. The Shevchenko Foundation will oversee 14 endowments set up by Peter and Doris Kule at four Canadian universities.

In their favour, community foundations continue to be community-controlled and have smaller administrative fees than do universities. For example, the Shevchenko Foundation charges a smaller administrative fee (up to 0.5 percent vs 1.0 percent). Moreover, unlike university investments, the Shevchenko Foundation has paid out returns of more than 6 percent when market conditions are suitable.

Greater co-operation within the Ukrainian-Canadian community will open new possibilities for growing IEUS in Canada. The need is evident, and this possibility deserves the attention of leaders in both the Ukrainian-Canadian community and academia. Future fundraising requires that the academy and community refresh and strengthen their relationship, which has proved so successful in the past. ■

NADIA JACYK

Petro Jacyk Education Foundation of Toronto

NADIA JACYK is the president and CEO of the Prombank Group of Companies, a leading Toronto-based land development company specializing in the industrial, commercial, and residential arenas. She is also the president of the Petro Jacyk Education Foundation. Philanthropic initiatives of the Jacyk family have resulted in educational programs at universities, including the University of Alberta, the University of Toronto, Columbia University, and Harvard University. These programs have contributed to the promotion of international awareness of Ukraine and its people. Nadia holds a Bachelor of Science degree from the University of Toronto, a teaching degree from York University, and a graduate degree in business from Harvard University.

The Petro Jacyk Education Foundation's views on community outreach

[SUBMITTED TEXT]

I would like to start by congratulating CIUS on its forty years of accomplishment and impressive contribution to the field of Ukrainian studies and higher education in general.

If the need in past decades was to establish programs with Ukrainian content within universities, today's need is to maintain, improve, and further develop.

Some of you may know about the Petro Jacyk Education Foundation (or PJEF for short) and what it does, and some of you may not. Although the foundation bears the name of its founder, we are not just a *family* foundation but specifically an *education* foundation. We are both a donor and a recipient charitable organization, with individual named funds from other donors, an impressive board of directors, and fundraising events. (I invite you to view our new and updated website, which will be up in the next few weeks.)

Founded in 1986 by Peter Jacyk, the PJEF is also celebrating a milestone anniversary this year—our 30th! My father headed the education foundation from 1986 to 2001, while I was a director from its inception and have headed it for the last fifteen years.

The PJEF is exclusively dedicated to helping establish a network of educational programs and academic centres at world-renowned universities. The founder, Petro Jacyk, strongly believed that centres and high-level scholarly programs in Ukrainian studies would provide scholarly interpretation and objective information about Ukraine and Ukrainians, thereby fostering much-needed international awareness.

Over the past thirty years, we have been funding significant programs in Canada, the USA, and Ukraine, as well as a variety of educational and publication projects in the UK, Brazil, and Poland.

Prior to establishing the Education Foundation, one of the first institutions of higher learning to benefit from Peter Jacyk's support was Harvard. In the late 1960s he dedicated a tremendous amount of time to raising endowment funds for the Harvard Ukrainian program through the Ukrainian Studies Chair Fund. The Harvard Ukrainian Research Institute (HURI) was launched in 1973, with Omeljan Pritsak as its first director. Three chairs were endowed, in Ukrainian language, history, and literature. Mr. Jacyk's work did not end there. Through the Education Foundation he went on to establish two permanent programs within HURI at Harvard:

1. The Jacyk Distinguished Fellowship provides gifted Ukrainian scholars, scientists, and politicians an opportunity to spend one year at Harvard conducting research, lecturing, and establishing contacts with other specialists in their field. Former Ambassador Yuriy Shcherbak and Professor Serhii Plokhii are among the past recipients.

2. The second is the position of a permanent bibliographer, the Petro Jacyk Bibliographer for Ukrainian Collections, at the Harry Elkins Widener Memorial Library (Harvard College Libraries). An example of an outstanding bibliographer who held this position at Harvard is Dr. Ksenya Kiebuzinski, who is now doing a fine job at the Petro Jacyk Resource Centre in the Robarts Library at the University of Toronto.

In 1979 and into the 1980s, Peter Jacyk was also very active on the fundraising committee for the publication of the *Entsyklopediia ukraïnoznavstva* by the Shevchenko Scientific Society in Sarcelles, France.

Since I am already speaking about programs across the border, the second institution of higher learning to receive a sizable donation was the Harriman Institute at Columbia University in New York, to endow its graduate program in Ukrainian studies; at its helm was Dr. Mark Von Hagen. One of its primary goals was, and is, to promote specialized knowledge of Ukraine among a critical constituency—graduate students preparing for professional careers in government, diplomacy, business, journalism, and NGOs. Peter Jacyk was a member of the Harriman Institute's National Advisory Committee in 1996. I have been a member since 2010 and have agreed to serve for another three-year term. I find that sitting on such an advisory committee provides a voice for Ukrainian studies.

Shifting across the border, the first Canadian institution with which the Foundation has closely worked is the University of Alberta.

Early in the 1980s, Peter Jacyk was impressed by the achievements of CIUS, as it was an academic arm that appeared to be focused on achieving significant and measurable results without being bogged down in the "ivory-tower" mentality. CIUS was very active at that time in publishing books and journals, developing other materials for Ukrainian-language education, organizing conferences and lectures, and awarding scholarships and research grants. It contributed to the cultural and educational development of Ukrainian community groups, and its work benefited Ukrainians in Canada and the world over.

Mr. Jacyk determined that CIUS would be the ideal facility to carry out the long-term project of translating and publishing Mykhailo Hrushevsky's *History of Ukraine-Rus'*,[13] along with other future publications. It engaged highly qualified academics—especially Dr. Frank Sysyn, who has worked tirelessly, wearing many hats, in this very important translation project. Prudently Peter Jacyk took advantage of an opportunity whereby the Province of Alberta provided two-for-one matching of approved educational programs in partnership with private supporters, and thus the Peter Jacyk Centre for Ukrainian Historical Research was established at CIUS. I must mention that Mr. Peter Savaryn was instrumental in helping to obtain this two-for-one funding.

The question arises: "Why history?" Hrushevsky's *magnum opus* was a definitive declaration that Ukrainians constitute a nation and that Ukraine was not an adjunct of Poland, Russia, or any other claimant. He felt that the world, through the international scholarly community, needed to know about Ukraine's history. The translation of his work into English was the best way to achieve this.

CIUS continues to be active and productive. In 2008 another matching fund opportunity presented itself, and a new Petro Jacyk Program for the Study of Modern Ukrainian History and Society was established. The first of its kind in the Peter Jacyk Education Foundation's portfolio, this is a co-operative venture between the University of Alberta and two universities in Lviv: the Ivan Franko National University and the Ukrainian Catholic University. Professor Yaroslav Hrytsak oversees this program. I am pleased that it continues to foster international collaboration in scholarship, research, and education.

Outside CIUS, the University of Toronto is home to the Petro Jacyk Central and East European Resource Centre at the Robarts Library (est. 1994), which supports the activities of five research chairs (Estonian, Finnish, Hungarian, Polish, and Ukrainian), the Department of Slavic Languages and Literatures, and the Centre for European, Russian, and Eurasian Studies. Thanks to another significant endowment provided in 2001, there is also a Petro Jacyk Program for the Study of Ukraine at CERES, University of Toronto. The program promotes scholarly understanding of government, economy, and society in contemporary Ukraine, as well as the country's history and culture. It has focused on issues such as building an effective state; foreign policy and international relations; and education, culture, and national identity. On a regular basis there are various workshops, conferences, lectures, seminars, and annual visiting scholars studying Ukraine who come to Toronto with further research goals. This is a very vibrant program.

Since 2008 the Petro Jacyk Education Foundation has funded a larger-scope project on a yearly basis, the Petro Jacyk Post-doctoral Fellowship at the U of T. Every year the Foundation announces a competition for the position. The objective of the fellowship is to support the most promising junior scholars studying contemporary Ukraine (within 3–5 years after receiving their PhD). The position provides a scholar with experience and allows him or her to apply for permanent positions. The special lectures and symposiums planned by the post-docs are often open to the non-academic community as well. The fellow also goes on a research trip to Ukraine.

Since this is a year-to-year project, it requires a significant amount of work, funds, reviews, and renewals. However, the results create academic dispersion of Ukrainian content to universities that do not have permanent programs.

"Universities have always been business or corporate entities, and successful ones at that. That is why we donate and/or endow with them. They have more longevity than any other organization focusing on the academic field. However, ... it has to be a two-way street: they have to benefit from our programs, as we must benefit from their management."

Among those who have been awarded fellowships are Olga Onuch (University of Manchester and Oxford University), Serhiy Kudelia (Baylor University), and Mayhill Fowler (Stetson University). Dr. Sysyn has already mentioned that five of the seven fellows have secured tenured positions. This is remarkable.

While year-to-year funding is more costly to a donor in the long run, this type of funding maximizes production. It keeps everyone on their toes, which is a good thing.

"Change is the only constant" and "nothing stays the same" are sayings that remind us to be nimble, adaptable, and look for opportunities. Over the decades, the PJEF has seen several changes at the universities as they pertain to its endowed programs, and we have always closely monitored their activities.

The issues raised about changes imposed by the university administrations and their effect on Ukrainian studies are nothing new. Universities have always been business or corporate entities, and successful ones at that. That is why we donate to and/or endow with them. They have more longevity than any other organization focusing on the academic field. However, in business it has to be a two-way street: they have to benefit from our programs, as we must benefit from their management.

Even as far back as HURI in 1973, there was a rude awakening about how university management works. Some in the Ukrainian community who were responsible for the funds raised were too timid to correct Harvard management for a grave error on the university administration's part. Others, like my father, took them to task. The result was that the three chairs were not lost but endowed "in perpetuity," and an apology was issued. Again, this demands knowledge and experience in the workings of administrations.

What I have seen since the 2008 financial crisis—when major universities, including Alberta, lost 30 percent of their endowment principal—is that it has taken many years to rebuild and the universities have not yet fully recouped their losses, at least not as evidenced by our endowments. Budget cutbacks to departments and programs have not encouraged much expansion of studies, and the PJRC is not seeing as many proposals for funding as previously. I hope this will change soon.

The U of A is one of our largest endowments, and we have been pleased to be working closely with the academics and university administration for decades.

There have been changes. When a 5-percent fee was imposed on future donations from the Ukrainian community (to fund development/advancement/fundraising departments of the university), I was informed by CIUS and acted quickly, sending letters of objection with valid reasons to then U of A President Indira Samarasekera. I viewed this as extremely detrimental to the work of the centres: in business terms, it would be similar to increasing your sales department but decreasing your products to sell—counterproductive at best. This 5 percent would be discouraging to donors, on whom the university so heavily relies. Within two years, donations dropped so significantly that the 5-percent fee was rescinded.

What this means is that donors, institutes, and programs need to be actively involved in protecting and pushing for what is good for them. In turn, this will be good for the university. Measurable productivity is what counts.

This brings me to the point that we need to select charismatic, hard-working, and passionate academics to head our programs and courses. Students gravitate to such professors/directors, and then enrolments increase. Most often, generating success is about the people one employs.

Now to the extremely important and crucial topic of succession. It affects every organization. We have had such dynamic academics for decades, as evidenced by many of the participants at this conference and celebration. It is imperative that institutions and programs be assured that there will be succession implemented by the university, and that the mandates and programs will be continued. Our Education Foundation is always concerned about this when considering funding.

Also, the donors of Toronto very much appreciate that CIUS is a national institution of Ukrainian studies. It is based in Alberta but has a Toronto branch that produces academically and interacts well with the community, keeping it very much informed.

In the past 30 years, the PJEF has been quite successful at receiving matching funds, negotiating clear contracts with universities, and monitoring the progress of endowments and their relevant programs. We have international outreach, with significant funds and impact. Therefore the PJEF has its own model of success in the expansion of Ukrainian studies.

Having solid experience in this field, we look forward to continuing to entertain academic proposals that have tangible, measurable results, and progressing in what we believe we do well. ■

PAUL GROD

Discussant, Ukrainian Canadian Congress

PAUL GROD is the president and CEO of Rodan Energy, a leading North American energy management company. Prior to founding Rodan Energy, Paul was a corporate and investment banker with CIBC World Markets and a lawyer with Gowling Lafleur Henderson LLP, practicing corporate finance and M&A law. Grod is the national president of the Ukrainian Canadian Congress and vice-president of the Ukrainian World Congress, and chairs its Council in Support of Ukraine. Paul holds a BA in political science, a law degree, and an MBA, and is a member of the Law Society of Upper Canada.

The Ukrainian diaspora's role in Ukrainian studies

I am sorry that I do not have any giveaways, but next time I am on a panel with Andrii [Hladyshevsky], I will make sure to bring giveaways. [Laughter.] I have lots of flashlights I can give out. I think those would trump the brochures, but we will save that for another time.

It is a real privilege to be here as a net recipient of the good work that all of you do. I am very pleased that I have been a student of some of you and have read many of your works. You have made an impact on the future of the Ukrainian-Canadian community thanks to your good work, so I just wanted to start off with that, because what you do is very important. As a discussant, let me just touch on some of the key themes here.

Andrii Hladyshevsky talked about outreach, the importance of knowing your stakeholders, and getting your message out. He talked about some of the pillars of the Shevchenko Foundation, and of course he made his pitch for you to give to the Foundation, at least once. [Laughter.] He talked about the need to promote Ukrainian education. I will touch on this a little later, but the theme of my presentation is: how do we do that? How do we get there with all these great ideas that have been generated? How do we—CIUS and other academic institutions—interact with student organizations and with the community? That was Andrii Hladyshevsky's message.

Olya Kuplowska spoke about the Canadian Foundation for Ukrainian Studies and some of the challenges that it is facing, as well as many new needs. She mentioned that rigid restrictions on the use of endowments cause problems because of ever-changing priorities in Ukrainian studies. There are also challenges in the administration of existing funds. She talked about donor development and the desire of some donors to focus on one area, which raises the problem of long-term limitations. There is an issue with attracting new donors, and we have to consider how to interest donors and demonstrate the value of Ukrainian studies to new donors.

I emphasize that Ukrainian-Canadian studies are not independent of the Ukrainian-Canadian community. That has been a theme throughout the discussions here, addressed in particular by Professor Lupul. It is really important for us, at this conference in particular but also on an ongoing basis, to review our successes and our disappointments and address them effectively.

Roman Petryshyn spoke about the governance of our foundation money and gave us an interesting description of our community as a "community of communities," which I fully support, because the Ukrainian-Canadian community is not a monolith. We need more endowments, because there is a correlation between endowments and the success of Ukrainian studies. We talked about endowments in community foundations—the value of having our endowments not with universities but with community foundations like the Shevchenko Foundation. That would not only add efficiency, which Dr. Petryshyn focused on, but also increase autonomy and enhance bargaining power with academic institutions. Talking about the $54 million of endowments in Western Canada, a large percentage are focused on studies of Ukraine, and the administration fees of $3.8 million are very large. That is money that could be put back into Ukrainian-Canadian education or elsewhere.

We talked about constant administrative change at universities and the challenges we face as a result. We have to be vigilant when administrative changes happen, and, as Nadia Jacyk said, we have to do something about them to protect the endowments.

> *"During the last three years, the Revolution of Dignity, the Russian invasion of Ukraine, and today with the ongoing conflict in Ukraine, an expectation has arisen that the academic community that focuses on Ukraine and Ukrainian studies should be at the forefront of ensuring that Canadians ... are properly educated."*

Other issues, such as recapitalization of endowments, are often not addressed, which also applies to the administration of endowments and teaching our donors to set them up properly. That is why the concept of a consortium of directors and a national network of fundraisers is very critical. It would ensure the efficacy of endowment agreements and other agreements we have with universities: these should not have to be relearned over and over again.

Another important theme was the strategic administration of endowments: what do we need from Ukrainian studies and how do we get there? Also some of the challenges with endowments: if there is no student demand, then professors could be reassigned, which defeats the purpose of the endowments. We talked about a national network of fundraisers and the importance of focusing on strategic priorities, which need to be explained to our stakeholders.

Nadia Jacyk talked about the vision of the Petro Jacyk Education Foundation as both donor and recipient, and Petro Jacyk's vision of supporting CIUS. A very interesting theme that she introduced, which I think after forty years we can be really proud of, is that CIUS's focus on education assisted in establishing Ukrainians as a nation [in the eyes of the Western world]. Forty years ago it was much more difficult to take that for granted: CIUS has delivered on it with support from the Petro Jacyk Education Foundation. Nadia also talked about funding programs rather than endowments: scholarships can make possible strategic placement and flexibility. She talked about maximizing the productivity of our funds, being adaptable, and being competitive. We constantly need to monitor counterproductive behaviour at universities, such as unilateral increases in administrative costs of fundraising, and take action against it.

Nadia mentioned that she and others have written, but often the community is not mobilized to support such initiatives. It is also very important, as Nadia mentioned, to hire charismatic, committed scholars and educators who will attract undergraduate and graduate students.

Succession planning is also very important: CIUS is and must remain a national centre for Ukrainian education. In conclusion, Nadia talked about tangible and measurable results.

A fundamental theme underlying this discussion is the importance of the Ukrainian-Canadian community and its connection to Ukrainian studies. Because the community has a vested interest in Ukrainian studies, it began to fund them. We must connect with those stakeholders and understand their needs—including future students. Are we reaching out to youth and student organizations? Are they participating in conferences of this kind? We have to go out of our way to ensure that they do. We also have to reassess what we have done well and what have we not done so well, and ask ourselves: does the community really understand CIUS's vision?

I will be frank: I do not think it does. There is a misconception in our community that CIUS is responsible for all education in Canada—for teaching, not just research, so we must ask ourselves: what does the community know about us? what does the community expect of us? What is the vision? Does it need to change for CIUS? Is it relevant to our stakeholders? What do community leaders want from the Ukrainian academic community? During the last three years, the Revolution of Dignity, the Russian invasion of Ukraine, and today with the ongoing conflict in Ukraine, an expectation has arisen that the academic community that focuses on Ukraine and Ukrainian studies should be at the forefront of ensuring that Canadians, those formulating public policy and decision makers, are properly educated. I understand the need for academic independence, but if you are knowledgeable about Ukraine and Ukrainian politics, there is an expectation from the community that you will be at the forefront advocating, participating, organizing conferences on these issues. Some are doing so, but the community does not see enough articles on these issues in the national papers and magazines. It has got to the point where our community has started to fund non-university institutions, such as think-tanks. For example, our community, through the Ukrainian World Congress but primarily from Canadian resources, is funding the Atlantic Council in the amount of $600,000 per year for their "Ukraine in Europe" initiative. That is what I consider an academic exercise, because they are discussing issues important to our community today. I think that is an area that Ukrainian-Canadian studies have missed out on. I am not being critical: I am looking at this as a future opportunity.

Again, our community leaders are looking to academia to help influence the public and policymakers, and I think the academic community can expect the Ukrainian-Canadian community to advocate on its behalf. Earlier today, Professor Magocsi called for advocacy on behalf of Ukrainian studies, which is, quite frankly, within our mandate, and we should be doing it. I would like to sit down after this conference to discuss it a little further.

I would also like to talk about different models. There are models such as the Sheptytsky Institute.[24] They have two endowed chairs and a foundation, and they are able to pick and choose. You may have heard, just a few weeks ago there was an announcement that the Sheptytsky Institute is moving from the University of Ottawa to St. Michael's College at the University of Toronto. [...] If you can pick up your foundation and move it to a university more conducive to you, then you have flexibility and bargaining power.

There is also the example of the Ukrainian Jewish Encounter.[25] I would argue that it is an academic initiative with maximum flexibility—a living and breathing initiative that accesses Ukrainian studies but is not committed to any particular institution. There are organizations such as CIUS's Holodomor Research and Education Consortium, and there is the Ukrainian Catholic University in Lviv, which has a very interesting model.

There are models we should be looking at and opportunities for us to continue to grow and be more effective. There is a sense, though, that the academic community does not want the community meddling in its activities, and asserts its need to have academic independence—which, frankly, I fully support. There is an opportunity now to change that paradigm and establish a much closer relationship between academia and the community. You should be looking to the Ukrainian Canadian Congress, and the Ukrainian World Congress, as your international and Canadian partners. There has been some discussion at our board table at the Ukrainian Canadian Congress as to whether institutions such as CIUS should be invited to become members of the UCC. I know that when I mention it here, there is probably an initial reaction and a fear that "uh-oh, that rabid Ukrainian diaspora, they just want to control us." By the way, "rabid diaspora," for those who do not know, was a phrase that Russian Foreign Minister Sergei Lavrov used not so long ago to refer to the Ukrainian-Canadian diaspora in some public remarks he made to the CBC. Some of us are very proud to be considered a "rabid Ukrainian-Canadian diaspora." But trust me, we are not going to be rabid with the academic community here in Canada.

First of all, the Ukrainian Canadian Congress has evolved. It is an organization of organizations. Our job is to bring together everything Ukrainian, whether it is the arts community, youth, religious communities, or academia. In fact, at our 25th triennial congress of Ukrainian Canadians, which we concluded just two weeks ago (where I had the privilege of receiving another three-year mandate), there was a session dedicated to CIUS's fortieth anniversary. I just want to quickly read to you the resolution that came out of that session, and I hope it is appropriate to what we have talked about.

> Whereas it is important that UCC have access to the most up-to-date scholarly information about Ukraine, be it resolved that an academic advisory [committee of UCC National] be established, consisting of scholars, specialists in Ukrainian studies in various fields, which could provide advice to the UCC President and Executive on matters related to their areas of specialty or expertise.

This is something that I fully support and endorse. I have had discussions with some of you, including Frank Sysyn and others, about the possibility of creating something like this. Whether it is a matter of CIUS becoming a formal member of the Ukrainian Canadian Congress or not, I think that is less relevant than bringing people together. I fully support and endorse the creation of a loosely affiliated council of scholars in Ukrainian studies that could come together as needed, with an executive committee made up of scholars that would address issues important to Ukrainian academic studies in Canada and even internationally.

This would be an opportunity to provide ongoing advice to the Ukrainian Canadian Congress, because our role has been to influence public perceptions and to influence policymakers. And that is why we are constantly developing policy papers on various issues, whether it is Canadian foreign policy vis-à-vis Ukraine and Russia, defence policy, technical and international assistance, or heritage. We have very well-developed policy positions that we have presented to government, and we continue to advocate. These are areas where we would love to connect—and we do, but perhaps not in a very organized manner—with academics in Ukrainian studies. But there is a great opportunity there, so I would like to end my remarks by calling on us—and I would like to hear your comments on this—for the creation of a council of scholars in Ukrainian studies within the Ukrainian Canadian Congress. ■

DISCUSSION

ANDREW HLADYSHEVSKY:

I think Pavlo raised it regarding the Sheptytsky Institute: unless you have clout, you will continue to be downtrodden by those who hold your money. The community has $54 million, according to Mr. Petryshyn, but you have little bang for your buck with the management of your money. That has to change.

Pavlo suggests some models, advocating with different universities, and that endowments start to be placed within the Shevchenko Foundation in perpetuity for particular programs in order to gain independence from universities, to be able to tell them, "If you do not like it, we will go somewhere else." The fact of the matter is that CIUS cannot say right now to the University of Alberta, "We are leaving for the University of Toronto." When Eastern Christian studies fell out of favour at St. Paul University, the Sheptytsky Institute eventually left with its money [funds at the Shevchenko Foundation], which gave it some power and authority to negotiate with the University of Toronto. So those models have to be considered.

The people in this room are beneficiaries of literally hundreds of millions of dollars of cash that has flowed to you, to a lot of you, to do what you have done. So for you to say that you are not part of the community, or that the community should not have a say in what you do, is quite frankly, for me, not in the cards. I think before you shuffle off this mortal coil, you should give back to your community in some way. I think Nadia would probably agree that we have put in processes for our organizations to last in perpetuity. So that is extremely important. Thirdly, your customers, your students, have to be convinced that even though what you may teach may not result in a particular career, somehow it is relevant in their lives, relevant enough for them to experiment with courses in Ukrainian education, relevant to talk to their kids about it and interest them.

OLGA KUPLOWSKA:

Where foundations are concerned, I think we do need some kind of loose networking to share information. Different foundations or organizations are informed at different levels, and we have all had our own experiences. We need to share some of those stories so that we may be better prepared to deal with whatever situations come up. Also, priority setting is needed without tying down; with each university, there are different priorities. We need a better sense of existing gaps and needs as perceived by academics and community members alike in order to deal effectively with donors and applications. So I am looking forward to networking and increased communications from all parties.

ROMAN PETRYSHYN:

Each university is in competition with every other, and Ukrainian programs at different universities are in competition. I regard competition as a good thing. The more competition, the more the message gets out inside the Ukrainian community about endowments or funding individual programs. We need to understand that we can trust one another in Ukrainian studies—we can operate as a national community of interest while competing. So that trust relationship, sharing of information, and transparency are the elements needed to create a much more powerful vehicle than we currently have. The models used in the 1980s, 1990s, and so on have shown what they can do. The time has come to envision a different model for fundraising. There are many people in Canada, not just of Ukrainian background, as we have heard at this conference, who are interested in what we do. But communication between the community, particularly donors, and the academy leaves much to be improved. We have the resources to do it. We just have to set that as a priority and focus on it.

NADIA JACYK:

With regard to Dr. Petryshyn's idea of a different model, I would just ask whether it would not be a good idea to study other ethnic groups that possibly have very vast and successful studies at different universities, and take what they do successfully and mimic it. Trying to create something ourselves may be not the most prudent way to go. If there is no example to follow, then you have to be a pioneer, and with pioneering come all kinds of challenges and risks. So I would urge that maybe somebody, and I do not know if it would be me. I am not volunteering myself for it—see whether the academic institutes know or can help us find out about achievements in Chinese, Russian, or East Indian studies, or anything somewhat similar to ours.

QUESTIONS AND COMMENTS

LARISSA BLAVATSKA (OTTAWA):

Thank you for this excellent, very informative panel, which addressed issues that I personally have been interested in for some time. I was very interested throughout the two days to hear that many of the issues that Ukrainian studies, whether scholars or administrators, are grappling with are felt throughout the humanities and social sciences. That is, the corporatization of the university system has hit the Faculty of Arts particularly at this university, which has also undertaken a very misguided effort to be in the top twenty universities internationally. This is an impossible goal, and it has disproportionately affected the study of liberal arts at the U of A.

One of my particular concerns is the status of the Institute here at the university. At one point, in my understanding, it was an independent institution affiliated with the university. It is now under the umbrella of the Faculty of Arts and reports to the Dean of Arts. I was not very happy with the comments made by the Dean of Arts. I did not feel that they were very reassuring—a lot of platitudes, but nothing very specific about what the university can do to continue championing the health of the Institute. I have a request, not a question.

My request would be that the Institute inform members of the community about three things. One is: what is the administrative status of the Institute? I know a lot of the administration has been taken over by the university, but what is the status of the Institute? And here I am not looking for pages of explanatory information but really what is the status of the endowment funds? There are a lot of stories. There was an email sent by a professor at this university a few days ago that I think many people have seen. My understanding is that the endowment funds specify how they are to be used. That is fair enough, so the Institute cannot take funds that the donor allocated for the study of poetry to fund a centre in Kharkiv or Ukrainian-Canadian studies. But my understanding—or at least I have heard various comments over the last few years—is that the endowment funds themselves have been taken over by the university for uses other than those specified by the donors.

Thirdly, I think of donors such as myself. I am not a large donor, but I have given enough money to be invited for lunch at one point by the Dean of Arts. I have not given money for the last two years because I have not been able to find out what is happening. I would ask you, Professor Kravchenko, to perhaps put the information on your website, perhaps send an email or letters to your mailing list, to clarify this for people such as myself. I am very happy to continue contributing, but I need reassurance that that money is going to be used by the Institute, and that it is not going to be taken over by the university for something that I was not planning to subsidize.

Lastly, I would like to congratulate the organizers. These two days have been very stimulating. I have certainly learned a lot. It was wonderful that both Professor Lupul and Petro Savaryn were here. It was wonderful that we heard from Bishop Gudziak. I think it was great that so many people who have been instrumental in furthering Ukrainian studies in Canada and abroad were here.

LARISA SEMBALIUK-CHELADYN:

I am the community liaison for the Kule Folklore Centre as of two weeks ago, and I have the task of helping introduce our new director, Dr. Jelena Pogosjan. My takeaway from today's session, actually from the whole day, was best expressed by Andrii Hladyshevsky with his passionate demonstration of how important it is to interact with our stakeholders. You actually walked down those steps and came down to our level, which is, I think, something all of us have to do. If we want new students in our classrooms, we have to go into the classrooms, recruit, go online, mingle with the students. If you want money, there are a lot of examples—six institutions that Dr. Petryshyn presented, with people who were actually interactive with their stakeholders. Bohdan Medwidsky, every one of you on the panel here, have gone out, had coffee with potential donors, explained to them why the money is needed, and how we will be responsible with the money they invest with us. We have to interact with them, make them feel comfortable with what we are doing. And lastly, I just wanted to comment on how Paul Grod interacted with the stakeholders. The UCC resolution for an academic advisory council is really worth considering, and I am glad it has been brought forward.

BOHDAN MEDWIDSKY:

You have three foundations represented here. My question is: would it be kosher if the three foundations gave one another the outcomes of their investment policies?

ANDREW HLADYSHEVSKY:

Well, we at the Shevchenko Foundation are pretty transparent. I think I just handed that out to everybody. One issue that I have, not with the people up here, but with many community organizations—some related to academics, others non-academic—is their unprofessional money management. The community could benefit from the expertise of some of the people up here in fund management. Community leaders could then lead without trying to be investment experts.

NADIA JACYK:

I am in support of what Olga Kuplowska said, that it would be good to have gatherings of interest groups with similar goals. I am not so sure that I am excited about another intermediary or organizational level exercising oversight. Let us see the foundations that are already doing good work. The jury is still out on whether that is something I would support.

OLGA KUPLOWSKA:

I actually wanted to support what Larissa [Blavatska] was requesting, not only with regard to CIUS. When we are approached by donors, they often do not have a clear enough idea of how things work within universities—budgeting and costs. Sometimes even we do not have full information. The more we can educate stakeholders about how universities work, the better. When people see that there is going to be a return on their investment, they are prepared to lend support. But they need that information, and you want to have an informed consumer. So I would ask whoever is in a position to share that information to do so—but that information does need to get out.

MANOLY LUPUL:

I made a suggestion earlier, when there was a Ukrainian-Canadian panel here—and we are very glad to see you here, Paul Grod. The suggestion was very simple: we should have more emphasis on Ukrainian-Canadian studies, and a whole day should be devoted to that subject at the next Ukrainian Canadian Congress, following an agenda prepared perhaps by the directors' consortium that was suggested, which is a good idea, or by your advisory committee. I do not care how the thing is structured. I do not care about models. Let us get going; that is all. But let us have that session, because the public needs to be sensitized. Public consciousness has to be aroused: they are giving money as Ukrainian Canadians, but there is very little study of them as people who are donating. I repeat, it would be good to have a whole day, with an agenda previously prepared, so that something concrete comes out of it.

PAUL GROD:

I fully support and endorse what you have just proposed, and I have to say that this is a new chapter in the relationship between the Ukrainian Canadian Congress and the directors and CIUS and the academic community of Ukrainian studies. I think there has been traditionally a misunderstanding, perhaps even a distrust of one another, and I think that this 25th congress was the first in my memory at which CIUS took such an active role. It is not just the community saying, "We need to bring together the academics in Ukrainian studies," which is not particularly effective if this [academic] community does not want to be involved. So, if I am hearing you correctly, there is a sentiment—I cannot say it is a complete consensus, but there is a strong sentiment here—that there is an interest in doing that, and we will take up that call.

Round Table V: Community Outreach.
L–r: Paul Grod (discussant), Nadia Jacyk, Roman Petryshyn, Olga Kuplowska, Andrew Hladyshevsky, Roman Yereniuk (moderator, at the podium).

VOLODYMYR KRAVCHENKO
CIUS Director

VOLODYMYR KRAVCHENKO is a professor in the Department of History and Classics and director of the Canadian Institute of Ukrainian Studies, University of Alberta (since 2012). His recent works include: "Ukraine: History confronts geography," in *The EU's Eastern Neighbourhood: Migration, Borders and Regional Stability* (2016); "Ukrainian historical writing in North America during the Cold War," in *East and Central European History Writing in Exile 1939–1989* (2015); "Ukraine faces its Soviet past: History vs. policy vs. memory," in *Mass Dictatorship and Memory as Ever-Present Past* (2014); and the monograph *Ukraïna, imperiia, Rosiia: Vybrani statti z modernoï istoriï ta istoriohrafiï* (Ukraine, Empire, Russia: Selected Articles from Modern History and Historiography; 2011).

Closing remarks

Your Grace Bishop Borys, Your Excellency Ambassador Shevchenko, President of the Ukrainian Canadian Congress Pavlo Grod, colleagues, friends: our conference is over. I am standing between you and the banquet, with just some observations and feelings I managed to collect and summarize while attending the debates.

First of all, it was really exciting. Our conference was enriched by more than six hundred visitors from all over the world, including those who attended in person here at the University of Alberta. I am really impressed with the intellectual level and openness of the debates. I believe most of us now better understand where we are with Ukrainian and Ukrainian-Canadian studies. I believe we better understand their context as well. That is why the conference title is "Texts and Contexts of Ukrainian Studies in Canada." That is what really matters. My impression is that, despite all odds, optimists prevailed over pessimists. *Shche ne vmerly ukraïns'ki studiï.*[86]

There were some interesting topics I would like to touch upon. For one thing, the balance between Ukrainian and Ukrainian-Canadian topics, our two main pillars. I do believe it is possible to develop both of them to mutual advantage—to bridge them. Just consider such topics as work ethic, social values, political culture, cross-cultural communications, urban studies, ethnic and nationalism studies, regional and border studies, diaspora, refugees, and so on and so forth. Forty years ago, Ukrainian studies revolved around a non-existent state and a nation with dubious credentials. The irony is that today, when the Ukrainian political nation is a reality and the Ukrainian state exists, I would say that Ukrainian studies are becoming important precisely because they are about a specific nation—a border nation located in the geographic centre of Europe, with complex geographies and identities. Dominique Arel sounded optimistic, and I am also optimistic about the possibility of interdisciplinary dialogue. It is interesting that political scientists are moving toward history, while historians are becoming contemporary studies specialists and experts in Canadian and non-Canadian aspects.

Basically Ukraine is a teenaged country, with all the complexes and complexities characteristic of that age. If our partners in Ukraine are ready to be treated as adults, let us establish a new mechanism of dealing with them. Let us treat them as real partners, not just recipients of some sort of humanitarian aid. Let us support Ukraine-based projects on the basis of open competition. We have received about 250 applications from Ukraine this year alone, which is a good sign. It shows that the Ukrainian academic community is active and gaining maturity.

"Our conference was enriched by more than six hundred visitors from all over the world, including those who attended in person here at the University of Alberta. I am really impressed with the intellectual level and openness of the debates. I believe most of us now better understand where we are with Ukrainian and Ukrainian-Canadian studies."

This conference was conducted on Canadian soil. Thus, all our findings and debates also contribute to Canadian

86 "Ukrainian studies live on," a play on words from Ukraine's national anthem.

scholarship; they will be published in Canada and become part of the Canadian humanities and social sciences. Dear colleagues, we are all involved in one way or another. I wish there were no issues with identity, no memory issues, and so on. However, Ukraine is still a work in progress. Canada is also a work in progress. Thus, identity matters. It is important for those who are discovering their Ukrainianness to understand their identity, to understand where they are and what is going on. We cannot predict the results and cannot impose our agenda on the course of events. [...] What we can do is keep our minds open, maintain academic integrity, abide by our professional norms and values, and be honest and tolerant with each other. One doesn't need to have a Canadian passport to do this. That is where I stand.

> *We are a part of the University of Alberta. Having said that, I would like to stress that it was our community support that helped us survive and maintain our academic identity. Let me tell you that no endowment, no amount of money invested in the Institute, no matter how small, has been used for purposes other than Ukrainian studies.*

By the way, I was intrigued by Mark Von Hagen's observation about the applicability of a model of a military democracy to Ukraine. And Rory Finnin is right to draw our attention to the ethical consequences of our activities. On another matter, in the course of the last two years thousands of texts about Ukraine have been published in different languages. So we can no longer complain that Ukraine is not visible in information space. However, when it comes to the issue of professional competence, sometimes I am really shocked to see respectable professors turning into propagandists and warriors. It seems to me that the world of academia should behave with greater decorum.

This is not to say that we should discourage those who become interested in Ukrainian topics. Let us not forget the non-Ukrainians who have been and are deeply involved in Ukrainian studies. To mention just a few: Canadians George Simpson, Watson Kirkconnell, and our colleagues David Marples, Heather Coleman, and Dominique Arel; and Americans Clarence Manning, Philip Mosely, William Chamberlin, and John Armstrong; and elsewhere, our colleagues Mark Von Hagen, Hiroaki Kuromiya, and many others. Of course, they do not need to be patriotic Ukrainians—they just need to be professionals. We should be happy to have all of them in Ukrainian studies.

In terms of our priorities, let me presume that you have read my introduction to the commemorative issue.[1] If not, please do, since I expressed some ideas there about the future development of the Institute, my vision of Ukrainian studies, and our priorities as well. Let me tell you that I am really attracted to the think-tank model, and I am sorry to say, I do not believe that any new institute of Ukrainian studies is possible in Canada in the nearest future. If you are really interested in the future of Ukrainian studies, let us build up new endowments, establish endowed chairs at the universities, and consolidate our resources, financial as well as intellectual.

Thirty-five years ago, after the Institute was established by the provincial government of Alberta, our founders decided to integrate CIUS into the University of Alberta. Our budget also became part of the university budget. I think it was the right decision. The Institute can function properly only if it is part of the academic environment and the academic world. We are a part of the University of Alberta. Having said that, I would like to stress that it was our community support that helped us survive and maintain our academic identity in research activities and priorities. Let me tell you that no endowment, no amount of money invested in the Institute, no matter how small, has been used for purposes other than Ukrainian and Ukrainian-Canadian studies. All of the Ukrainian endowments in the Institute are safe. However, I do admit that we have problems in using some of our endowments with their very specific terms of reference. We have too many restrictions to be able to operate according to our changing priorities. That is why we are well-to-do on the one hand but short of money on the other. That is a paradox, but all that is Ukrainian is always full of paradoxes, is it not? That is why two of our three main units, the Peter and Doris Kule Ukrainian Canadian Studies Centre and ULEC, the Ukrainian Language Education

Centre, are underfunded. We cannot even afford to hire a full-time coordinator for each of those two units.

As for collaboration, I am ready to collaborate with any organization in Canada and worldwide on the basis of academic autonomy. If you need our knowledge, our expertise, our experience, please say so: we are ready to help.

Has CIUS fulfilled its mission to become the main coordinating centre of Ukrainian and Ukrainian-Canadian studies in Canada? That is a rhetorical question, but I would ask you all: how many centres of Ukrainian and Ukrainian-Canadian studies do we really need to avoid the impression that Ukrainian studies are overrepresented? As for the community, of course I wish it were better informed about our activities. Let me say, then, that we have created a "Contemporary Ukraine Studies Program." Two young Stasiuk fellows, specialists in contemporary topics, as well as two distinguished specialists, Taras Kuzio and Bohdan Harasymiw, were also engaged by CIUS in order to help us developing the program. They produced many valuable texts (interviews and special publications) and delivered many presentations in an attempt to explain what is going on in and around Ukraine to Western audiences. So do not try to persuade me that CIUS doesn't pay attention to contemporary Ukraine. Above all, the mandate of CIUS is to produce expert knowledge published in professional journals. That is where we stand, and that is our identity.

We completely reorganized our website, which gained 2,000 followers in just a year and a half. The fact that our conference was live-streamed to Australia, Ukraine, the United States, and Europe shows that we are increasing our visibility and influence as we provide reliable information and produce and distribute expert knowledge about Canada and Ukraine.

A couple of words about Ukrainian studies at the University of Alberta. For now, we have two centres: the Canadian Institute of Ukrainian Studies and the Kule Folklore Centre. We have two chairs in Ukrainian studies, and CIUS has the largest cluster of endowments of any centre or institute at the University of Alberta. So I would say that rumours about the death of Ukrainian studies at the University of Alberta are a bit exaggerated. Last but not least, we are going to transcribe and publish the proceedings of this conference. Once again, let me express my deep gratitude to all our participants for their hard work, to our sponsors—especially to the *Tovarystvo sen'ioriv*[87]—and to our team and our volunteers. Thank you very much. ■

87 Ukrainian Senior Citizens Association of Marko Boyeslaw (Edmonton).

INDEX

A

B

C

N

O

P